Voices From Minnesota

Drew

Christmas 2017

Jerry Abraham

Voices From Minnesota

Short Biographies

From Thirty-two Senior Citizens

by Jerry Abraham

 **DeForest Press**

Elk River, Minnesota

Published by:
DeForest Press
P.O. Box 154
Elk River, MN 55330 USA
www.DeForestPress.com
Toll-free: 877-441-9733
Richard DeForest Erickson, Publisher
Shane Groth, Editor in Chief

Cover design by Linda Walters, Optima Graphics, Appleton WI

ISBN 1-930374-13-5

First printing November 2004

Printed in the United States of America
08 07 06 05 04   5 4 3 2 1

Library of Congress Cataloging-in-Publication Data

Abraham, Jerry, 1946-
  Voices from Minnesota : short biographies from thirty-two senior citizens / by
Jerry Abraham.
     p. cm.
  ISBN 1-930374-13-5
  1. Minnesota—Biography. 2. Older people—Minnesota—Biography. I. Title.
  CT242.A27 2004
  920.0776—dc22

2004021086

This book is dedicated to the people of Minnesota and the United States of America who grew up and led productive lives during the twentieth century. In the process, they influenced the lives of sons, daughters, and many other relatives and friends. They are to be commended for making life better for those who followed.

About the Author

 Jerry Abraham was born and raised in Minnesota. He and his wife Lois have been married since 1968. They have three grown children; Michelle, John, and James. Jerry taught social studies in the Elk River School District for over thirty years. Most of his tenure was spent teaching American history at the junior high school and senior high school levels. During the last few years of his career, Jerry taught mainly on twentieth century American history. His experience as a teacher played a major role in fostering an interest in the historical roles of average American citizens.

Contents

Preface

According to *Webster's New Twentieth Century Dictionary* (second edition), an oral history is "an account of what happened, narrative, story, tale." Oral histories have been important for passing on information from one generation to the next since the beginning of time. These "stories" spread and perpetuate historical information, culture, language, philosophy, and more. If we lose historical accounts of those who came before us, we lose important connections with our past.

All of the above brings us to the contents of these pages. Thirty-two senior citizens, residents of Minnesota, have told the stories of their lives. These stories can be seen in light of the historical context of the last eighty plus years of the twentieth century and the beginning of the twenty-first century. The tone of the stories emphasizes the human element in the realm of history. This human element is important as we recognize that history is a record of events, most of which are driven by people. History is alive and ever changing.

During our lives, we become part of history as observers and actors. Whether a person is rich or poor, powerful or weak, famous or anonymous, that person helps shape the time in which he/she lives. By recognizing and recording the individual histories of our fellow people, we may be better able to see how we are touched by others and in turn touch people ourselves. We may be better able to see our interrelatedness in history and develop a better sense of our importance on one scale and the importance of history on another scale.

The interview process used in obtaining the histories was quite open ended. One of the primary objectives of each interview was to encourage the person to speak freely with as little interruption as possible. However, at the beginning of each interview, each person was told of the parameters of the interview. Each person interviewed was encouraged to discuss parents, childhood (especially in relation to the 1920s), adolescence and young adulthood (especially in relation to the Great Depression of the 1930s), life during World War II, and life after World War II to the present. The purpose was to create a story that had a sense of chronology. As such, questions were asked only as a guide to help get a more complete lifetime picture of the person.

Results of the interviews varied greatly. Some people were quite detailed in describing their lives, while others spoke much more generally. One reason for the differences had to do with sharpness of memory. Another important reason had to do with how much information the person chose to share. Some people were more cautious in what they wanted the public to know about them and their families. In addition, some people chose to dwell more on a specific part of their lives. Some, for example, spent more time talking about their education than about their adult life. Others spoke in greater detail about war experiences or their vocations than about family lives. Some left gaps in their stories, while others were more consistent in discussing each chapter in their life histories. While such differences may leave some questions unanswered in the minds of the readers, they project the personalities and humanity of the individuals who were interviewed.

To give a better picture of the environment of the interviewees, a thumbnail description was given of the geographical areas in which they live. Thus the reader can get a sense of a person growing up in a rural or city area, or in some cases both, and get an idea of the cultural and economic tenor of the area.

In addition, an effort was made to cover a variety of ethnic groups. The goal was to obtain representation of western European, eastern European, African American, American Indian, Hispanic, and Asian American people. In some cases, it meant interviewing someone who was new to the state, but newcomers are always part of our population. While many residents of Minnesota have lived most or all of their lives here, the state does have a significant number of recent immigrants. Some groups may have been over or underrepresented. This was mainly due to the fact that participation was voluntary.

This effort will be considered successful if it leads more people to seek out our senior citizens to find out about their lives. It would be especially helpful if sons, daughters, nieces, nephews, and other extended family members would talk with their elders. What a great way to experience how our ancestors helped build the United States into what has been termed a "superpower"! What a great way to help us learn who we are and how we fit into this ongoing story! What a great tribute we pay to our seniors for leading the way for us and for being important contributors to our society! We need to understand that it was not just leaders like Benjamin Franklin, George Washington, Abraham Lincoln, Franklin Roosevelt, and Martin Luther King who shaped the country. It was not just state leaders like Alexander Ramsey, Floyd B. Olson, and Hubert Humphrey who shaped the state of Minnesota. It was also the cumulative efforts of the many so-called "average citizens." These citizens may not think of themselves as heroes, but they certainly can be described as hard working, strong willed, and sometimes even courageous.

It is equally important for our senior citizens to be willing to share their lives. They are important people and their life experiences are important. All people experience successes and disappointments in life. When these experiences are shared, they can help others gain new insights into contemporary history. Our seniors have contributed much and continue to contribute. These contributions should not be diminished.

Acknowledgments

So many people have contributed to this effort that it will be impossible to thank them all. Obviously, all the people who chose to share their life histories were important—this is their book. However, in each community, other people helped in making this an experience that will not soon be forgotten.

In September 2002 I knew in a general way what I wanted to do, but did not have a very good plan to carry it out. I knew that I wanted to interview people from different parts of Minnesota, so I made the first of many telephone calls to the Polk County Historical Society in northwestern Minnesota. From that call, I was able to contact Alta Hermodson. Alta was kind enough to supply information about the senior center in Crookston, which led to the first set of interviews. I regret that I did not get the opportunity to meet Alta in person.

Soon after that contact, Michelle Reichert provided information about the "how to" aspects of writing oral histories. As a social worker who had worked with seniors, she had an understanding of how to elicit information from seniors.

A couple of weeks later I arrived in Crookston, walked into the Chamber of Commerce, and met Jeannine Windels, the president and CEO. She graciously supplied background information on the area. In addition, she gave me clear directions to the senior center. Ms. Windels was even kind enough to supply specific names of people to contact as potential subjects to be interviewed. Dee Myerchin, director of the Golden Link Senior Center, did a great job in helping me contact people for interviews.

After the first set of interviews was completed, it was time to find seniors in a western Minnesota town. After several misses in several towns, I contacted the Historical Museum of Stevens County. I talked with Tami Plank who gave me information about the senior center in the town. Later, I talked with

Randee Hokanson from the museum who gave me the lead to contact her father-in-law. Judy Nord and Coleen Dogotch from the senior center were very helpful in allowing me to talk with the seniors and get some great interviews.

Then it dawned on me that if I wanted to get this bountiful information published, I had better get each person to sign a release. I enlisted the help of Cindy Fennig to come up with a legal release form, which was accomplished. Then I revisited the people I had already interviewed. I made sure they had the opportunity to read their stories and approve what was written. Then they were asked to sign releases. At the same time, I needed to continue the interview process.

So, it came time to find a town to represent southern Minnesota, and it turned out to be New Prague. Mary Vacarro referred me to Lucine Wendorf, who gave me the opportunity to speak at the senior center. Later, I was able to talk to Mary Whitmer, Housing Director at Mala Strana Assisted Living. She was very helpful in all stages of the interviewing process. She introduced me to wonderful seniors living at Mala Strana. She also helped coordinate interviews and the signing of release forms. I am very thankful for the use of a case study written by Kathy Huber for her master's program. The case study was helpful in reinforcing information and filling in gaps from an interview with Anne Juni.

I made several different contacts in the Twin Cities. John Abraham, an assistant professor at the University of St. Thomas, introduced me to two colleagues who had great stories to tell. Janet Stately from the Office of Indian Ministry was very helpful in helping make contacts with American Indians. I am especially grateful to Barbara Bester for allowing me to interview her while she was recovering in the hospital from injuries suffered in an automobile accident. She exhibited a good deal of patience and grace. Two more people who were very cooperative were Annie Turman and Judy Dworsky from the Jewish Community Center in St. Louis Park. Annie gave me names of possible contacts and Judy allowed me to make my presentation to seniors at the center and to set up interviews. I also want to thank Kris Niebler and Diane Knutson from the Coon Rapids Senior Community Center. Kris helped set the stage for my presentation to seniors at the center and introduced me to some wonderful seniors. Diane followed up with many other referrals. She not only gave me local referrals, but also gave me names of contact people in other parts of the Twin Cities and greater Minnesota to help me obtain ethnic and cultural diversity among the interviews. Two people from Our Lady of Guadaloupe Catholic Church helped a great deal. Artemio Alvarado did well in lining me up with two wonderful Hispanic women to interview. Corinne Bruno was very helpful in the process that allowed me to complete paperwork. Finally, contacts with Dean Potter and Tom Hara were very helpful in helping obtain the interview with Kimi Hara.

Last of all, I would like to thank my wife Lois for ignoring my protestations and overall stubbornness in getting her to read every page of this work to help make it more readable. She quietly went about reading very carefully, doing the best job she could. I hate to admit it, but whenever we disagreed about sentence structure or clarity, she was right the vast majority of time.

Northern Minnesota

Crookston

Downtown Crookston at Main and Robert Streets

Crookston represents the economic and cultural nature of northern Minnesota.

This community is located in Polk County in northwestern Minnesota on the plains of the Red River Valley of the North. It is the county seat, about 290 miles northwest of the Twin Cities, with a population of 8,192 as of 2000.

According to the *Crookston Membership Directory and Community Service Guide* (Crookston Chamber of Commerce, 2003), Crookston was named after Colonel William Crooks, a railroad man. Colonel Crooks was credited with bringing the first steam locomotive to Minnesota. People of Scandinavian descent made up most of the early population in the area. Scandinavian heritage seems to dominate present day Crookston as well.

The economy is based mostly on agriculture and related agribusiness. Leading agricultural products in the area include wheat, barley, sugar beets, and potatoes. In fact, Polk County leads the state in the production of those crops. Other important crops in the area include sunflowers, rye, flax, soybeans, and corn. The strong agribusiness nature of the area is reinforced by the presence of agricultural processing plants. There are four processing plants in Crookston. Most have national and international markets.

There are other major industries that are important to the Crookston area. Some of the major industries include a fiberglass fabricating company, a maker of aluminum castings, and a manufacturer of buses.

In addition, The Crookston area is a regional educational center in Minnesota. A new high school was completed in 1997. The school, which includes grades eight through twelve, has been described as "state of the art." A branch of the University of Minnesota also is located in Crookston. It is a well-respected school that offers associate and bachelor degrees. It also offers outreach programs for citizens through workshops and provides information referral for a variety of subjects.

Medical facilities are extensive. Riverview Hospital was expanded and updated with state-of-the-art equipment in 2003. The city also has a modern clinic, two nursing homes, and centers for treating mental health issues and chemical dependency.

Crookston also boasts a fine cultural environment. It is home to the Polk County Historical Museum which has a great selection of historical items that include old buildings and railroad equipment. The Ox Cart Days Festival is held each August and commemorates the Red River ox carts that came through the area as they traveled between Winnipeg, Canada, and St. Paul. Other cultural events are presented during the year by the Crookston Community Theater, the Civic Music League Artist Series, and the University of Minnesota, Crookston.

Eliza (Liz) Weiss

Liz began her narrative by talking about her parents, stating that they came from Germany. Her mother was five years old at the time and her father was "a little older." They came over separately. Their families both settled near the town of Sabin, which is a small agricultural community a few miles east of Moorhead, Minnesota. Her parents met and married in Minnesota. Liz was born on August 21, 1906.

The family was tied to the land. Liz's parents were homesteaders, starting out with 160 acres. They began with a small house; however, the family grew. Eventually there were six boys and seven girls, and the family outgrew the house. Liz said that when she was eight, "Dad built a new house. There were four bedrooms upstairs and four rooms downstairs."

As farmers, her parents raised cows, chickens, sheep, and pigs, and grew a variety of crops. This type of farming was typical for the day, in contrast to the specialized farming of today. Over time, Liz's father bought more land. In fact, rather than asking his own wife, her father asked Liz if he should buy more land. With a smile, Liz said she used a Ouija Board, and from that, encouraged her father to buy the land.

The children also were called upon to help with the farm work. Liz remembered threshing and shocking grain in late summer. She noted that when harvest time came, neighbors helped one another. Neighbors gathered at one farm, did the harvesting, and then moved on to the next farm and so on until the area farms finished their harvesting. Then Liz remembered that potatoes were one of the main crops when she was growing up, and she joined the rest of the family in picking the potatoes. Digging the potatoes, putting them in a basket, and then dumping the basket into large gunny sacks was hard work.

Liz was never bored in her childhood years. She loved to play games, and neighbor kids often came over to play ball games. Playing cards was a favorite winter pastime. The family also had a player piano that was played for family entertainment.

However, household chores were required too, and Liz often helped do housework. She also took care of the smaller brothers and sisters. By the 1920s, Liz worked outside the house and voluntarily helped her neighbors.

The family was among the earliest in the area to have some of the newest conveniences of the time. Liz said they had their first telephone before she could remember. The first car, a Ford, was purchased when she was ten. Liz said it was nice, but "you had to be careful driving because of the roads." Electricity came into the home when she was thirteen. Liz said they had a Delco plant that produced enough electricity to light lamps in the living area. This was a primitive system for producing household electricity before major power plants came into being.

Since the family was among the earliest to have electricity in the area, neighbors often came by to socialize.

Times of rationing, such as during World War I, did not greatly affect Liz's family. The family always had enough to eat. Her mom was not only a good cook, but did canning. They always had enough sugar for making baked goods, and a large garden helped provide vegetables for canning. They churned their own butter, and wheat was taken to the mill in town to be ground into flour. Her dad made graham flour at home. This was a very self-sufficient family.

Liz was married in 1932. She and her husband established their first home in the small town of Sabin. Soon they moved to Moorhead, where her husband got a job driving a truck. He was able to keep this job throughout the Depression. In 1940 they moved to Thief River Falls, and in 1943 they moved to Crookston.

Liz also worked during this time. She got a job candling eggs at a company called Peterson-Bidekk in Thief River Falls. Candling involves holding an egg to a light to see if the egg is fertilized and if it is fresh. She worked there for thirty years. This first marriage ended in 1959 when her husband, a diabetic, died. Liz enjoyed farm life. However, like most other wives of the time, she followed her husband when they married. Since he was a truck driver, and since it was the Great Depression, this took them to Moorhead. A transfer took them to Thief River Falls. When the company went out of business, the move to Crookston resulted.

Life must go on. Liz got a job as a second cook at the country club in Crookston. She continued this work until retirement. She remarried in 1964. Her second husband, who worked for the city, died in 1998.

At the time of the interview, Liz believed that having the University of Minnesota, Crookston, had changed the town; she said there were more young people around the town. She was proud that two grandsons attended the university and a great grandson started in the fall of 2002.

Life is still full, though sometimes confusing. Two daughters live nearby, so there is much opportunity to talk and visit. Liz still does volunteer work, such as sewing for the hospital and fixing "trauma bears" at the Senior Center. Besides that, there are the regular lunches and card games at the center. With all this going on, Liz does not have to worry too much about the latest technology such as computers and cell phones. She said, "A lot of times I wonder just what is what." Liz does not have any desire to learn about the new technology.

Finally, Liz mentioned that her parents' house was purchased in 2002 and moved a few miles northwest to the town of Perly. She said the house still looked pretty good, and the land on which the house originally stood was still in the family and was being farmed.

Josephine (Jo) Dewhurst

Jo's parents came from Illinois. They first moved to the Williston area of North Dakota where they made a homestead claim, but it failed and several moves followed. They moved back to Illinois, then again to North Dakota. From there it was south to Florida, and finally back to North Dakota. For most of this early time, her father was a farmer. He later became a cattle buyer. Jo's first memories included the time that the family lived in Florida. Josephine Trump was born on November 6, 1913, during the family's second stay in North Dakota.

The family had four children, two girls and two boys. Jo remembered always having enough food to eat as a child. This was mainly due to a large garden that her parents kept and to the fine cooking of her mother. Jo enjoyed playing cards as a child. Her father would not allow the children to play cards with a full deck, fearing the children might play poker, and he did not think it was an appropriate game for children. However, the children were allowed to play games such as Rook, French, and other card games that did not require the use of face cards.

Jo felt that her family, though not rich, was not really poor. Food was plentiful. She said the family had a telephone from as far back as she could remember. Their home did not have electricity or indoor plumbing, which was common in rural areas at that time. She pointed out that her family was the first to pay income taxes in Buxton, North Dakota.

Education was a little different during the first third of the twentieth century when Jo graduated from Buxton High School. In those days, a person could accelerate learning and finish school two or three years early. She did that and graduated after attending elementary and secondary schools for nine years. Her twin brother graduated three years later.

One story from this period was an incident that occurred on the way home from school one day. A horse and buggy was their method of transportation. As they were going home, the horse died. Imagine walking home and telling your parents that the horse died!

Jo went to Mayville College after high school. It was there that she earned a certificate to teach school. She began teaching at the age of seventeen in a one-room school near Cummings, North Dakota. Jo started teaching without a license because, at seventeen, she was too young to have a license. Because of her November birth date, the superintendent let her teach anyway. She taught for four years to students from first through eighth grade. She did everything from building the fire to scrubbing the floor in the school house, which did not have electricity or indoor plumbing—definitely bare bones!

After quitting teaching in 1935, Jo and four teacher friends left in her Jewett car for the state of Washington. When asked why she went to Washington, Jo replied, "Oh, for the fun of it." Jo noted that she thought she would teach again, but she never did. She stayed in Washington until January of 1936. During her time there, she did housework, bakery work, and worked in a confectionary store. Jo sold her car for twenty-five dollars before she left Washington. The day before she left, someone stole the money out of her purse. Jo was sure it was the man that bought the car.

California was to be the next stop. However, without the twenty-five dollars, Jo was in a fix as to how to get there. She read an ad in the newspaper that asked for riders to go to California, and she answered the ad. The man told her he was going to leave the next morning. When he arrived, he had two other men in the car with him. Jo was a bit surprised, but noting that "It was a long time ago and things are different now," she decided to go along with them. They ended up driving straight through to Los Angeles.

Jo was dropped off at the door of a girlfriend who was earning money by doing housework, and the friend helped her. The friend snuck her into another house in which she was doing housework, and she gave Jo her paycheck. Jo recalled how she had to sneak out of the house early in the morning before the family awoke, and she walked about two miles to a bank to cash the check. "Everything got straightened out," and she got a job as a maid.

At this point, Jo mentioned that during her time in Washington she lived in Yakima. She had a boyfriend in Yakima, and they became engaged to be married. A breakup resulted instead. However, Jo found out she was pregnant, and she knew that she would have the baby and adopt it out. She and two friends of hers took a roadster car and went to Helena, Montana, where she had her baby. The baby was adopted out. Her daughter found Jo twenty-five years later. Since her daughter lives in Oregon and Arizona, they do not see each other very often but do stay in touch. Jo said, "We are so much alike, its pathetic." They are very close.

The next stage in Jo's life came when she moved from Helena back to the state of Washington. She had a sister who lived in South Bend, Washington, and Jo went out to visit her. She ended up staying for two years. During her time there, she met her future husband. He had come down from Canada to work in a lumber mill. Jo and her husband Elwood were married in 1937. The young couple decided that there was no future in the lumber mill, so they moved to Spokane where her husband took a job in an electric power plant. They lived there until 1954. During this period of time, they adopted two children. A boy, Ross, was adopted in 1943, and Rita was adopted in 1947. Both children were adopted as infants. Rita, who also found her biological mother, lives in the Crookston area. Ross just returned to the United States after spending three years working in China.

A move in 1954 brought the family to North Dakota near the Minnesota border. Elwood found a job at a Crystal Sugar plant where he worked until he retired in about 1973. When they adopted the children, Jo became a homemaker. She remained a homemaker from then on. Jo said that she never went back to teaching. She added, "I wouldn't now. I would rather scrub floors."

During their later years, Jo and her husband often took winter trips to Texas to visit their son, and to Mesa, Arizona, to visit their daughter. Her husband died in 1997 and a "very good marriage" of sixty years ended. Jo always said that she would never stay in their house alone. After a year and a half, she moved into an apartment, and in our last conversation said she loved it.

Jo was involved in several hobbies and other activities over the years. One hobby was making pine needle baskets. She was a long time member of the Eastern Star, which is associated with the Masons. Her favorite pastime is playing cards. She said she plays as often as she can.

Jo collected antiques during the last twenty years of her marriage. She decided to auction off the collection before moving into the apartment. She felt that she received good value for each of the pieces she sold. Jo noted that a North Dakota pottery vase sold for $900. She also mentioned that a round oak pedestal table sold for $900 and then the auctioneer sold each leaf separately for fifty dollars a piece! The one antique piece she kept was a spool cabinet.

Jo has remained active over the last several years. She did oil painting for fifteen years before giving it up, saying, "I didn't want to become another Grandma Moses." She maintains the motivation and willingness to always try something new.

Henry Gredvig

Henry began his story by talking about his paternal grand-parents and their relatives. They came to the United States from Telemark, Norway. They first settled in Iowa, and moved from there to southern Minnesota. When the Red River Valley in northwestern Minnesota opened up, a brother of one of his grandparents decided to start a farm near Fisher, Minnesota, about nine miles west of Crookston. However, it was a flat, wet prairie, and the land could not be worked with the oxen. A move back to southern Minnesota (near Albert Lea) followed. Henry gave a one-word reason for this movement: "Wander-lust," the idea that life always looks better elsewhere.

Finally, one brother from Henry's father's side moved to Fertile, Minnesota, located about twenty miles southeast of

Crookston in the Red River Valley. This was an area family members had tried previously, an area near the old ox cart trail that had been used by fur traders. Instead of being located on the flood plain of the river valley, Fertile was located on a ridge above what once was part of ancient Lake Aggasiz. The location included sandier soil and was not subject to flooding like the flood plain. This area also provided wood for fires and for fixing carts. Around 1880, the brother of Henry's grandfather urged other family members to come to Fertile. His grandfather settled south of Fertile. The family was among the first immigrants in the area.

Henry's maternal grandmother's family came from Bergen, Norway. His maternal grandfather first built a dugout along the river bank to use as a temporary house while they cut logs and built a permanent house. Henry pointed out that many Norwegians settled in the Fertile area. Family members helped settle the first township of Fertile. To top it off, his grandfather founded the first Norwegian Lutheran Church in the area.

Henry's family was typical of the time. His father was a farmer and ran a grist mill and a dairy. Henry's family growing up included six boys and six girls. Henry was the third oldest of the boys. He was born on November 12, 1918. He has one living sister who resides in Seattle, Washington, and two brothers who are living in the Fertile area.

Henry had several memories of his early life. For one thing, the family had a telephone for as long as he could remember. Telephone calls to each house had a different number and/or pattern of rings. The telephone in their house had three rings. The house was built with a Delco unit which generated some electricity. In about 1927, the house was rewired and hooked to a transformer, which brought neighbors to visit on many occasions.

His dad had cars during Henry's youth. The first car Henry remembered was a Model T Ford. Then, in the town of Mahnomen about fifty-three miles southeast of Crookston, his father traded the Model T for a Studebaker. It got stuck three times on their way home from buying it. This was because the car was built lower to the ground, which was a problem when traveling on the rutted rural roads of the time. In addition, the Studebaker Company used a 1929 transmission in the 1930 model, and it was not reliable. They had to carry a spare axle with them due to the problems.

Another memory for Henry was learning to swim in the local mill pond. He used to enjoy jumping in the mill pond after harvesting. It was a good way to wash off the dust and grime.

Speaking of driving, Henry learned to drive on the farm. This, of course, replaced the usual method of travel by horses. His first car was a Model A, which he drove almost to the time he was drafted into the military.

Being a farm family during the Great Depression helped. They milked and processed cows. Henry mentioned that milk sold for seven cents a quart in those days. Family members delivered the milk door-to-door. Henry also was involved in 4H. He raised sheep and hogs for 4H projects. Having a farm meant the family always seemed to have enough food.

Henry completed his schooling during this period. He graduated from high school in 1936 and went to work helping to run the family's mill for three years.

World War II brought the depression to an end and signaled major changes for the family. Five of the boys were drafted. Without the necessary help to keep things going, his father sold the mill which he had bought in 1918. His father also sold the dairy and basically retired.

Henry's military experience was interesting. He received his basic training in Rockford, Illinois. He took training in animal husbandry, which he hoped he could use in farming after getting out of the service. From there, he was assigned to work with pack mules for moving artillery and other equipment in the mountains of Colorado. He spent his first winter in Leadville, Colorado. Henry expected that his overseas assignment would be in some place like Norway in Europe. However, life always seems to have unexpected twists. The movement of artillery became mechanized, so he became an ambulance driver and medical technician.

Instead of being sent to Europe, Henry was stationed in the Pacific. His first assignment was in Australia, where he drove military personnel who needed to be transported to the hospital. He worked at this job while United States forces continued the island-hopping strategy in the Pacific. Henry's travels during this time took him to New Guinea, the Admiralty Islands northeast of New Guinea, and Leyte in the Philippines. It was on Leyte that Henry saw General Douglas MacArthur come ashore when he returned to the Philippines as he had promised. Finally it was on to Luzon until the Japanese were pushed out of Manila.

Henry talked about one specific incident on the Admiralty Islands. The men had to dig fox holes or dugouts near their tents or hammocks. During attacks, they were supposed to leave the tent for the dugout. One day, a fellow not far from Henry decided that he was not going to get out of his hammock. A Japanese bomb exploded in his dugout. The soldier was wounded by shrapnel but probably would have been killed if he had gone into his dugout. Maybe that soldier had a premonition that day which ended up saving his life.

As the war neared the end, Henry had another historic experience. He stayed in the Philippines for a while. Then his company was sent to Japan, and his ship was in Tokyo Harbor on the day that the Japanese signed the surrender on the USS Missouri. Henry went on to spend a month in Japan. He described it as "all burned up . . . It looked very tough in there."

The road back to civilian life started with a trip on a liberty ship to Australia. He had served a total of about thirty months. As he looked back on the war years, Henry remembered that Australia was the only nice place. Most of the time they had to sleep in dugouts. Weather was hot and wet, especially in Leyte. "You couldn't get around because of the mud," he said. "Everything got wet and moldy." To avoid trench foot, he tried to wear dry socks as much as possible. Many others were not as successful and ended up with severe foot problems. Boots had to be kept under netting at night to keep the bugs out of them.

With the war over, Henry finally got his discharge from the army and life really changed. By the time he arrived home in November, his two younger brothers had already come home and were working on the family farm. On December 31, 1945, Henry married a young lady named Mernie. She and Henry had grown up together. She, too, grew up on a farm near the Gredvig family farm. She became a nurse during the war; she had taken nurses training and tried to enlist in the WAVES (Women's Reserve of the United States Naval Reserve), but was not accepted. She returned home and became a nurse in Crookston and remained in the profession for forty years.

Henry wanted to get on with his life. He and Mernie went to Chicago so Henry could learn a trade. He used the GI bill to study refrigeration and electricity. Mernie worked in a Chicago hospital while Henry went to school. Soon the Crookston hospital wanted Mernie to come back. To encourage the couple to move back, the woman in charge of the hospital talked to a friend in the appliance business in Crookston, who hired Henry to work for him. So the couple moved back home to Crookston. Henry held that job for eight years until his boss died suddenly from a heart attack.

Henry did not have enough money to buy the business, so he had to look for other work. The first thing he tried was selling insurance, but said, "That wasn't any fun." Then the new sheriff in the area asked Henry if he wanted to work as a deputy. He did that job for two years, but did not like the fact that most of the work was done during the weekends. Henry's next job was as a juvenile probation officer. "That was about as bad as being a deputy sheriff," he said. It lasted two years. Nevertheless, it was interesting.

The next job turned out to be his vocation for twenty-five years. In 1959, the county assessor was retiring and was looking for someone to take his place. He thought Henry would do a good job, so talked him into applying. As county assessor, he had jurisdiction over forty nine townships and fifteen villages and cities. The job of the county assessor was to supervise the local assessors throughout the county. A high point of Henry's career was being elected President of the State Assessors in the 1960s. He served a two-year term. This required trips to cities in different parts of the state to attend meetings. Henry retired in 1984.

Henry did not mention farming during the account of his work life. Did he not want to be a farmer? He said, "No, I thought I would farm." As a matter of fact he did buy a 177 acre farm that had a lake on it. He and his wife farmed on the weekends. His nephew rented the land and did most of the farming. Henry had planned on building a retirement home out there, but this plan was not fulfilled. The property was eventually sold. First he sold five acres to his niece. Then he sold the rest of the land to his brother, who planned to give it to his daughter (the niece who had purchased the five acres earlier) in the future.

Over the years, his life stayed full in many ways. Henry talked about his oldest granddaughter who was a graduate of Concordia College. Henry described his wife as a "true Norwegian" because she could speak and sing Norwegian. Mernie wanted to pass on the Norse heritage to the grandchildren. She asked the grandchildren if they wanted to take lessons in Norwegian at a camp near Bemidji. The oldest one got connected to Concordia College through this camp. In the process, she went to Norway for a year and received college credit for this. So the heritage has been passed on, at least to the eldest granddaughter.

Henry got involved with the Polk County Museum in Crookston. He was president of the museum for ten years. The museum closes down each year after the town's fall festival. The museum includes a big ox cart stand which celebrates the importance of the ox cart trail through the area. One building is full of tractors and farm machinery made in Minnesota.

Another building is filled with retired fire trucks from the county. Also, there is a schoolhouse which is open to classes in the fall and spring. It is used for showing how rural education was conducted in the late 1800s and early 1900s. They also have a log house to show people how settlers used to live. There was a "little house" owned by a man that lived on the nearby prairie. Since there weren't any trees, he had lumber hauled in to make the house. The man raised four children in that house.

Another item of interest in the museum include a communications booth with a television from 1945.

Mernie died in 1999, and life changed. Henry sold the house and moved into an apartment in Crookston. His daughter lived in Minneapolis and got an apartment for him in the city, where he spends his winters. Henry suffered two strokes, which affected his speech and ability to walk for a time. Perseverance helped him make almost a complete recovery. One thing that did not change was the fact that this active man still enjoys driving a car as confirmed by our most recent conversation.

Gladys Peterson

The story of Gladys Peterson started out similarly to others who live in the Crookston area. She began by talking about her grandparents who came from Norway because of the slim economic conditions in the home country. In Norway, tradition meant that farms were split among the children; this eventually left too little land to make a living. Thus, it was on to the land of opportunity!

Gladys's parents found it difficult to make a living. Success required hard work and a few moves between North Dakota and Minnesota. First, her parents filed to homestead land in western North Dakota. They joined her dad's sister who had settled near the town of Arnegard. Gladys said the agreement was that if they lived on and worked the land for eighteen months, it would become theirs. After facing difficult conditions in North Dakota, her parents moved to Minnesota to earn money. Her dad worked until he had enough money to buy needed farm machinery and cows. Then it was back to North Dakota. Gladys was born on December 27, 1909, and lived in North Dakota until she was ten. It was then that the parents returned to Minnesota. They bought land near Fisher, Minnesota and started farming again.

Gladys had some good memories of her early life. She said the family house did not have plumbing or electricity, which was pretty common for the early 1900s. Since the family farmed, she recounted how they did not have to buy many staples. Sugar, flour, and salt were among the food staples bought at the store. Memories of fruit were clear in Gladys's mind. Common fruits of today, like apples and oranges, were not common around her house. The family did have some apples during winter months, and the children often got an orange for Christmas. But wild plums and rhubarb were plentiful. She remembered picking wild plums in the fall during her time in North Dakota. The plums were most often turned into sauces and jelly. One food she remembered not liking was oatmeal. Another memory of her early life involved an uncle who was in World War I. Gladys mentioned that he often wrote letters to the family, and she wrote back.

As the 1920s rolled by, Gladys noticed some of the cultural changes that were taking place. This was the period of Prohibition. Nevertheless some family members, as well as others in the area, were involved in making moonshine. Gladys thought that her father and uncle knew about the moonshining but never told her mother because she did not approve of such activity. Gladys said a lot of the liquor made in the Crookston area ended up in East Grand Forks, which became notorious for its illegal bars. She also mentioned that styles for women changed. It was a time of short skirts and bobbed (short) hair. Gladys said her mother allowed her to wear skirts and dresses that were a little shorter than what had been worn earlier. However, she could not wear the really short skirts. On the other hand, her mother did not care if she wore her hair short since it seemed more practical.

The 1920s marked growth into adulthood. Gladys graduated from high school in Fisher in 1926. She went on to complete a one year teacher-training program in Crookston. She then taught for six years in area schools. These were the typical one-room rural schools, which did not have plumbing or electricity. The teacher taught grades one through eight. In many ways, the teaching was difficult because of all the lessons that had to be prepared. Yet one thing made it easier—the children often worked to teach each other.

As the 1930s rolled around, the Great Depression hit, and times became harder. Gladys was earning ninety dollars per month as a teacher in the early 1930s. In 1933, she married Vincent Peterson. Wages fell in 1934 and in 1935, but Vincent was a farmer, which helped in terms of putting food on the table. However, opportunities for women were minimal. Jobs were not available for women unless there were dire circumstances. With little money, they rented the land they farmed and borrowed machinery from Vincent's father. For a while, they would take a case of eggs to town, and the money they made from the eggs was used to buy their groceries and gas for the car. At that time, eggs sold for twelve cents a dozen, and they did this on a weekly basis. The money they earned had to be applied to groceries first. At times, it meant they might have only about a dollar left to buy gas.

During the Depression, many farms faced foreclosure, and many farms were taken over by the state for back taxes. Although the owners were given a certain amount of time to buy the farms back, many could not afford to do so. That meant some farms were available for purchase in the Crookston area. Also a New Deal program called the Farm Security Administration was started. This program helped the Petersons buy 240 acres for a little over $8,500; they were not even required to make a down payment or put up collateral.

Two sons were born during the Depression. They came into the world only thirteen months apart in 1937 and 1938. Her husband was against the sons becoming farmers, because he felt it was awfully hard work. Nevertheless, they both took agricultural programs in college and went on to become farmers in the area.

By the early 1940s, more changes took place. Plumbing was eventually installed in the house. They had a very good well on the land, and they pumped the well water into the house with a gasoline engine. The water was pumped through pipes into a huge tank in the basement. Pressure was then used to push the water up to the bathroom on the second floor. Gladys said of the indoor plumbing, "That was wonderful." Electricity followed in 1947 through the Rural Farm Electric Cooperative. Before that, the family did not have the convenience of electricity.

At the same time, World War II was raging in Europe and the Pacific. Gladys said her husband served on a rationing board for farm equipment. She mentioned that two big problems facing farmers at the time were shortages of tires and gas. This was especially important for the farmers who had the newer tractors with rubber wheels, which were replacing the slower ones that had steel wheels. However, people did not suffer a great deal in the overall scheme of things. She mentioned that the family was lucky because neither her husband nor her children were involved in war. Her husband had been too young for World War I and too old for World War II. Their sons were in the National Guard, but again, they were too young for Korea and not needed in Vietnam.

Gladys had a couple of interesting observations as she looked back over the last few years of the twentieth century. She was not surprised by the fall of Communism saying, "I never thought it would succeed." She also felt the space race was interesting and surprising. When she was in school, she thought things such as a man walking on the moon was "another world." Gladys did not think it could ever happen. She felt that people in the Crookston area have not changed much over the years. Many have northern European ancestry. Gladys said the area was stable with a good support system.

At the time of the interview, Gladys was still going strong. She said she read a lot. In addition, she loved to do volunteer work such as sewing caps and mittens for poor people. It was something she did for several years. Then there were visits to sick people. Gladys said the people really appreciated the visits, and it made her feel that she was still good for something. Attending activities at the Senior Center, such as the lunches, was another important element in her life. All of this added up to a pretty active lifestyle for a person who truly enjoyed living in a rural community like Crookston.

I returned to Crookston almost a year after my first visit and had a nice talk with Gladys. She passed away about a month after that last conversation. She left me with the lasting impression of being very kind and generous.

Georgine Arness

Ms. Arness conducted a fantastic picture tour through her apartment in Crookston. Items such as photos, news articles, and certificates adorned all the walls in the apartment. It was apparent from the beginning that she had great pride in her family. Most of the interview revolved around the work and accomplishments of her family.

Georgine's story began with her great grandfather Gunder G. Dale. Mr. Dale was an immigrant from Norway who settled in Minnesota. He entered the army during the Civil War, where he served in Company C, 2nd Minnesota Regiment, from May of 1864 to June of 1865. Of 1,100 in the regiment, he was among only seventy that returned.

Georgine then began talking about her father Lewis Wehus. He too served in the military. During World War I he fought in the Meuse-Argonne Forest with the 33rd Division. According to Georgine, he saw the first allied airplane shot down in Germany. She noted that during the war, a ship he was on was torpedoed. After the war, Mr. Wehus spent a year in Germany doing guard duty.

She had a farm background and remembered picking potatoes with her aunt. Georgine said, "Boy, that was work!" She talked about bending over all day picking three hundred bushels of potatoes that sold for ten cents a bushel. The farm produce gave them most of their food.

Georgine also remembered studying by kerosene lamp because her family did not have electricity in their home. They did not have indoor plumbing, so water had to be carried in from the well, and the bathroom was an outhouse. She mentioned that the well was also used as a refrigerator to keep fresh goods cool. Georgine mentioned that the family did not even have a telephone. Horses were used to get to school; in the winter, the horses pulled a sleigh and the children had straw and foot warmers to keep warm.

Being poor contributed to one of the few regrets that Georgine had. She had been a good student and graduated third in her class at Climax. However, because the family did not have enough money, she could not go to college.

Georgine met her husband Alton in high school. They knew each other even though they did not go to the same schools. She noted that Alton went through grade eight in a school across from the family farm and skipped two grades on the way to graduating from high school. They even went to the prom together. Her future husband graduated from the Northwest School in Crookston that later became the University of Minnesota at Crookston.

Georgine talked a bit about their honeymoon. They borrowed Alton's father's car and went to Detroit Lakes for three days, which is roughly ninety miles south of Crookston. The newlyweds had sixty dollars in their pockets. After paying for food and lodging, they had enough money left over to buy Georgine a sweater and a pair of shoes. How times have changed!

The early years of their marriage were not marked by convenience. Alton did not have a car when they were first married; he had to borrow his father's car to get around. They also did not have their own house. They lived with Alton's parents on the Arness family farm for the first year. Then Georgine and Alton made an apartment out of the upper floor and lived there for six years. After that, his folks moved into town, and the younger Arness couple took over the house and farm.

The couple spent their whole married life on the farm. It was homesteaded property, and they were the third generation to live on that farm. Alton's grandfather was the first to homestead and live on the land. The house was built in 1914 for $1,500. When she left, the house was still in excellent condition.

Georgine also had three brothers who were in the military during World War II. One was a technical sergeant in the Air Force. He ended up serving for over twenty years. A high point of his career was being on a mission in 1958 that found the ship, Lady Be Good, which went down in 1943. A second brother, Lawrence, served in the United States Navy. He took part in eight invasions in the Pacific during the War. He too made the military a career. The youngest brother, Wallace, was in the paratroopers. He did not take part in fighting during the war, but was part of the occupation forces in Japan after the war ended.

Alton was a "car nut." He restored a 1957 Ford with a retractable hard top and also restored a 1962 Thunderbird. Both were sold after his death. The 1957 Ford was bought by an acquaintance in California and the Thunderbird was purchased by a local Crookston area resident.

Georgine's sister died at the age of twenty-nine and left two children behind. Georgine and her husband took them in when they were five and six years old. They cared for the children for two and a half years until their father remarried and took them back.

Son Craig is a source of great pride to Georgine. He was involved in a variety of activities as a youth. He practiced tap dancing for five years and played the trumpet, piano, and snare drum. Both parents encouraged his efforts.

Craig went to Carlton College for his undergraduate degree and Yale for his masters degree. During his time at Carlton, he went to Russia on a study tour. During the tour, he went to Czechoslovakia and witnessed the Russian invasion which crushed the Czech democratic movement that took place in 1968.

Craig worked for the United Nations for four years. Then he started working as a diplomat. Working in the State Department had been a dream of his since he was in fourth grade. It was this work that took him to several countries around the world. The fact that Craig worked in different parts of the world led to several exotic trips for Georgine and Alton.

As noted, the Arness family did a lot of traveling over the years. They spent a month in India visiting their son. Georgine and Alton rode elephants, saw the Taj Mahal, and basically visited the country from north to south. Craig spent two and a half years in India and married an Indian woman. She went to college in the United States, but she and Craig met in India. She still works as a diplomat.

Another trip took Georgine and Alton to Thailand and then to Nepal. Other countries they visited included Pakistan and Russia. She showed off a variety of treasured gifts and purchases from their travels. In addition to all these trips was a Caribbean cruise and several other trips within the United States and Canada.

Alton was a farmer who loved musical activities. He was a meticulous farmer. One of the important crops on the farm was sugar beets. Alton retired from farming in 1985, and the family auctioned off the farm equipment. He was good at playing the piano, organ, trumpet, and saxophone. Besides these talents, he loved to dance and was very good at it. Dancing appeared to be a recreational highlight for many years.

Alton died of lung cancer in March of 1998. Four months later, Georgine sold the farm and moved into an apartment in Crookston. Looking back, she described him as "personality plus." The loss of her husband of fifty-five years was difficult for Georgine. The loss was made more difficult with the breakup of the house they had shared for so many years. Georgine did not want to stay in a big house by herself and could not take care of the large yard. She had to reduce the amount of possessions from the four-story home in order to move into a one-bedroom apartment. Deciding what to keep and what to sell or give away was hard. Nevertheless, she completed the task and is now very happy in the apartment. Georgine stated, "I will stay here until I kick off."

The apartment has much more than the wall hangings and possessions from trips. Georgine has about 130 ceramic figures that she made herself. They are found throughout the apartment. In addition, she has several silk flower arrangements decorating the apartment.

She expressed great pride in her two granddaughters. Both were in college at the time of our interview. One was studying to be a doctor and the other a lawyer. Both had varied talents in the arts. The oldest had the privilege of playing the flute at the White House. Both were described as excellent students.

Georgine and Alton were very active in retirement. They received several awards for their volunteer work in the community. One award she received for volunteering was Outstanding Woman of Polk County. Among their activities was being in a band at the Golden Link Senior Center. Georgine was also responsible for doing the decorating for special events and seasons at the center. She said, "I love doing it."

The last thing Georgine talked about was her battle with cancer. She developed breast cancer in 2000. She found the lumps herself and had a mastectomy in 2000 and had twenty-four lymph nodes removed. A year later, cancer recurred, this time in her shoulder. She took radiation treatment and the cancer disappeared. She described herself as cancer free at the time of our first interview. Her goal in the fall of 2002 was to make her granddaughter's graduation in May 2003, and she did! Georgine came across as very optimistic and spirited.

Victoria (Vicki) Irwin

Vicki described her parents as " hard working, honest, and good Christians." Both parents grew up in southern Minnesota. Her father was Ernest G. Frank. Besides being a dedicated farmer, she said her father played the banjo and the harmonica and could dance the jig. She added that her mother, Emma, did a lot of canning and was a very good cook. She was especially famous for her chocolate cake.

Each parent had relatives living in northwestern Minnesota. They often urged Ernest and Emma to come north to settle. Daughter Vicki was born on July 27, 1915. When she was two and a half months old, her parents decided to make the move. Her mother, sister Louella, and Vicki came north by passenger train. Her dad and uncle came by freight train. The two men brought the stock and all the other belongings with them. The trip was hard—it took two and a half days. Meanwhile, Vicki, her sister, and her mother reached their destination and were waiting. One crop her father brought north was potatoes. However, when he found out how good the northern potatoes tasted, he fed his to the hogs.

There would eventually be three brothers and two sisters in this close-knit farm family. Vicki described herself as a tomboy who loved to work with her father. She said he was fun to be with and she liked to be a gofer for him. Vicki said that with all those kids, they had to help their dad. The children regularly did chores, such as milking the cows before school and cleaning the cream separator. Chores were not only expected of the children, but they were to be done without complaint. Vicki was very thankful that her father taught her the importance of work.

Their farm was not specialized. Besides dairy cows, the family raised chickens, pigs, and turkeys. Vicki noted that the turkeys were not very bright. When it rained, they just stood outside getting wet. Family members had to bring them in the house, put them in boxes by the stove and dry them off. Her mother kept a large garden and canned several types of produce from the garden. Between the garden vegetables and the meat they processed, there was always enough to eat.

Vicki related several tidbits about her economically poor childhood. She mentioned that they had neither plumbing nor electricity in their house. Most evening chores and studies were done by kerosene lamps. Her mother made and packed their school lunches in two gallon syrup pails. After being emptied of syrup, the pails were used for storing lard and for lunches. One day she was in a rush to get to school and picked up her lunch pail where she thought it had been placed. Needless to say, she got the wrong pail—she took a pail filled with lard! What a big surprise! Then Vicki talked about how she loved to get to school early. Instead of taking the horse-drawn wagon, she and a brother usually ran to school to get there more quickly. Being a tomboy, she loved to play ball with the boys.

Vicki had two dress outfits for school that had to make do. Otherwise, she wore overalls on the farm. Her mother made clothes out of old flour sacks and had to boil them to get the print out. One day, Vicki was playing ball with some other children and a boy said, "Hey Vicki, I see the Gold Medal" (the label from the flour sack). Another time, her mother hired a woman to sew clothes for the children. The woman made Vicki a beautiful gingham dress with blue and white dots and trimmed in red. When the dress was about done, she had to try it on for size. Although her mother told her to take it off before going out to milk the cows, Vicki did not obey. She went right out to the barn, grabbed a one legged stool, and started milking. The cow kicked at something that sent Vicki sprawling on the barn floor, then it stood on her new dress. She yelled for help until her mother came, and her mother was not very happy to see the mess made of the new dress.

Vicki also told a story about working the beet fields when at about age fourteen or fifteen. Vicki and the other children worked for a farmer to earn money for school clothes. After he cultivated, the children went into the field to thin the beets. This meant crawling along the ground and holding on to a beet while picking away other beets growing around it. This was very hard on the hands and knees. In the fall the children helped pick the beets. The farmer went ahead and loosened the plants. Then the children picked the beets, hit them together to knock off the dirt, and later cut off the green sprouts. Vicki said their goal was to earn a dollar each per day.

The children put their money in the Eldred Bank to use for school clothes. They ordered their clothes from a catalog in those days. Unfortunately, the effects of the Great Depression took its toll on the little bank in Eldred and it went under. Luckily, the banker was a family friend, and he made sure the children received their hard earned money. When the clothes arrived, they were able to pay.

The town of Eldred had the first consolidated school in the northwestern part of the state. Vicki said with glee that "it had everything." It had separate bathrooms for boys and girls. It had manual training (industrial arts), sewing, cooking, and other subjects. The school house had "all the grades," one through twelve. Four grades were taught in a single room; the teacher had students sit around her on stools for reading or discussion. This was the only school that Vicki attended. Though doing well in school, she got caught up in the work around the farm and did not graduate.

Vicki's teenage life was busy. Besides the love of playing softball, she took part in school plays and 4H. She also followed her father's interest in the playing of horseshoes.

Another story dealt with the building of a church in Eldred in 1930. The elevator man became critically ill; on his death bed, he asked the minister to build a church in the town. The townspeople really did not have any money, but the people got together and bought the carpenter a suit of clothes when it was finished. She said the dedication of the church made her feel proud. The church was right next to the school. In addition, the ball field was just across the road. The minister would often go over to the ball field after Sunday service and umpire a ball game.

During the period of Prohibition, farmers in the area made liquor and soft drinks. Vicki's father made beer, but drank it only occasionally. What she did remember with a relish was that her mother made root beer. Vicki said, "That was so good." It was a real treat, especially when there was not much money to buy goods.

As noted earlier, most purchases in the 1920s and 1930s were catalog orders. That does not mean they bought things regularly, but when they did, it was through a catalog. Vicki remembered that they bought their first radio in the 1920s, and their first phonograph came in the 1930s.

In another story from about that time, Vicki mentioned that they had a lot of cattle on the farm and the family produced quite a bit of skim milk. One day a farmer friend was plowing in a nearby field. At the end of the day, he asked if he could keep his horses in their barn. Her family fed the horses skim milk and the horses loved it!

Although it was the time of the Great Depression and the family was poor, they did not lack for food. They churned butter and had all the milk and cream and poultry they wanted. Also, they butchered livestock one week a year. She mentioned that they might butcher one head of beef and five hogs in a week. Aside from the different cuts of meat, they made sausage and smoked their own bacon and ham. Besides that, she described her mother as the "best canner." According to Vicki, "We had so much to eat we did not suffer at all." The only things they bought were sugar and flour.

One of the problems with farms were the wild critters in the area. The family often fed skim milk to the chickens. One day, some baby skunks got into the chicken coop to drink the milk. Unfortunately, they could not have the skunks staying around their chickens, so her father had to kill them. Then the mother skunk showed up. He had to dispatch her too.

Another fact of farm life was the well. The children had to haul water from the well to the house and to the barn for the animals. This was hard work. The way some of the bigger animals could drink meant that several trips had to be made to the well daily.

On June 30, 1937, she married Andy Dragseth. They had known each other for a long time, as they attended the same church. They had three children. Vickie called them a treasure to her. She described her husband as a "good farmer" who owned his own farm. Thus, farming was the family occupation when they were married. Andy was very trustworthy and clean. He kept his farm in good repair. His trustworthiness led to bartering or trading as a way of doing business. So instead of using precious money to buy farm equipment, he got it through trades. But Andy was not just a farmer. Andy's father had been a mailman and as his father aged, Andy helped deliver the mail.

Farming during the first half of the twentieth century was more diversified than it is today. Vicki recounted how her husband was urged to put a lot of acreage into sugar beets. At first, they could not make money at it, and debts mounted. Finally, however, the prices turned around and they started making a profit.

Improvements continued in the 1940s. Andy's work as a farmer meant deferral from the military, and he did not serve in World War II. The couple had three young children to raise. Nevertheless, improved farm prices meant that home life became a little easier. They built a new home which had two bathrooms. What an improvement to go from an outhouse to two indoor bathrooms! The family farm continued to prosper during the 1950s.

Major change took place in the 1960s. Andy died in 1966. By the time of his death, son Allan was old enough to take over the work of the farm. Vicki described Allan as smart and creative. He went to agricultural school (now the University of Minnesota at Crookston) because he always wanted to be a farmer. Besides Alan, the other two children are Jane and Judy, with Judy being the older. Both live nearby, have families, and have successful careers.

In 1973, Vicki married George Irwin. He ran the Farmers Union Elevator in Eldred and also helped out on the farm. She described him as a very good man, but he passed away from cancer in 1990.

Although Vicki was facing some physical challenges at the time of the interview, she recounted a continuing active lifestyle. Osteoporosis limited her physical activity and sapped her strength. It meant she had to quit driving in 2001. It also helped lead to the move to an assisted living apartment in the spring of 2002. The move made life a little bit easier. Still, she was able to rattle off several activities that she was doing. She was a member of the local Hospital Guild. As secretary, she was in charge of planning programs. She also was a member of a homemakers group. In addition, she was a member of the

Elder Ladies Aide that did charitable projects. Moreover, she was associated with the Polk County Museum. Vicki was an active member of the Golden Link Senior Center. She was a member of the birthday club and announcer for the senior center band. She was not done yet. She said she was a member of the Crookston Garden Club. Last but not least, she announced community activities on a local radio station. The sparkle in her eyes showed that she enjoyed all of these activities and enjoyed life.

Western Minnesota

Morris

Downtown Morris

Morris represents the economic and cultural nature of western Minnesota.

This is a pleasant city located about one hundred sixty-five miles northwest of Minneapolis-St. Paul. It is the county seat of Stevens County and boasts a population of 5,453. The *Morris Area Centennial Historical Album 1871-1971* was used to provide the following information.

This area of western Minnesota was originally occupied by the Dakota and Ojibway nations. The Dakota lived west of the Pomme de Terre River and the Ojibway to the east of the river. The United States Government obtained the land that became known as Stevens County in 1851 from the treaty of the Traverse de Sioux.

The first permanent settlers arrived in 1866. The community was named Scandia and later became known as Framnas Township. The first settlers were Scandinavian families, and their shelters were dugouts and shanties made from brush and sod. Some even lived out of their wagons for a time. Permanent shelters followed as the families became more established.

Morris itself was founded in 1871. It was named after Charles F. Morris who was the chief engineer of the St. Paul and Pacific Railroad. The town was built to accommodate the railroad construction workers. The town became incorporated in 1878, and at that point, a municipal government was set up that helped bring an orderliness to the area. The railroad helped the city grow and thrive throughout the last part of the nineteenth and all of the twentieth century.

Agriculture also developed in the area with 160 acre homesteads being common. Such farms were the backbone of agriculture in the area. Wheat was the dominant crop during the early 1900s. Farming became more diversified as the twentieth century progressed.

Today, Morris is known as an agricultural and educational center. While the population of Morris has been declining gradually over the last few years, it still has vitality. Agriculture is still important in the area. In addition, it claims a branch of the University of Minnesota. The University of Minnesota, Morris, is a small liberal arts school with a big-time reputation. It has been long recognized as one of the best public liberal arts colleges in the country.

The city offers interesting diversions for most of its residents. There are high school and college sporting events, and plays, concerts and other cultural events sponsored by the high school, college and community. The activities generate interest for the different demographic groups in the area. Added to this are the special activities that occur on an annual basis. One of those is Prairie Pioneer Day which takes place the second week of July and celebrates the agricultural heritage of the area. Then there is the Stevens County Fair which rolls around in

August. A third event is the Harvest Holiday Festival which is held the second Saturday after Labor Day and celebrates arts and crafts.

I found Morris to be a very welcoming place. When I first visited, it was in the dead of winter, not the best time to be in a small prairie city. Yet, the layout of the city was interesting and filled with the bustle of people. The people I met were great, and much was to be learned from those I interviewed.

Marlys Alm

The story of Marlys started with her parents. Her father, Emil LeSage, was born in Illinois. Her mother, Verenna Bloom, was born in Pennsylvania. An interesting note about her mother was that Verenna was a descendent of one of the Mayflower passengers. The family was able to trace its roots back to Henery Sampson (sic) who landed with the other Mayflower passengers in Massachusetts.

The families of both parents moved to Minnesota before the children reached adulthood. Her mother's family settled in a small town near Morris called Tinta. Her father's family also moved to the Morris area. Her parents met, married, and settled in the Morris area.

Her parents were farmers. Marlys described her dad as a "dirt farmer." He grew a variety of crops and raised a variety of animals. As will be noted later, farm life was hard in those days. It was in this environment that Marlys LeSage was born on February 19, 1915. She was the second of four children. Marlys had two brothers and a sister. Wayne was the oldest, followed by Marlys, June, and Donald.

Marlys noted that everyone worked hard on the farm. She said that the family never owned a tractor. All the field work was done by real horse power. Water for use in the house had to be brought in by pail from the windmill. Of course, the used water also had to be hauled back outside too. Corncobs were collected for fuel. She stated, "It wasn't a good idea." It was very labor intensive. She said that temperature was controlled by the number of corncobs put into the stove. As an example, her mother made angel food cake with one corncob because, "she didn't want it very hot." The family certainly did not have comforts such as indoor plumbing. They also lacked electricity. She mentioned that she was about twelve when the family got its first telephone. The kids learned to eat whatever they had. A large garden provided much of their food, and it was either eat that food or go hungry. They also had a supply of meat except for the period of the Great Depression.

During her early years, Marlys stated that they often made their own entertainment which meant making up games and activities. Besides that, she mentioned some of the games they played. The children like playing cards. A game she remembered was Rummy. They also played spin the bottle at parties. A couple of the outdoor games were run sheep run and hide and seek.

Like many children, the LeSage kids could be daring and creative. According to Marlys, the family bought its first car, a Maxwell, when she was about seven. Road conditions meant the car did not get driven often. She remembered learning how to drive in the family's pasture. She drove alone by the time she was twelve years old. Her first driver's license cost twenty-five cents. She pointed out that she never took a driving test because in those days it was not required.

Of course, school was an important part of her life at this time. Marlys started out in a small country school. This was the typical one-room schoolhouse in which the teacher taught students from kindergarten through eighth grade. Marlys remembered playing games in the school. Like the typical rural school, it did not have indoor plumbing. She felt the education was good because the younger students learned by listening to the lessons of the older students. The kids used to carry their lunches which sometimes included potatoes and soup. A potato would be placed in the front part of the stove in the morning, and it was baked by lunch time. The soup would be heated on the top of the stove, and they would have a baked potato and soup for lunch. She completed two years at the country school and then attended the elementary school in Morris through sixth grade. Then it was back to the country school for grades seven and eight. She completed her high school years at Morris Senior High School. Since the family lived outside of town, she and her sister and a brother stayed at a house in town during the winter. The children could not afford the school lunches, so they would run back to the house for lunch every day. They lived on corn soup, tomato soup, and salmon soup. When not in school, she did babysitting to pay for necessities. Marlys graduated from high school in 1933.

Marlys made a couple of other observations about schooling in Morris. She noted that during the warmer weather, her main method of transportation to and from school was a bike. She also pointed out that each of her five children graduated from Morris High School. As a result, when there is an all-school reunion, the whole family can attend.

Her high school years took place during the early part of the Depression, and times were hard. Her mother did a lot of sewing. She sewed clothes for the children. It was hard to keep up with the town kids. Most of their parents had jobs and regular incomes. The farmers had to live on what they could sell. During the Depression, the farmers made nothing. The family was not even able to have much meat during most of that time.

At first the government gave them feed for the livestock to keep them going. However, the government eventually took control over the livestock and would not allow the farmers to butcher the animals. This reduced the meat supply to chickens and turkeys that the family raised. One thing Marlys remembered very well was eating egg plant as a substitute for meat. They prepared it by soaking it in salt water and then rolling it in cracker crumbs.

Marlys had an interesting story about how she came to know and fall in love with the man that became her husband. She first met him when she was in the eighth grade when he came to the country school to take exams. She added, "Of course, I did not pay any attention to him." Then when she was in ninth grade, she saw him again. This was the first time she really met him, and there was a spark. They went together for five years before getting married. Marlys was nineteen and Parnel Alm was twenty-one when they eloped. She said her parents did not have the money to pay for a wedding, so eloping was the polite thing to do.

Early years were not extravagant. Parnel had to borrow his father's car when transportation was needed. They did not buy their first car until they already had their second child. That first car was an old one which burned oil. Marlys said her children used to yell "Goose her, Daddy, goose her," and look out the back window as the smoke came billowing out. Parnel did a variety of jobs. He worked for his father's elevator shoveling coal and lining boxcars for grain. He also did work for the WPA and received commodities (food supplies) from that. After a few years he went to work for the railroad as a laborer. He started out making twenty-eight cents per hour. He ended up working for the railroad for thirty-two years. Illness caused him to retire in 1974.

Marlys also did a variety of things. When her first two children were young, she took in sewing. People often brought in old clothes to make over. However, one time a women brought in three yards of new material to make a dress. Marlys was thrilled to get something new to work with. Marlys charged the women one dollar for the dress and the woman thought it was overpriced. This for an item of clothing that took three days to make. In addition she went out and did housework for others, and she brought her small children along so she could watch them. Later Marlys cooked at the school in Donnelly, Minnesota. In those days the government supplied many items like flour and meat. She was the only cook. That meant getting to the school at 4:30 AM to start making the bread. She even made cinnamon rolls for the teachers. Later Marlys worked in several restaurants in the area. She did both cooking and waitressing and rarely got tips. The exception was during the hunting season. She said the hunters did give tips. Eventually, Marlys worked as a helper in the Donnelly Post Office. That job lasted for twenty-three years. Loss of hours helped Marlys decide to retire, which she did in 1975.

The family did not suffer great and lasting hardships from World War II. Parnel did not have to go into the service because he was considered too old. However, a brother was in the Battle of the Bulge. He was in a foxhole when artillery fire came in. His partner was killed and he suffered from many shrapnel wounds. Her brother had nineteen holes in his helmet from that incident but he did survive. Marlys also remembered rationing things such as sugar and gas, and she said she still had some of the ration books.

Housing was very basic to start with. At first they rented for five dollars per month. The house lacked indoor plumbing as well as many other conveniences. Marlys carried water from her in-laws across the road. The Alms bought their first house in 1959. The three room house had electricity but no plumbing. The two oldest daughters had left by then, but the family still included five members at home. This house was located in Donnelly. Her dad was a carpenter, and he helped Marlys add two bedrooms to the house. She borrowed money through the lumber company to get the materials to add to the house. Marlys stayed in this house until after her husband died. She then moved into an apartment in Morris. The move to Morris came about because the city was bigger and it was easier to get around.

Her family grew steadily over the years. With four daughters and one son, Marlys described the combination as "one onion in amongst those petunias." The oldest child, Connie, was born in 1934. She was followed by Barbara in 1935, June in 1942, John in 1943, and Pamela in 1949. At the time of the interview, the girls all lived in Minnesota. The closest was in Chokio which was only about fifteen miles from Morris. Her son lived in Ohio and ran his own office supply business.

Since the family was not rich, the children had to pitch in. Marlys mentioned that the kids had to work to get money. When she worked in the restaurants, the two oldest girls took over the house. They made supper, put the younger children to bed, and kept the house clean.

The Alms were married for fifty years when Parnel died from lung cancer in 1984. He had fought this disease for a long time. He did not wish to leave home during his sickness, and Marlys honored this wish by doing her best to keep him comfortable through the last stages of the illness.

The city of Morris changed greatly in Marlys's eyes. She said she used to know everyone in the town. She said she "couldn't tell you who lived in Morris now." She even remembered roller skating on a sidewalk by the courthouse with a friend. One day a lady came out of her house and told them not to skate there any more because sparks from the roller skates could start her house on fire. How times have changed!

Marlys was still driving in 2002. In over seventy years of driving, she has only had one fender bender—in 2002. This happened as she backed out of her driveway one day when cars were parked nearby. She did have two cars totaled. In each case, a daughter was driving, and those accidents were the fault of the other drivers. When we talked later, a back problem was keeping her from driving.

Marlys's main hobby was crocheting. She loved to do it and actually taught it for seventeen years. She made many table cloths and baby afghans over the years. This meant a lot of work to supply the family, because she had twelve grandchildren, twenty-four great grandchildren, and four great great grandchildren when we last talked.

Her family was very important to her. Most of the family got together every so often. The sparkle in Marlys' eyes showed the loving feelings she had for her family, and she also recounted how her father mentioned that when he moved to California from Morris he really missed being a dirt farmer and being with the grandchildren.

Volunteer work was a part of her life for quite a while. She worked for the Senior Federation in Morris and the Nutrition Assistance Program for Seniors. She also used to work in the kitchen at the Senior Center but had to stop because of arthritis.

Marlys concluded the interview by saying, "It was a tough life all along." The family never had extra money, but they lived through it. Her children truly appreciated how their parents sacrificed and worked hard to bring them up well.

Katherine Gausman

Mattie Lewis, Katherine's mother, was born in New York. The family soon moved to Michigan, where Mattie spent most of her formative years. Meanwhile, Katherine's father, Arthur Douglas Hale, was born and raised in Nebraska. Eventually both families moved to South Dakota and set up homesteads. According to federal law, a family could claim the land as theirs if they improved it and stayed for five years. The Black Hills area of South Dakota was where her parents met and married.

It was in South Dakota where Katherine's life began. She was born on March 24, 1913, in Custer County. The family eventually numbered eight members. Besides Katherine, there were three girls; Daisy, Ruth, and Nellie. The boys were Willard and William.

The family moved to Rock County in southwestern Minnesota when Katherine was only five months old. Using a team of horses to move their belongings, she said she thought it took about two weeks to make the move. The family stayed in Rock County until 1919. Katherine described Rock County as a "dog-eat-dog kind of a place" because so many people were farming. The local banker encouraged them to go to the "great wheat country of Stevens County." So Katherine's father and an uncle put their belongings into boxcars and took the train north to western Minnesota. They ended up renting farms, because they did not have the money to buy.

The first farmhouse was still in Katherine's memory. She said it had a telephone—a real rarity in rural Minnesota at that time. However, it did not have electricity or indoor plumbing. Light was produced mainly by kerosene lamps. Cooking and heat was provided by a coal stove, as will be discussed later. When the children were young, "There was a pile in each bed." Two slept at the head of the bed, and two slept at the foot. The farm that they lived on while she was growing up was a quarter section (160 acres). It was for sale for $12,000, but her father did not have enough money to buy the farm, and they rented instead.

Memory of the farm helped Katherine recall her school days. She walked to school, a distance of over two miles. She mentioned that some school districts were consolidated at the time, but her school rejected it because it would have required a one-half mile walk or more just to reach the bus stops. Her school voted against consolidation, so she went to the typical country school of the time—one room and eight grades. Kids brought their lunches to school in half gallon or gallon syrup pails. The pails often contained the lunches of every child from a family that attended the school. She noted that the lunches were probably not the most nutritious. Apparently, many of the students ate "syrup sandwiches" for lunch. She went on to high school for two years.

Katherine added an interesting anecdote about her school days. On one occasion she came to school driving a horse-drawn wagon. The horse stumbled and the shaft or axle on the buggy broke. So Katherine unhitched the horse and rode it to school. When she got to school, she realized that she had forgotten her lunch. All the students offered her some of their food, but so did the teacher. She thought I must have the teacher's sandwich because it must be something right out of heaven. She took the sandwich, but found it was so salty she could hardly eat it.

The first family car was probably purchased in the early 1920s. Katherine remembered that she was in grade school when her father bought a used 1914 Model T Ford. She noted that most families did not own a car at that time. Only the people with money, such as bankers, could afford to buy cars. Even though they had a car, they did not use it a lot. Her father did not have much mechanical ability and probably did not have the confidence to make repairs if the car broke down on the road. Instead, the parents often hitched up a team of horses to a wagon to make the four to five mile trip into town. With the parents gone, the kids would get mischievous. The front seat of the Model T had to be taken off to get at the gas tank. Then they took a stick and dipped it into the tank to check the level of gas. Next, they got into the car and drove around the big driveway. Katherine estimated that she was in grade school at the time. The kids were never caught. One reason was that they could always see the parents coming from a long distance. The horses and wagon created a lot of dust along the road, which gave the kids advanced warning. In addition, when the kids put the car back in the barn, they swept the tracks away from the barn.

She went on to explain the workings of the Model T. It had a crank (which was dangerous to use) to start it. It also had three pedals. The first pedal was to rev it up. A shift was used to put the car into a high gear. The middle pedal was reverse.

The last pedal was to stop the car. From this early beginning, Katherine continued to drive until 2001.

Bootlegging also took place in the area during the 1920s. Katherine was a little hesitant to talk about it at first. Then she told about a neighbor who was a bootlegger during Prohibition. It was bootlegging that helped the family not only get by, but also to do pretty well economically. She said they were very nice people. Bootlegging was common in the area and added that a road west of town became known as "Moonshine Trail" because so many used it to run liquor.

The family grew a variety of crops on the farm, but her father was best known for his yellow dent corn which was admired by many. People often wanted to buy his seed corn. The family also grew grain such as oats and wheat. Katherine and her sister Ruth had to shock the grain (put the sheaves in piles). She mentioned that at first they had to take water and food out to the workers in the field, but they got "so smart" they were given a job.

Katherine's father even got them a job helping a neighbor. The neighbor had an eighty acre grain farm, and he needed help shocking the grain. Her dad suggested Katherine and Ruth, saying that the two of them could work faster than one field hand and would not charge much money. The two girls ended up shocking eighty acres worth of grain for five dollars. They thought they were rich!

The diet in the 1920s was probably more balanced than what many eat today. She said they ate mainly the same things as others in the area. Oatmeal was the breakfast food. Meat (often salt pork) and potatoes were eaten for dinner. Without refrigeration, most food was kept in dirt cellars. Cooking was done by a stove fueled with coal, wood, or even corncobs. Her father even collected old railroad ties to throw into the stove. The same stove also was used for heating the house.

Talking about her house and the food the family ate made Katherine think of an interesting story. In the 1920s, few couples had big weddings. Fancy weddings were for the wealthier people who advertised the event in the society pages. Well, one of the ladies in the neighborhood had a wedding. The bride generously gave some of the wedding cake to the local teacher who chose to share it with the students. Now Katherine did not have much knowledge about weddings. Remember, she was a child and fancy weddings with the trimmings were rare. When she found out that she was going to get some wedding cake, she became quite excited. A wedding cake was special, so it must taste special. She thought she was going to get "something divine." When she bit into her piece of cake, "It tasted just like cake!" It wasn't "divine" or special after all!

Once out of school, the time had come to support herself. Katherine took a job doing housework. She made three dollars and fifty cents per week during the warmer months. The pay scale changed during wintertime when it was one dollar per week and room and board. It may not have been much money, but she managed to get by. Katherine felt it was a disgrace to owe money.

She was able to save money from doing the housework and used it to go to cosmetology school, and she went to Minneapolis for the training. Then she worked for another beautician to gain advanced training. However, she did not work at cosmetology right away.

It was the housework that led Katherine to meet her future husband. She was working for him, his first wife, and family. Emil Gausman's wife had heart trouble and died. After a time, Katherine and Emil became romantically inclined and were married on January 8, 1938. With the marriage, she got an instant family with two stepchildren. In 1939, Katherine and her husband had their own child named Gerald (Jerry).

Her son was married and still lived in the area. He was a farmer and also ran an Arctic Cat dealership. His wife, Doris, taught thirty years in the Chokio-Alberta School District and retired. Both helped look after Katherine.

We decided to spend a little more time talking about the 1930s, the period called the Great Depression. When asked if she was affected by the depression, Katherine replied that she probably was but did not realize it. The family always had enough to eat, but not always what they wanted. She said that one year all they ate during the winter was corn bread and corn mush. Potatoes, salt pork, and homemade bread were other staples during the 1930s. Katherine referred to the decade as the "Dirty thirties." It was because of the constant wind that blew the dirt around all the time. The dirt would pile up along fences in drifts. Dirt and dust got into everything including the houses. During this time, when people set the table to eat, they put the plates upside down which helped keep the dust off the eating side of the plates. They were turned over only when people were ready to eat.

Katherine's marriage to Emil led to the next stage in her life, being a farming partner. They farmed until 1954. As time went by, life became a little more convenient. She remembered getting a radio for the first time. They had a telephone, but in the rural areas, all the calls went through the operator. It was in 1954 that Emil died from an accident. He was helping a neighbor fix his well when he cut his thumb on some equipment. He developed tetanus and died.

After his death, Katherine went to work for Jackie Ann Hairstylists in the Twin Cities. After working there for a while, she returned to Morris. She had a house built that later included a room for her to use as a beauty shop.

Katherine mentioned that living back in the old days made the people "ever so much more appreciative of what they had." New conveniences such as electric lights, refrigerators, freezers and such made people feel like they had died and gone to heaven. These conveniences are all taken for granted today.

This energetic lady was involved in many hobbies and projects over the years. She was a painter (of rural landscapes), a quilter, made ceramics, explored genealogy and local history, and was into gardening. Many examples of her work were on display in her apartment. She had completed several quilts. Among them were friendship quilts and other theme quilts.

The paintings were quite good. Declining health forced Katherine to abandon these hobbies, but her works will be enjoyed by others far into the future.

Katherine passed away in March of 2003. Her quilts, paintings, and other crafts will bring lasting memories to her loved ones. I wish I had known her better.

Robert (Bob) Rose

Bob has truly lived an interesting life that has been full of twists and turns and many major accomplishments. His recollection of life's events was admirable.

Bob's mother, Ruth Dunphy, was born in Eau Claire, Wisconsin. Her family was involved in boat building and saw filing, which brought the family to Little Falls. Ruth's father was hired as the chief filer at a Weyerhaeuser saw mill on the Mississippi River at Little Falls.

The Rose side of the family came by way of Newfoundland and Nova Scotia. Bob's great grandparents came from this area and probably migrated from Scotland. Bob did not know how the family came to Minnesota, but probably through Wisconsin to central Minnesota. Grandfather Rose was a blacksmith and ran a livery stable in Hancock (eight miles southwest of Morris) before settling in Burtrum, Minnesota (about thirty miles southwest of Little Falls). Charles Raymond Rose, Bob's father, was born in Burtrum. Charles held a variety of jobs during his career. He worked for the Great Northern Railroad, worked on a surveying crew in North Dakota, and was manager of a Tanner Company elevator in Swanville, Minnesota (about twenty-five miles west of Little Falls). Bob remembered that the elevator not only stored grain, but also handled potatoes.

Bob's parents attended school in Little Falls. His mother remembered Charles Lindbergh attending school at that time. She had said that he attended school most of the time—when he wasn't tinkering with cars. This, of course, was the same Charles Lindbergh that flew solo from the United States to France in 1927.

The family moved around the state as his father took new jobs. Bob was born on January 7, 1923, in Little Falls, although the family lived in Swanville at the time. The Roses moved to International Falls (a town on the Canadian border) when he was about three years old. At that time, Charles took a job at Minnesota-Ontario Paper Company.

Charles's brother, Jessie, was a customs agent at Rainier, the port of entry into the United States from Canada. Jessie knew of openings at the paper company in about 1925 or 1926. He told Bob's father about an opening, and the family went to the border town. Not much later, Charles took a civil service exam for the United States Postal Service. He received an appointment to report to St. Paul and began work as a mail clerk on various trains. Eventually the family moved to Thief River Falls when his father became a mail clerk on the "Wheat Line." He sorted mail between Thief River Falls and Kenmere, North Dakota. He got his forty hours a week in two days during the out and back run. When the snow hit and the trains could not run, he had to take the mail into the hotel with him.

All these moves led to memories of several houses. The home in Swanville was located near railroad tracks. In those days, a local train called a "puddle jumper" went by regularly. Its run was between Little Falls and Sauk Center. The train carried freight, passengers, and mail. The draymen then delivered the freight by horse-drawn wagon. The house in Swanville did not have electricity, so kerosene lamps provided light. The house also was with-

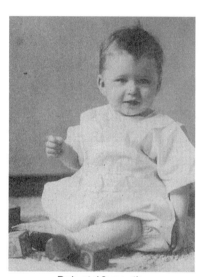

Bob at 10 months

out plumbing. Bob remembered a chicken coop in the yard. The house in International Falls was modern in that it had electricity, plumbing and hot water heat. The family stayed in International Falls for about a year, then moved to St. Paul at about the time Bob was ready to start kindergarten. They ended up staying in St. Paul for twelve years. Bob remembered one house having a pot bellied stove that was fired with briquets (compressed coal dust). They moved three times in St. Paul, and his parents always rented until they moved to Thief River Falls. The family had a telephone in all the homes from the time they lived in International Falls, and also had a radio as far back as he could remember.

Bob did not remember his mother being a cook of traditional foods. As such, he did not list any particular foods that he liked or did not like. He did mention that his family knew the Larsen family (of the Larsen Boat Works), and the grandmother made some very good Swedish rye bread.

Many of the games he played were popular for the time. Some of the indoor games he played as a child included Parcheesi, checkers, and Uncle Wiggly. He played outdoors a lot, and playing in the snow was a fun wintertime activity.

The family was affected by the Great Depression, but not as bad as many other families. His father took a fifteen percent wage cut during the Depression, but "he always brought home a check." Bob felt this was one of the benefits of working for the government. His father managed the money well. His mother was also a good manager, and the family never had to skimp for a meal.

Bob at age 13

World War II became an important part of Bob's life, and the memories were still vivid at the time of the interview. He was a student at North Dakota Agricultural College (now North Dakota State University) during the early part of the war. He was a sophomore in the Pharmacy program. Bob and seven other pharmacy students went to the ROTC headquarters on campus and signed up. The idea was "that they were going to stay together." He said, "Well that didn't happen." Personnel cards were issued that listed each person's specialty. Bob's specialty was supposed to be pharmacy technician. Upon arrival at Fort Snelling, he found out that he was placed in a personnel group and was shipped to Camp Lee, Virginia. He found himself in a barracks with professionals with advanced degrees. These people were assigned to do interviewing and counseling. He did not know what he was going to do in a group like that, so he complained, and it paid off. Bob was sent to Camp Pickett, Virginia, for medical basic training, which he completed.

Bob wanted to go to OCS (Officers Candidate School). He was told the Army had a quota to fill for ASTP (Army Specialized Training Program) and he had qualified, so it was on to VPI (Virginia Polytechnic Institute) for training in engineering. Again he was detoured from medical work. He completed two quarters at VPI. By this time, the planning for D-Day was reaching an end and the landing was near. As a result, all those in the ASTP program were "cleaned out" of VPI and other colleges and sent to Camp Claiborne, Louisiana. He was assigned to the 84th Infantry Division and was classified as a machine gunner in a heavy weapons platoon. Bob knew that such an assignment meant a short life expectancy. He asked for and received a reclassification.

He was assigned to the 335th Regiment as a medical aid man. He knew that being a medic was dangerous but said, "I thought that as a machine gunner you were not going to last too long. I was playing the percentages."

Then came the time to go overseas. Bob's regiment occupied one of three ships that left from New York. Each ship also carried the field artillery and divisional medical units. The personnel and equipment from each ship was to fight as a separate unit. The British ship, Sterling Castle, was headed for Cherbourg, France. Not long after leaving port, the troop ship was engulfed by heavy fog. Somewhere near the Nantucket light- house the ship sliced into an oil tanker and had to return to New York for repairs. This made the regiment a week late in making the eleven-day crossing and required the entire 84th Division to land in England and assemble near the town of Winchester. The 335th Regiment set up quarters near a small town called Crowley Court. (Bob noted that Crowley Court does not exist any more and a large British Broadcasting facility occupies the area where the town was.) It took another two weeks for all the equipment and the regiment to arrive and get organized.

Next, they crossed the English Channel and "motor marched" to the Dutch border where they joined the 9th Army. They lived in basements from then on. The division's job was to put a wedge between the 1st Army and the 2nd British Army as they advanced toward Germany to the east. In other words, they filled a gap between the two armies that was created as they advanced against the German lines. Bob's regiment was on the front lines by the middle of November 1944.

Before continuing the description of his war experiences, Bob explained about the 84th Division. It was formerly an Illinois National Guard Division. Its insignia was an axe splitting a log and the men were known as the rail splitters. Bob explained Army units as follows: there were three battalions in a division, there was one aid station per battalion, and the aid stations were sometimes ahead of the front lines.

The experiences of being on the front lines were many. With the help of his high school German, Bob became the interpreter for his medical unit. The medical aid station was often set up in houses that were still standing, and the men lived in basements for protection from German artillery fire. The fire from the German's infamous 88's (.88 caliber artillery) often hit these buildings and caused quite a concussion. Light was provided by a lone Coleman lantern or by candles.

The 84th Division was confronted by the fortifications of the German Siegfried Line. Numerous pill boxes and trenches were now encountered. The 84th was working its way to the Roer River. This is a small river that flows north through western Germany into Belgium, where it flows into the Maas River. By mid December, the 84th was detached from the 9th Army and assigned to the 1st Army in what came to be known as the "Bulge."

The Battle of the Bulge began on December 16, 1944, with a German offensive that was directed towards the port of Antwerp, Belgium. Bob's whole division made the move south in two days. They ended up defending the town of Marche, Belgium. In probing for the enemy, commanding General Bolling's jeep drove up to a "roundabout," only to be confronted by a German MP. They quickly circled the "roundabout" and drove back down the road, much to the amazement of that MP. The 84th Division stopped the German advance outside of Marche and kept it out of German hands, contrary to American newspaper accounts.

In an aside, Bob talked about Hitler's attack in the Bulge. The German army had moved through the Ardennes (a forested area on the border between Belgium and Germany) in 1940 on the way to attacking France. Hitler felt he could do it again to reach his objective, which was the fuel depot at Liege, Belgium. However, the area he attacked meant crossing a lot of little bridges on a lot of narrow roads. This route, combined with the winter weather, did not lend itself to fast movement, especially with huge Panther tanks and heavy artillery. Bob also said in referring to Hitler that "he did not count on the ingenuity of the American soldier." Americans dynamited gas supplies, which meant vehicles had to be abandoned. Without the gas, the Germans had to park many of their vehicles along the roadsides.

Bob's division was under the command of British General Montgomery at the time. After securing Marche, they leapfrogged a number of times and ended up just north of Luxembourg. At that point, they got a few days rest in the town of Ville. They lived in a castle. During the rest period, he received his only injury. He was using a pen knife to put blankets over windows to create a blackout situation. The knife snapped out after he wedged the blanket into the wood. It flew up into the air and hit him in the top of the head. There was no purple heart for that wound!

The division was part of the push east once the German offensive was broken. They went back to where they started on the Siegfried Line and crossed the Roer River in March. It was here that he experienced a scare. He was blown down the stairs of a building from the concussion of an exploding artillery shell. Luckily, he landed on a sergeant coming up the stairs and was not hurt. Of course there were casualties along the way. One night, they rescued a young soldier who had a broken leg and had lain in a foxhole for two days. Frostbite was a major problem in the Bulge. Another time, he was called because soldiers manning an antitank gun had been buried by debris caused by an exploding shell. An .88 caliber shell hit the side of a foxhole and the concussion brought a lot of dirt down on the men. Bob mentioned that it cost the rescue about thirty minutes to get to him and take him to where the explosion took place. By the time he got there and they dug away the dirt with their hands, the soldiers were dead. When enemy medics or doctors were captured, they were often called upon to help with the wounded before being sent back as POWs. The 88th Division finally reached the Elbe River in late April of 1945. He remembered the end of the war in Europe in May because he was on rest and relaxation in Nice, France, when it happened.

Bob was asked if he remembered problems in getting supplies as the front lines advanced farther from the supply depots. He said, "I never had any problem." As a matter of fact, one of his functions was to get supplies to the battalion aid stations. He said he became very popular when he went to get rubbing alcohol, but with none to be had, took a five-gallon can of ninety-proof ethyl alcohol.

Bob had many other experiences as a medic during the last offensive push into Germany. In Belgium the civilians helped in many ways. The Belgians tore up sheets and gave them to the soldiers for camouflage in the snow. One woman even sewed jackets and hoods from army blankets.

After entering Germany, fraternization became a problem. With this freedom came the social diseases of gonorrhea and syphilis, which were treated with penicillin. On occasion, a German woman might see a couple of soldiers walking nearby and she would yell, "Rape!" This would bring the military police and result in arrests of the GIs. Efforts were made to treat the civilian women as well as the GIs, but officials had to rely on GIs being able to identify who they fraternized with before they contracted a social disease. This method did not turn out to be very successful.

Wartime experiences were not over yet. Soldiers such as Bob wondered if they were going to be rotated to the Pacific theater to fight against Japan. At the time, the 84th Division occupied an area around Heidelberg, Germany. However, a break came his way. The United States opened two universities in Europe staffed by American professors. One was near Oxford, England, and the other at Biarritz, France. Bob was given the opportunity to attend one of the universities, and he chose the one in France "because it was warmer." Still, there was some wait before he could go to France. A few days later he was told that there was already an opening in England, and would he like to go? He said, "Sure." So in September of 1945 he was on his way to Shrivenham University near the town of Swindon, England, not far from the city of Oxford.

Bob was allowed to take two academic subjects at the school and one recreational subject. He took organic chemistry and psychology for his academic courses. His recreational course was wrestling. He was able to complete one quarter of study, and the credits were transferred back to North Dakota State University as electives.

His decision, upon returning to Minnesota, was to go back to pharmacy school. This came after trying to get into the University of Minnesota medical school. The dean had discouraged him, and he ended up returning to North Dakota State University to complete his pharmacy studies.

He had already known his future wife by this time. They had met at a church camp before he went to war. They wanted to get married before he left for the service, but her parents in particular were discouraging. So the young couple went along with it and waited. Bob and Joan Lawshe were finally married in September of 1946.

Her father had quite a reputation. Mr. Lawshe taught printing at South St. Paul High School and was curator of a museum in South St. Paul. He started the museum in the basement of city hall. By the time he died, a museum building was completed and named after him. Indian artifacts were his forte. He also had a theme idea for setting up a town scene. It included a blacksmith shop, shoe shop, pharmacy and the like. Bob pointed out that Mr. Lawshe got a lot of his artifacts from Morris. He basically got the materials for the shoe shop from Morris. Bob also gave him many old pharmaceutical objects.

After getting married, he had to finish his degree. Bob was back in school in Fargo, North Dakota, while his wife was taking nursing education—a four year program at the main campus of the University of Minnesota. She still had a quarter to go in school, and they had a commuting relationship during the time that she completed her studies. He took the train to visit her on the weekends. Then she moved in with his parents in Thief River Falls and took a job in a hospital because they could not find student housing in Fargo. By the winter quarter of 1948, he had earned a straight A average and their first child was born. The child was named Bob. He pointed this out as an example of how World War II helped mature many men who had not done particularly well in school before. He felt it changed the outlooks of many and made them determined to work harder.

Bob graduated from North Dakota State in 1948. Graduation meant it was time to get a job. The family grew during these early years. He was recruited by the owner of Countryman Drug in Fergus Falls, Minnesota. Bob took the job and stayed there a year. During this time a second child was born. The child was born under hypnosis, an experimental procedure for which his wife volunteered. The second son was named Charles. Then Bob heard about a job in Alexandria at a pharmacy called Boston Drug. He took that job, and it lasted two years.

A new opportunity opened up in Raymond, Minnesota, a small town south of Willmar. The pharmacy was for sale. The owner had been letting it run down. The doctor in the town wanted a pharmacist, so the doctor co-signed the note for Bob to buy the pharmacy. The doctor ended up delivering two children for Bob and Joan for forty dollars a piece. The Rose's had a girl and another boy. In 1958, Bob sold that store and went to Morris. A key to the move was that people he knew from Alexandria bought the store in Morris and they wanted him to run it. He also knew the University of Minnesota was soon to open a branch in Morris and felt that made it a good opportunity. He managed the Rexall Drug in Morris for about three years. Then the owners wanted to sell out, and although Bob wanted to buy it, he was outbid.

Another career shift was in order, and Bob interviewed at the State Hospital in Willmar. Then a Morris doctor told him to stop at Hancock, Minnesota, to check out an opportunity there. He ended up working out an arrangement in which he would work at the Hancock pharmacy for three days and the Morris pharmacy for three days. Over time, he worked more in Morris and less in Hancock. Eventually the Hancock portion was down to an on-call basis. The job kept evolving. Messner Drug in Morris opened a pharmacy in a clinic building near the local hospital. Bob was involved in running it for a couple of years. That led the hospital administrator to hire him to run the hospital pharmacy. He took the job and moved from the clinic across the street to the hospital. His tenure with the hospital went from pharmacist to purchaser to assistant administrator to administrator of the hospital. It was a position he held for ten years. All the while, he continued his pharmacy work.

In 1978, Bob added a $2 million addition to the hospital. It included new operating rooms, an emergency room, and an intensive care unit. It was now a fifty-four bed hospital. The cost of construction, including the loss of patient space during construction, led to loss of profit. The hospital board decided to hire a consultant to help Bob. The consultant was the administrator of the hospital in Alexandria. This consultant seemed to want to add the administrator position of the Morris hospital to the one he held in Alexandria. The result was that Bob did not want to deal with all of that and asked to go back to just being a pharmacist. The board agreed, and he continued in that position for another ten years.

Bob's first wife, Joan, died in January 1980. She had a liver problem that had resulted from an infection. They went to the Mayo Clinic and she received a spleenal renal shunt. The purpose was to stop the build up of blood in her esophagus. The procedure helped her live for another nine years.

Bob remarried in 1982. He met a woman from Little Falls that had taken care of his father's affairs when his father passed away in 1981. Marian had been divorced about ten years previously. Marian also had known Bob's first wife, so they were not strangers. They had twenty years together before physical complications led to her death on October 1, 2002. She died from complications of a perforated bowel that was from a staph (MSRA) infection while in the hospital. The infection could not be overcome. She had other physical problems by that time, including a heart condition and blindness.

Bob completed his work at the hospital but was not ready to retire. He went to work for one of the pharmacies in town and also did relief work in the surrounding area. He went to Wheaten, Benson, and Graceville, Minnesota, to work and give the regular pharmacists a day off.

He was still active at the time of our first interview. He was the president of the Senior Club at the Morris Senior Center at this time and was a consultant for the University of Minnesota Morris Health Services. He ordered and packaged the medications that the doctors wanted to use in the health services area. He did this one hour a day, five days a week. He has been a member of the Red Cross for fifty-two years, and in 2003, was the manager of the local Red Cross chapter. When he lived in Raymond, he was trained as a first aid instructor. He taught the first ambulance personnel, police, and firemen first aid in Morris. He was no longer active in the training at the time of our interview. He was on the State Health and Safety Committee for the State of Minnesota Red Cross.

Another area of interest that carried into retirement was related to dogs. When Bob married Marian, she had a cockapoo. It died after about two years so they were without a dog. A hamburger restaurant opened in Morris and the owner had three Samoyed dogs. Bob got excited about these dogs, and he and Marian would visit the dogs and feed them snacks. A drawing was held for the dogs and Marian was one of the winners. They picked out the smallest of the Samoyed puppies, but he turned out to weigh 125 pounds as an adult! He was named Lucky after their good fortune in winning him.

Bob's oldest son was running a motel in Grand Marais, a small resort town on Lake Superior in northeastern Minnesota. His son said, "Ya gotta come up and see the Beargrease Sled Dog Race." The experience of seeing the race got Bob and Marian interested in a sled dog operation. Lucky's first harness was from a man who started the Beargrease Race. Later they were on a trip to Montana and met a woman who made harnesses. She made two or three harnesses for Lucky. Bob and Marian taught the dog how to pull a sled. Then they started going to schools and gave rides to kindergarten students. They also demonstrated how to harness a dog and gave the students hands on opportunities with Lucky. The dog traveled from coast to coast with them in their motor home. This was also a time when Bob and Marian regularly attended the Beargrease Race.

Lucky was involved in many other family activities. One of the trips took Bob and Marian to Alaska. They met Mary Shields on the trip, an experienced musher who wrote a book and made a video tape about the sport. Bob had been writing to her and had been using some of her material (with her permission). She even had Bob help her during one of her presentations. Lucky was often taken into classes and was especially calm around special needs students in Morris. Bob and Marian even took an interest in the big Iditerod Sled Race in Alaska, and they got students interested. Bob tried to help the students become knowledgeable about the mushers, the dogs, the route, and the terrain that was covered in Alaska.

Bob still lives in his own house. He has much in the house that needs to be sorted and some of it thrown out. He also has an idea in the back of his mind to write a book about the medics in World War II. Bob has many stories that he collected from other members of his medical detachment. One story included the experiences of an acquaintance who was a POW. This POW was part of an incident in which American planes strafed railroad cars that held the prisoners. The American prisoners broke out of the rail cars, immediately took off their shirts, and with their bodies spelled out "POW" in an adjacent field. The planes acknowledged them by wiggling their wings, and flew off. Another story involved a medic who commandeered a jeep to evacuate wounded to an aid station. He ended up getting captured. Bob has many other stories that would interest people and expose a little known aspect of the war. He also has regularly attended infantry reunions of the 84th Division.

Bob has been involved in taking the story of World War II into classrooms for a long time. He had interviewed with or spoken to students from elementary school levels up to the college level. His wealth of knowledge stemmed from the more technical aspects of fighting and being a medic on the front lines to the more personal issue of staying alive. This type of information made Bob a valuable resource. He gave people more than a glossed over view of World War II. His stories brought a human aspect to the war. He is truly a remarkable man.

Walter (Slim) Hokanson

Walter Hokanson left the farm, but he never left farming. His school housing and his home throughout his working career were the same. As will be seen, these two unusual statements help explain the life of this remarkable man.

Walter's father, Olof Hokanson, was born in Skane, Sweden, and immigrated to the United States. His mother was born only a mile from where she and Olof farmed. The Hokanson's worked a 120 acre farm located northeast of Morris and about eight miles from the town of Hoffman. The farm was pretty typical for the day—they milked cows, raised chickens and pigs, and grew a variety of crops. His father died at the age of fifty-four after suffering a heart attack.

Walter was the second of three children in the Hokanson family. A sister was born in October of 1908. Walter came next on April 9, 1910, and he was followed by a brother who was born in December of 1911. One sister died a few days after being born. Both siblings are still living and reside near Walter. His sister lives in Alexandria, which is northeast of Morris, and his brother lives in the small town of Evansville, about thirty miles north of Morris.

Growing up, he remembered that the church the family attended was about a mile from the family home, and they attended every Sunday. Then he mentioned something about the church that followed a tradition from colonial times in the 1600s and 1700s. According to Walter, the men sat on the right side and the women and children sat on the left side. He said of the church, "It was the only place that I know that did this."

The school, part of District 49, was located about one and a quarter miles from his home. He said, "I don't ever remember getting a ride. We walked every day regardless of the weather." The school was a typical country school in that it was a one-room school that included grades one through eight. He graduated from the country school in 1924.

The family house was also typical for rural Minnesota during the early 1900s. They did not have indoor plumbing, which meant no running water in the house and the need for an outhouse. The house also did not have electricity or a central heating system. Although the family did not have a phone when he was very young, Walter did remember a telephone after a few years. He noted that it was on a country line, and their ring pattern was two long and one short. Being on a country line meant people could listen in on each others' conversations. Cooking was done on a wood-burning stove, which also provided some heat during colder weather. Refrigerators did not exist at the time, and the family did not have an ice box, so a cellar was used for keeping some foods from spoiling rapidly. The house had a kitchen, dining room, living room, a bedroom downstairs, and two bedrooms upstairs. A separate stairway led up to each bedroom.

The first family car was a Model T Ford purchased in 1917. It was a four-cylinder with side curtains. To start the car, a person had to pull a wire to choke it and then turn a crank. In those days, cars did not have heaters, so winter driving was cold. Use of the car was sometimes limited because roads were not paved and poor weather like heavy rain made travel difficult. Travel was even more restricted by snow and cold in winter. Plowing of roads was not done in those days, meaning the car stayed home after a heavy snow or blowing snow with drifts. That meant a key method of transportation was still real horse power.

Growing up on a farm meant doing a variety of chores. Walter mentioned that their barn was quite a distance from the house. He had to go out every day to milk cows. Then the milk was brought into the kitchen to be separated. That is where the Hokanson's kept their cream separator. He and his grandfather had to cut down trees to get the firewood for the stove. They each took an end of a crosscut saw and sawed a tree down. Then the trunk and branches were cut into usable lengths and split. Imagine doing all of that by hand! It was the major pastime in the winter. He also mentioned that they sometimes used corncobs to start fires in the stove. While he was growing up on the farm, all the plowing and other heavy work was done by horses. Horses were used the entire time he lived on the farm.

Walter arrived in Morris and entered West Central Agricultural School on October 1, 1927. It was an agricultural vocational school run by the University of Minnesota. As such, students specialized in farming practices, but took other courses as well. The program was set up for three years, and to get the equivalent of a high school diploma, a student had to go for four years. He noted that the first class graduated in 1912. Walter specialized in animal husbandry and graduated in March of 1930; he did not go on for the fourth year.

Since he lived at the school, he had to pay room and board. When he started in 1927, board was fourteen dollars a month and room rent was five dollars a month for a total of nineteen dollars. The cost for room and board went up to twenty-one dollars a month by his senior year.

Walter started working at the school between his junior and senior years. He worked in the dairy barn, which became his place of employment for the rest of his working career. He started working full time the day after he graduated.

Walter worked about four years before getting married. He was not too specific about their courting, but did say that he and another guy ran into his future wife Lily and her sister. The guy Walter was with ended up marrying the sister, and Walter married Lily in 1934. She had been a school teacher and quit teaching for a time while they raised four children. The oldest is Sheryl who is married, lives in Kensington, and does day care. Robert, who is a retired teacher in California, came next; Rolland is a CPA and lives in New Brighton, Minnesota. The youngest son, Steven, is retired from UPS and lives in Morris.

At West Central Agricultural School, he lived on the school campus the entire time he worked there. Before he was married, he lived with other single men in what was called the "farmhouse." It had six bedrooms upstairs and two bedrooms down. Two women, the cook and the housekeeper, lived downstairs, and they fed the men and cleaned their rooms. Shortly after marrying Lily, they lived on the third floor of the dining hall. They rented two rooms across the hall from each other for ten dollars a month. They did not have a refrigerator, so they put their food on the window to keep it cool during the colder months. They lived under this arrangement for about three years before making a move back to the "farmhouse." The men living in the "farmhouse" all married and had moved out. This made the house available to Walter and Lily, and they took advantage of it.

Walter noted some interesting facts about the "farmhouse." One was that the house was moved from the time he lived there as a bachelor to the time he and his wife moved in. The move was less than a block, and the house ended up across the street from the dairy barn where he worked. When Walter and Lily moved into the house, rent was thirty dollars a month and included all utilities. When he retired in December of 1975, the rent had gone up to the princely sum of sixty dollars a month. It was one of the reasons he did not build a home until after he retired. As an aside, Walter mentioned that the house was torn down about a year or two after they moved out and college apartments were built on the site.

As noted earlier, he graduated in March of 1930. In June of that year, the herdsman working for the school quit, and Walter took over as acting herdsman. Eventually, the acting part of the title was dropped and he continued on the job until retirement. Starting salary for the herdsman's job was forty-five dollars a month plus room and board. The salary increased to sixty-five dollars a month by 1934, but pressures of the Great Depression caused a cut to fifty-five dollars a month a few months later. His original responsibilities put him in charge of the dairy cattle, beef cattle, hogs, and sheep. As herdsman, Walter oversaw the complete feeding and care of the animals, meaning he managed the workers who had the jobs of feeding, cleaning stalls and pens, milking cows, and the like. As time went on, the school expanded each department, and he eventually was left with responsibility for dairy cattle only.

World War II created some added hardships in the barn. The war had created a manpower shortage, and Walter had to rely on students to fill in. He was the only full-time worker, and this was when he still had responsibility over dairy cattle, beef cattle, pigs, and sheep. He said, "We had to be up and ready to go at 4:00 in the morning," because milking had to be done early. Sometimes he had to go to the dorm and wake the students up. He admitted that it was hard for students to get up so early, but they did not have any money and had to work for their room and board. Walter said that he worked many eighty-hour weeks, but that was what you did.

In discussing the war years, Walter mentioned that he had spent that time in the National Guard and was never called overseas. Actually, he joined the Guard in October of 1927, starting out as a private. The government paid the men one dollar a meeting, and the National Guard met every Monday night. As a result, he and the other members each received a twelve-dollar check every three months. He said, "We needed that twelve dollars." Walter stayed in the National Guard for twenty years and worked his way up through the ranks to retire as a second lieutenant. He mentioned that the government viewed his job as important enough to the home front effort that he was not called up for active duty or sent overseas.

During those early years on the job, a specific routine was followed for milking. After milking the cows, the milk was taken directly to a walk-in cooler at the West Central Agriculture School. In those days, people from the area could come in and buy milk and cream directly from the school. In 1942, they raised the price of milk from five cents to seven cents a quart—or twenty-eight cents a gallon—and they raised the price of cream from thirty cents to thirty-six cents a quart—or one dollar forty-four cents a gallon. Skim milk was given away. In addition, people who bought the milk and cream came with their own containers.

In the year 1960, the University of Minnesota opened a branch campus in Morris which included the site of the West Central Agriculture School. The agricultural school and the University operated as separate institutions for the first two or three years. Then the agricultural school was phased out, and the property and program were taken over by the University. After a time, the University moved its experiment station (where Walter worked) and called it the West Central Research and Outreach Center. Thus, he ended up driving to work the last few years before retirement. He noted that his middle son started at the University of Minnesota at Morris the inauguration year of the school.

This energetic man is not only defined by his job and family, but also by his avocations. One of his early hobbies was being a beekeeper. Walter started during World War II when he took over the operation from an acquaintance who was drafted. He did not know much about beekeeping when he first started, but read books and talked to experienced beekeepers in the area; soon his efforts started paying off. Once Walter got things off the ground, he was shipping clover honey to customers in several states as well as Canada and England. In discussing beekeeping, he described how he used an electric knife to cut off the wax. Then the comb was put into a centrifuge to extract the honey. The wax was put into a melter, which separated the wax from any remaining honey. He then sold the wax to a dealer in South Dakota to be made into candles. Enough honey had to be left in the hive so the bees could survive the winters. He used to leave sixty pounds of honey per hive for his bees. Walter pointed out that the beekeepers today send the bees south or to California for the winter. The keepers rent out the bees to people who need the bees to pollinate their orchards to get bigger crops. As time went on, many of the beekeepers moved their operations to North Dakota because there was not enough clover being raised in western Minnesota. As a matter of fact, when Walter quit beekeeping in about 1980 and sold his equipment, a beekeeper from Alexandria took over his locations. Now that beekeeper does his beekeeping in North Dakota.

Walter had to have a place to extract the honey from the combs, so he bought over four acres of land in 1959. He paid $1,500 for the land and put a honey house on the land in 1960. The land was later used for his own home, which he had built in 1976. In 1993, he sold off a portion of his land to another person for $15,000.

Walter also became involved in the nursery business. He worked part-time at a nursery and raised evergreen trees on his own and sold them. He said, "I planted the trees by the thousands." Once the seedlings became big enough, he sold them to nurseries; trees that became too big to sell to nurseries were sold as Christmas trees. He estimated that he sold about fifty to sixty Christmas trees a year. The building of his home meant the end of the evergreen tree business.

Activity continued after retirement. Though his nickname is "Slim," Walter said, "I wasn't always slim. I weighed 240 pounds." So at the age of sixty-five he took up walking. One day, he was walking down the road by the University of Minnesota Morris, when two female students passed him as they jogged. He thought to himself that he could do that, too. Thus, he went from walking to jogging, and the combination of exercise and a better diet allowed him to drop his weight to 160 pounds. His routine was to run early every morning and do about five miles a day. By the age of seventy- two he started competing in races, usually ten-kilometer races. He remembered wondering if he could complete the distance of his first ten kilometer race and admitted to being happy to see the finish line. Apparently, it was a good experience, because he ended up with several age group ribbons and trophies for winning or placing in races. He even ran seven and a half miles on his seventy-fifth birthday. As he looked back on his years running he said, "Oh, I enjoyed running. Ah, what a great sport."

His running years came to an end in 1994. He needed both knees replaced, and wanted the doctor to do the surgeries during the off season so he could go back to running and not miss races. Well, the doctor told him that if he intended to keep running, he would have to find someone else to do the surgery. Artificial knees wear out over time, and exercise such as running shortens the lives of the artificial parts.

Even though his running days were over, Walter continued exercising. He went back to walking and continued biking, another activity he had taken up. With biking, he became involved in touring. His first one was a ten-day tour through the Black Hills. He hooked up with a bicycling club from San Diego. The trip started in Wall, South Dakota, and went through some of the legendary towns and sites in the Black Hills. He also participated in some of the "Jaunt with Jim" bicycling tours led by retired Star Tribune columnist Jim Klobuchar. Whereas his South Dakota trip was rather luxurious because they stayed in nice hotels, this eighty-plus-year-old man was tenting it on the Klobuchar trips and loving it.

Walter had not stopped as of the time of the interview. Though he did not bike in 2003, he did not say that he had given it up. He continued walking and working out at the University of Minnesota Morris fitness center. In addition, he did all the yard work on his three-plus acres. Besides regularly mowing the large lot, he planted dozens of plants in 2003. Walter also took care of his small orchard on the property, though he did cut down some of the trees. Then there was the house maintenance. He had recently painted window trim and stained the whole house. Winter was a little slower, but he still shoveled his own snow, and he had a long driveway. Though he owned a snow blower, he enjoyed shoveling and only used the snow blower after deep and heavy snows.

Besides all the physical activity, he had a great collection in his garage and his old honey house. It was a collection of 185 antique cream separators. The separators were in mint condition. He said he still collected them if he could find them but had not found any in quite a while. At the same time, he was looking ahead. In the summer of 2003, he took some separators to Iowa to be placed in a museum. In the fall of 2003, he placed an ad to sell the rest of the collection. When asked about this, he said that he knew age would require selling the house in the future with a move to an apartment. He knew his collection would have to be gone by then.

Walter is a very energetic, optimistic and interesting person. He believes in making the most of each day. Also, he and his wife Lilly are proud of their four children, eighteen grandchildren, and twenty-six great grandchildren. To say that he has lived a full life is not an adequate description.

New Prague

Main Street in New Prague

New Prague represents the economic and cultural nature of southern Minnesota.

This community is located about forty miles south of the Twin Cities in the heart of farm country. The town was founded by Anton Philipp in 1856 when he was thirty-five years old. He was responsible for platting the early village. By the time Anton Philipp died in 1888, New Prague had developed into an agricultural and business center. The town was officially designated as a city in 1891.

The early settlement was dominated by people of Czechoslovakian descent. Many of the first settlers were direct descendants of immigrants from the area of Czechoslovakia known as Bohemia. A large number of Germans also populated the area. This is a city that truly celebrates its cultural heritage. Many murals and other landmarks around the city stand as bastions to the historical make-up of the city.

The dominant feature on Main Street is St. Wenceslaus Catholic Church with its twin spires reaching 110 feet. The original church was started in 1857, just a year after the founding of the town. It is the oldest Czech parish in the state of Minnesota. The present church was started in 1906 and dedicated in 1907. It is patterned after a church in Prague, Czechoslovakia.

Another landmark on Main Street is Schumacher's New Prague Hotel, designed by Cass Gilbert, the same architect who had designed the Minnesota State Capitol. The hotel was built by W.S. Broz in 1898. It was originally a favorite overnight stop for visitors taking the train to and from the Twin Cities.

One of the newer landmarks is the New Prague Gateway Tower located on the eastern end of the city. The tower was designed by the New Prague Chamber of Commerce and built in 1988. It was patterned after the arches and spires of "old world" Germany and Czechoslovakia. It stands as a welcome to visitors and as a commemoration of the area's ethnic heritage.

Another recent landmark is a sculpture by the famous Czech sculptor, Milos Vlcek. It was presented to New Prague by Mr. Vlcek in gratitude for the wonderful experience his son had as an exchange student at New Prague High School in 1993. The sculpture is made of white oak and incorporates several symbols.

Several other historically significant buildings dot the city. They include the First National Bank Building, built in 1895, the Bean Mansion, built in 1906, and the Railroad depot, built in 1877. Many other important historical buildings can easily be seen in a walk around the city.

In addition, several murals around the city commemorate significant people, organizations, events, and the like. For example, one mural is a portrait of Anton Philipp, noted above as the founder of the city. Another mural commemorates the Bohemian Brass Band that was popular in the area during the early 1900s. Then there is a mural of the map of Czechoslovakia. Several other murals are found around the city and help give it a unique flavor.

Several communities are located near New Prague and also are based on agricultural economic concerns. The other communities include Jordan—about ten miles to the north, Lonsdale—about twelve miles to the east, and Montgomery—about ten miles to the south.

The New Prague Chamber of Commerce provided materials helpful for gathering the above information. Visitors would find the *Walking Tour And Recreation* pamphlet, along with other materials from the Chamber of Commerce, helpful.

Hilda Bruzek

The interview with Hilda Bruzek from New Prague, Minnesota, was delightful. According to Hilda, her mother, Anna Mary Labert, and her father, William Temple, were born and raised in Pesotum, a small town in the very south of Champaign County, Illinois. Their ancestry stemmed from the Germanic regions of Europe. They met and married in Champaign County.

Later, the Temples moved to Sherburn, Minnesota, a small town west of Fairmont in the southern part of the state. William and Anna settled on a farm at first, but soon moved into town. William worked in construction, building houses, and Anna was a housewife. They had ten children, five boys and five girls; the first of the ten children was adopted. Hilda said that the local parish priest announced that there were two children that needed adoptive parents and the Temples adopted one of them. Hilda was the second youngest child, born on December 29, 1918. In 2003 she was the only surviving child.

As she was growing up in Sherburn, Hilda remembered living in two houses. She had little memory of what the first house was like, since the family moved from the house when she was only three years old. Still, she was able to remember that it had an outhouse but did not remember it having electricity. It could be assumed that it was a pretty basic house for the time. She was able to describe the second house a bit better. It was across the street from the first house, and she said it was quite big. It had five bedrooms upstairs, with a kitchen, dining room, parlor, and the parents' bedroom downstairs. She also noted that it had two sun porches. The home was equipped with amenities such as electricity, plumbing, and a furnace.

Her mother was a very good cook, and Hilda recounted the Sunday meals with relish. The main entree was often either fried chicken or roast beef. For herself, she said, "I liked everything!"

Hilda was in her teens and early twenties during the Great Depression. She felt lucky because the family was not greatly affected by the economic times. She mentioned that one brother worked as a butter maker and another worked in a grocery store, so the family at least ate well. Also, her father was able to work during this period; however, she noted that he did not work as much in the winter. (This may have been due to the effect of weather on construction, as well as the poor economic conditions.) Hilda's description of how her family managed showed the importance of family cooperation with the children chipping in.

Hilda loved going to the town school. She also mentioned that she had an older brother who suffered from several childhood illnesses and was held back. He ended up going through school with Hilda. At one point, they each skipped a grade. The elementary school went through grade six and the secondary school went from grade seven through grade twelve. She liked all subjects in school—except physics. Hilda also was a good basketball player for the girls' high school team, one of the few sports available to girls in those days. Cheerleading was another activity that involved her time during high school. The love of school went hand in hand with the desire to be a teacher. It was a dream of hers from as far back as she could remember. Her love of school probably helped her achievement because she graduated as valedictorian. Besides that, she worked part- time in the superintendent's office during the school year, earning ten dollars a month.

After high school, Hilda continued her dream of becoming a teacher by attending Mankato State Teachers' College (now Minnesota State at Mankato). She completed a two year certificate program and later took more classes. Completion of the program at Mankato allowed Hilda to take the next step of becoming a teacher, which was accomplished when she took an elementary position in New Prague. She taught third and fourth grades over a period of four years. Her favorite subject to teach was math, but she loved music and also enjoyed being involved in teaching that.

Then came a new point in her life; Hilda met Benedict, her future husband. They met at a church festival in 1936 and dated four years before getting married in 1940. She told a short anecdote about their different backgrounds. Ben was Czech and spoke his ancestral language very well, as it was likely spoken around the house. Hilda, on the other hand, did not know German (her ancestral language) because her parents did not want the children to speak it. She said her parents took the attitude that they were Americans and English is what they would speak. At any rate, the young couple was married at beautiful St. Wenceslaus Church in New Prague.

The marriage occurred soon after war broke out in Europe. The war was starting to have a big affect on the United States. Hilda said Ben did not have to go into the service due to problems with kidney stones. As a matter of fact, no one from her family was called to serve in the military during the war. She did remember the rationing stamps for sugar, but did not feel the family suffered during World War II or any war that followed.

Marriage changed much in her life. Ben was a mortician in town and Hilda quit teaching because the school district did not hire married teachers. She indicated that while there may not have been a written policy, "It was not recommended." She also noted that she did a lot of subbing, which she loved to do. Besides subbing, she obtained a funeral director's license which allowed her to help Ben in his work. In addition, the family grew by four, with David, the first child, being born in 1942. He was followed by Deborah in 1944. Then there was a gap of eight years and Mary was born in 1952, followed by Mark in 1954. Hilda continued subbing during the years that her children were growing up. When the grandchildren started arriving, she retired.

Hilda pointed out an interesting fact about her childrens' careers. The two boys became dentists and the two girls became nurses. In 2003, three oldest children still lived nearby in New Prague, and Mark lived in Wisconsin.

For many years, the Bruzek's lived above the funeral home. That fact brought to mind a story about a couple of pets they owned. They sometimes put the family bunny and dog out on the roof in the wintertime. One day, the dog chased the bunny, and unfortunately, the bunny fell off the roof to its death. The youngest child at the time, Mary, was quite upset by the whole episode. Hilda said Mary was so hurt she thought the poor girl would never stop crying.

Substitute teaching and raising children were very important and time-consuming activities in her life. However, Hilda found time for more. She had lead roles in two community theater plays during the late 1950s. First, she played Bernadette in the play, The Song Of Bernadette. About two years later she played Lucia in the play, The Lady Of Fatima. Besides that, she sang in the church choir for many years and became one of the first lay eucharistic ministers for her church. She also took leadership positions in both the Boy Scouts and Girl Scouts. Her four children were all scouts, and she maintained these positions the whole time they were in scouting.

During their years together, Hilda and Ben traveled quite a bit. They took many car trips within the United States and also traveled to Europe three times. They traveled in many countries such as Portugal, Italy, France, Germany, Switzerland, and the Czech Republic. One of the highlights in Europe was climbing to the top of the dome of St. Peter's Basilica in the Vatican. Another highlight was viewing the shrine of Fatima in Portugal. Within the United States, trips to Colorado and California stood out. Actually, she had been to California several times because she had a very good friend who lived there.

Over the years, Hilda and Ben enjoyed a variety of activities. Dancing and roller skating were among them. She remembered going to the local ballroom for dances as well as for skating. She said even her father-in-law liked to roller skate into his seventies.

Besides the activities that involved her time while her children were growing up, Hilda continued participating in local organizations after they reached adulthood. For one thing, she was a member of the New Prague Historical Society and wrote a short history of New Prague. In addition, she was a member of Friends Of The Library and enjoyed baking for the group's activities. Not to be forgotten was her membership in the Queen of Peace Hospital Auxiliary where she did a variety of tasks.

A favorite hobby was sewing. She took a good deal of pride in her skills as a seamstress. She specialized in making clothes, and of course, her children were the recipients of most of her efforts. She remembered a time when she received a wool coat, cut it to a smaller size, and remade it for her son, David. She was even known to cut out her own patterns. She continued this hobby even after her children were grown and out on their own. It took a broken wrist a few years ago to stop her from sewing.

Hilda long enjoyed playing cards, including bridge, svik, and euchre. At the time of our interview, she only played euchre because she could not hold many cards in her hands, but she did play on a regular basis. She could not remember how to play svik, but it did remind her that her husband made a svik table many years ago. She said he liked to work with wood and often refinished wood pieces.

Although she did not do it so much any more, reading used to be a favorite past time. She did not have a specific category of books that she preferred, but probably read novels the most.

Although Hilda did not go into a lot of specifics about her life, she came across as a gentle person who cared about people. She and her husband appeared to have a strong marriage, and his death in 1993 was hard. But she has persevered and continues to be an active person.

Anne Juni

Both of Anne's parents were born and raised in Minnesota. Her mother, Mary Simek, spent most of her life in the New Prague area, although she did attend St. Joseph's Academy in St. Paul through eighth grade. Mary had one brother and one sister. Anne's father, August Sticha, was the youngest of ten children. Of the seven boys and three girls, the first seven were born in Czechoslovakia, and the last three were born in the United States. He and Mary were wed in 1889.

August was a blacksmith and a wagon maker, and had his shop on Main Street in New Prague. Anne remembered the sounds of the pounding of metals and the products created by her father.

Anne was the fifth of six children born to Mary and August. The children, in order of birth, were Celia, Mary, Alice, George,

Anne (born May 29, 1907), and Gus. She was born in the family home which was still standing in 2003. The home was located behind her father's shop. She remembered that it did not have electricity when she was little. Light was provided by kerosene lamps and candles. It was a time of family joy when electricity was brought to the house in 1914. Her mother thought it was the greatest invention. For the children, it meant they no longer had to clean lamp chimneys or trim candle wicks.

All of the family food was made at home. Her mother was a good cook, and Anne said, "She made bread and kolackys all the time." Baked goods were among her favorites, but she did not recall any foods that she did not like.

New Prague of the early twentieth century was much different than today. For one thing, the streets were not paved. The main form of transportation was by horse, which meant hitching posts were located up and down each side of Main Street, the center of activity in the town. Main Street was where most of the businesses were located and was the site of parades and political events.

Anne remembered many of the events and activities of the early 1900s. For example, she remembered that the first car in the area was purchased by a local doctor, and she even had the pleasure of being given a ride in that car. She also remembered the different peddlers that came into town by train or wagon during the summer. They often stopped by her family's house to sell their goods or services. A rag man might stop by one day, or a person who mended umbrellas. The chimney sweep or the man selling notions or the woman selling lace might stop by on other days. The stream of peddlers went on and on.

Anne's family was very close and shared strong religious beliefs. The family always managed to come together every day to eat their meals, and each meal started with the family members standing to say grace. Both parents spent a lot of time with the children, and the children often played together.

In 1914, Anne entered first grade at the local Catholic elementary school. She had a strict routine that began at 7:30 AM when she left home for school. She attended Mass at 8:00 AM and then went to classes. At noon, the students were given an hour for lunch, at which time she walked three blocks home to eat with the family. She then returned for afternoon classes, and school was finally dismissed at 4:00 PM.

Public high school was the next step in her educational life. She continued to do well in her classes, and also played a sport that she really enjoyed—basketball. Very few athletic opportunities were open for young women during the 1920s. Basketball was one of them, and it was very popular among the young women of New Prague. Anne played all four years of high school. However, playing was not always easy since they did not have a gymnasium for practice or games. Instead, a local saloon, Nickolay's, was converted for both practice and games.

Anne graduated from high school in 1925, and was ready to prepare for a career. Her intention was to become a nurse, so she went to St. Paul and was interviewed for a nursing program at St. Joseph's Hospital. A career in nursing was not to be, because her father had a different idea. He was a member of the school board and he told her she could get a year of teacher training at college for nothing.

The program was given in New Prague. She ended up taking the teacher training program and received her teacher's certificate after the one year. She said, "I never got into nursing because I got a job teaching and taught for twenty-one years!"

That first teaching job was in a rural school. The one year certificate limited teaching to rural schools. It was the typical school in which a single teacher taught grades one through eight. She was paid one hundred ten dollars per month and the major expenses were four dollars a week for room and board and fifty cents a day for transportation to and from school. She was able to save money and bought two fur coats during her early teaching career. After a few years of teaching, she completed a second year of education at Winona State and continued to teach in rural schools.

Anne made a change in the early 1940s when she decided to advance her own education again. She moved in with an older sister in Atlanta, Georgia, and enrolled in Atlanta University. She completed a degree in Commercial Science, which would be comparable to Business Education today. The program was centered around teaching subjects such as typing, shorthand, and bookkeeping. She liked teaching that subject because "classes were small and you could give the students individual attention."

After completing her degree in Atlanta, Anne took a position in Florida teaching Diversified Cooperative Training. She also continued her education at the University of Florida at Daytona Beach and earned another certificate. Then Anne went back to Atlanta to teach, and after a time, she returned to Minnesota.

Back in Minnesota, Anne became reacquainted with Howard Juni, her future husband. While she was studying and teaching in the south, he was in the military and fought in World War II. They first met at a festival in Montgomery, Minnesota, called Kolacky Days, before she originally left for Atlanta. They met again when Anne returned to teach in Jordan, Minnesota, and he ran a hardware store there. The couple married in 1946.

Anne and Howard made their home in Jordan, and he continued in the hardware business. Anne, however, left teaching as the family began to grow. They had three children: Mary Ann, Howard, and Carolyn Cecilia. Anne decided not to return to teaching until the children were pretty independent. However, she did earn certification in the area of Special Education—this time from Mankato State College (Minnesota State at Mankato).

In 1960, Howard sold the hardware store, and the family moved to New Prague. The children were in sixth, seventh, and eighth grades, respectively. Ann applied for and was hired to teach special education. She stayed in that position for eleven years and retired in 1972. However, she continued as a substitute teacher in the local Catholic school—and did it on a voluntary basis until 1982!

Of all her years teaching, Anne probably got the most satisfaction from teaching special education. She taught at the elementary school level through eighth grade. She said that she taught all the children how to type. This was a skill over and above what she was required to teach. The successes she had with specific students were special. In one case, parents told her about how their son came home from school one day and said he had learned to type. They did not believe him and told him to stay away from the family typewriter. Yet, he kept pestering them about being able to type. One day, in exasperation, they told their son to sit down and show them he could type. When he actually showed them, they were flabbergasted! In another situation, a student came from Faribault who could not speak, read, or write. With a lot of work and patience, she taught that student all three skills. She ran into him years later and found that he was gainfully employed and doing well.

Over the years and especially after retirement, Anne and Howard enjoyed traveling. They took several trips to Europe and visited most countries on that continent. Their trips included two visits to Czechoslovakia (where she was able to speak Czech) and a visit to Medjugorje in what was Yugoslavia. They also took a train trip across Canada.

The travel pretty much came to an end when her husband became ill and was diagnosed with cancer of the pancreas. Much of his treatment was at the regional Vets Hospital. Anne visited daily during those difficult days of treatment and surgeries. During the later stages of his illness, he entered Queen of Peace Hospital in New Prague, and it was there that he died. Although the death of a loved one is always difficult, his illness allowed Anne to be somewhat prepared when the end came.

Some time after her husband's death, she moved into Queen's Court, an apartment run by the local hospital for people who can independently care for themselves. The building had one and two bedroom apartments with a laundry on each floor and community rooms for social activities. More recently, she moved to Mala Strana, a very nice assisted living complex on the north end of New Prague.

Retirement and widowhood could have left Anne with an empty life, but she had a lifetime of volunteer activity that carried her through this period. During her early days as a rural school teacher, she started the first local Girl Scout Troop. She said some girls came to her house asking for an organization for young girls. Anne went out and bought a Campfire Girls book and a Girl Scout book, gave them to the girls, and let them pick which organization they wanted to join. A major reason the girls wanted to join an organization was to go to camp. Anne said the girls went to a Boy Scout camp that the girls were allowed to use during part of the summer, and it was there that they learned to swim. She also earned her swimming certificate at that camp.

Since those days, Anne has been involved in a long list of volunteer organizations. Anne was a member of the first local church board after Vatican II. Later she took part in a fund drive for St. Wenceslaus, her local parish. Anne also belonged to the local chapter of the Red Cross. Related to her professional life was her membership in the Legislative Committee of the Minnesota Association of Retarded Citizens. Not to be forgotten was her activity in the New Prague Senior Citizen's Club, in which she served as vice president and president. Anne also took part in several other activities such as Mittens To Go, which involved knitting and distributing mittens during the holidays. She also helped senior citizens with tax preparation. Finally, Anne served as the "Sunshine Lady," where she sent get well cards to the ill.

Over the years, she lost a little independence because she stopped driving in the early 1990s. In respect to driving, she was different than most younger drivers. For one thing, she did not learn to drive until later in life and never really enjoyed it. Anne did not like parallel parking, so she always tried to park near a corner, which was limiting. She also was nervous about having car trouble and being left stranded somewhere. Still, it was an adjustment to give up driving and the independence it gave her.

In 2003, she was no longer involved in a lot of volunteer activities, though she still enjoyed being active. Over the years, she enjoyed playing cards. Anne belonged to a club called Card-o-rama when she lived at Queen's Court. It was a card club that began play each fall. At the time of the interview, she still enjoyed playing a variety of games including bridge, euchre, and 500.

In addition, she did a lot of crocheting. She crocheted over fifty doilies and worked at it pretty regularly through 2002. She estimated that it took about fifty hours to complete each doily. Crocheting was still an important activity when we talked, as she had started on some pot holders that she intended to finish.

Anne learned from her father to plan for the future. As a result of planning ahead, she was able to receive retirement income from a variety of sources, and that allowed her to live comfortably in retirement.

This active lady made it a point to exercise her mind and body. In addition, she said, "I have a great deal of faith. I grew up with the idea that everything was the will of God." These characteristics helped Anne better adapt to the adjustments she had to make in life. With her sharp mind and good physical condition, her activity level remained high. While she may have lost a little independence over the last few years, she was still a person in control of her life.

Ed Sticha

Ed's work life was devoted to agriculture. He was born to a farming couple and spent most of his life on the same farm. His father was Frank W. Sticha who was born and raised in the New Prague area. His mother, Elizabeth, also was a lifetime local resident. They became a full-time farming couple, working eighty acres of land. Frank did much of the farm labor, and Elizabeth helped and did the cooking, They both played important roles in raising their children.

The Sticha's had four children: Julia, Ed (born January 18, 1913), Adeline, and Elsie. The children were expected to do farm chores as they grew up. They also had the benefit of eating their mother's cooking. She cooked and baked from scratch almost everything the family ate. She also did a lot of canning, and much of the canned food was eaten during the winter months. Ed noted that his favorite food was apple pie, but there were not any foods that he did not like. He said, "I ate everything."

The Sticha house was a large two story with three bedrooms upstairs and a kitchen, dining room, and living room downstairs. While he was growing up, the house did not have a telephone, electricity, or plumbing. Heat was provided by a wood burning stove and a cellar was important for storing canned goods.

An eighty-acre farm meant plenty of chores during those days when modern farm equipment was just beginning to come on the scene. It was a time when teams of horses were used for doing the field work, and dairy cows were milked by hand. Feeding the animals and cleaning out stalls were some of the chores Ed did while growing up. He also did things such as plowing fields, milking cows, and helping do repair work as he got older. These chores were typical of what any growing boy would do on a family farm during the 1920s. He seemed to take the attitude that the chores were a basic part of farm life, and one did not complain or try to get out of doing them.

Ed's education took place mainly in a rural school. The typical rural school had one room with students from first through eighth grade. It appears that he attended the rural school through about fifth grade. Then, at the age of ten, he transferred to the Catholic school in town for a couple of years. This was done in order to complete the religious training necessary to receive First Communion and then Confirmation. Next it was back to the rural school where he finished his education.

Like most rural children, he learned to drive at a relatively young age. When he was twelve years old, his father first took him out to drive on the country roads where they went slowly. Ed remembered the car—a Model T Ford with a crank start. He said it was sometimes hard to start the car with that crank. He said that sometimes it was easier to start by raising the rear end and putting it into gear and then cranking it. He said, "It was dangerous." Imagine having the car jacked up and in gear and then standing in front to start it. A person had to be quick if the car came off the jack. After getting some time behind the wheel, he was allowed to drive the car to church. He also was given the responsibility for driving his sisters to school.

When Ed was twenty, he met his future wife, Anna Pexa. They met at a dance, and courted for some time. They were married in 1933 and lived on his family's farm and worked the farm with his parents.

They were just getting started during the depths of the Great Depression. Prices for agricultural products were very low, especially in 1933 and 1934. During those two years, he was selling milk for eighty-five cents a hundred and pigs were selling for only three to four cents per pound. He remembered getting a seven dollar check for milk and then using all of it to buy silage. Ed mentioned that after Franklin Roosevelt took office and his New Deal Program was operating, prices began to go up. Even during those tough times they were able to keep the farm going. The family garden produced much of the food that sustained the family during those years and after.

Matters became even worse when drought hit during the depression. He said, "The crop was so poor that we did not have enough hay for the cattle." They actually had to cut down trees so the cattle could eat the leaves from the branches. They had to thrash all of the straw in the barn because it was all they had to feed the livestock. Then they had to get rid of some of their cows—for only seven dollars a head. It was truly a rough time.

In 1935, his father decided to retire and move into town. Ed paid his father about $5,000 and took over the farm. That piece of land would remain the home to Ed and Anna for much of the rest of their lives. It also was where they raised their two children, Gladys and Wilfred. Both still lived nearby, Gladys in Montgomery and Wilfred in New Prague.

The family farm was gradually improved over the years. Ed bought his first tractor in 1941 or 1942. Since it was during World War II, he had to deal with the rationing of products that were important to farmers such as gas and tires. He re-membered having ration stamps for the gas. As a result, Ed said, "A person did not do much driving." As a matter of fact, he still used his horses quite a bit. The tractor was only used for plowing the fields, and the horses were used for all the other field work. Ed said, "At that time practically everybody used the tractor for plowing and horses for everything else." Conveniences were gradually added to the farmhouse too. They had a telephone by the mid 1940s, and also upgraded with electricity, plumbing, and central heating. He recognized the need to increase the size of the farm and bought an addi-tional 23 acres to bring the total to 103 acres. More mechanization came to the farm in the late 1940s. They added milking machines in 1948. Up to that time, they were milking about seventeen or eighteen cows by hand. When he added a new and larger barn, they were able to milk twenty-six cows. He added structures such as the new barn in 1958 and then a chicken house and a pig house as time went on. The old barn was used for a couple more years and then they took it down.

Ed and Anna continued to work their farm for many years. During the last several years, he rented out some of the land but kept pasture land and livestock. Retirement finally came when the couple sold the farm in May of 1998. Most people say they spent their lives doing this or that, but when Ed said he farmed his whole life, he meant it. When a person is a fam-ily farmer and does not rely on a lot of help, it becomes all-consuming. There is often little time to develop hobbies, which was true in Ed's case.

Ed's farm was really too small for either child to take over and hope to make a profit. As a result, both went into other lines of work, and sale of the farm meant that after about 100 years, it was no longer in the family.

Ed and Anna moved into an apartment building in New Prague called Queen's Court. They enjoyed playing cards and going on organized day trips. He noted that he enjoyed his time there and had made many friends. Then Anna became sick and died on October 14, 2002.

He continued to live at Queen's Court for a while, then decided to move to Mala Strana—an assisted living complex. The facility provided two meals a day and provided weekly housecleaning services. These things made life much simpler for him. At the time of the interview, Ed still enjoyed playing cards—euchre was his favorite and he looked forward to reading the daily newspaper. Ed also had friends to visit with everyday. Besides that, he closely followed sports.

This man was truly an example of the family farmer of the 20th century. The farm was not large, nor was it specialized. He learned on the job as he grew, and the farm was not highly mechanized. Given these circumstances, farming was a hard and all-encompassing job. Yet, if one looked into Ed's eyes, one would see a person who probably would not have traded that life for anything else.

Olive Cemensky

Anyone who enters Olive's home would quickly be able to detect the two greatest passions in her life—her family and her music. One wall of the living room is dominated by portraits of her four children. Looking about the room, one cannot miss the cabinets and shelves filled with dozens of miniature pianos—sixty and counting. Her story clearly defines the importance of family and music.

Olive's parents, Max and Mathilda Haack, were of German ancestry and lived in Pettis Station, south of St. Peter, Minnesota. The community was so small Max owned the only store, a grocery. The family lived in the part of the building behind the store. The railroad ran by the store, and people brought their milk to the store to be put on the train to St. Peter. Her mother was apparently of delicate health. Before she married

Max, her family sent Mathilda to California for a time, thinking that it would improve her health. Unfortunately, Mathilda died only six months after Olive's birth on October 2, 1919. Her mother wanted Olive to be raised by her grandmother, Theresa Schmidt, Aunts Mary and Emma, and Uncle Gus. Olive said she thought the request was made because her mother wanted to make sure she would be raised as a Catholic. She did not have much contact with her father after the move and could not provide a lot of detail about either parent. She did say that her father eventually married a widow who had several children, and they had two of their own.

At first, Olive, her grandmother, two aunts, and uncle all lived on a farm near St. Peter. She remembered that the farmhouse did not have running water or electricity. It had three bedrooms upstairs with the kitchen, dining, and living rooms downstairs.

When Olive was six, her uncle Gus married. She noted that she was the flower girl and it was the only wedding that she was ever in because after that, she always played the organ for friends' and relatives' weddings, so she could not be a bridesmaid.

After the marriage, Gus bought the farm, and Olive and her grandmother and aunts moved to St. Peter, which is where she spent her formative years. It was during this period, she remembered, that when the man came with ice for the icebox, she and the other children in the neighborhood ran after him to get little shavings of ice, which were treats in the summer heat.

Olive said she was really spoiled as she grew up. She was able to get pretty much whatever she wanted, even during the poor economic times of the Great Depression. Some of these examples will follow, but an immediate factor from Olive's upbringing happened when she was five years old. That was when her Aunt Mary won a piano in a raffle. Olive took to the new instrument almost immediately. It was not long before she could play some simple tunes by ear.

She talked a bit about how she was spoiled. One year, she did not want her aunts to take down the Christmas tree after the holidays, so the tree was left up until all the needles fell off. She said she always had clothes and accessories to match. To this day, she does not know how her aunts were able to give her so much when they were not very rich themselves.

Her musical involvement really took off when she entered John Ireland Elementary School. Nuns at the school taught piano lessons, and her Aunt Mary signed Olive up. She took lessons at the school for two years but did not like the way the nuns taught. So she quit and decided to teach herself. That was when Olive also started applying her skills to the organ. By the time she was eight, she was playing the organ for the daily masses at her church. She said, "I played an old pump organ in church—one song in the morning." Within a couple of years, she started playing the big pipe organ at St. Mary's Catholic Church in St. Peter.

After completing her years at John Ireland, Olive went on to St. Peter High School, and her playing expanded. In addition to playing for masses, she started playing for all the weddings and funerals at the church. At about the same time, she started playing for the Golden School of Dancing in St. Peter. She said, "I would sit at the piano and play all day." She also began playing with two local dance bands, which lasted until 1936.

When she was sixteen, some of her girlfriends wanted Olive to teach them how to play the piano. Since she did not know how to teach them, she went to the MacPhail Center for the Arts in Minneapolis for about three weeks and paid a dollar per lesson. She said, "It was the first time I had been away from home." They taught her that chords were important to teach because you play the chords with your left hand.

When she was seventeen, the Archbishop of the Minneapolis/St. Paul Archdiocese wanted all the church organists to earn a certificate because he felt some were playing music that was not appropriate for the masses. All the organists were to attend the College of St. Thomas to earn the certification, so she went to St. Paul for three weeks and earned her certificate.

In 1937 she graduated from St. Peter High School and continued playing. She joined a local orchestra and also began giving piano lessons. Along with playing for masses and church functions, her musical plate was kept full.

Then she met a young man by the name of Ambrose Cemensky from Lexington, Minnesota. (It is a small town a few miles west of Montgomery.) They were married on April 28, 1942. Olive mentioned that during the wedding shower, her choir members made him promise to never take her music from her. The Cemensky's lived in Lexington after their marriage, and Olive became organist at St. Joseph's Church in that town.

She finally learned how to drive after her marriage. Her aunts did not own a car, so she did not get the opportunity to learn as a teenager. As a matter of fact, even if they did own a car, they probably would not have let Olive drive. She said they did not even let her have a bike because they were afraid she would get hurt. At any rate, she continued driving through 2003, but it was been much more limited after she suffered a heart attack in December of 2002.

World War II brought great change to the couple. Ambrose was drafted in 1943 and saw action in Italy. His time away from home during the war was the only time that Olive did not play—she was just too sad and worried. A friend noticed her state of mind and encouraged her to be active and productive. So Olive moved in with a relative in Minneapolis and worked at the Munsingwear plant as an instructor of sewing.

Olive said she bought many clothes while working there, but as things turned out, she ended up getting pregnant and could not wear the clothes. It was about this time that she took up sewing for herself and later for her family. Over the years she ended up sewing clothes for her children, including all their costumes during the years they took dance lessons. She also sewed items for their homes such as drapes and bedspreads.

The tragedy of war soon hit home—Ambrose had his jaw shot off during battle at the Anzio beachhead in Italy. He received emergency treatment and hospitalization in Italy for a couple of months and then was moved to a military hospital in Springfield, Missouri, for two and a half years of surgeries and rehabilitation. During that time, they chiseled a piece of bone from his hip and grafted the piece of bone to rebuild his jaw. Skin also was grafted to the jaw to complete the reconstruction. Olive moved to Missouri to be with him during the rehabilitation, and as noted above, became pregnant with their first child. After his rehabilitation, he was given a medical discharge, which turned out to be the date of their oldest daughter's first birthday.

Olive and Ambrose raised four children. In order of birth, they are Donna, Kathleen, Dale, and Trudy. All of the children learned to play the piano and took dance lessons, but not all with the same enthusiasm. Years later, son Dale, a six-footer, still says, "Ma made me take that ____ dancing." On the other hand, Trudy graduated from Mankato State (Minnesota State University at Mankato) with a degree in music. Olive played with an orchestra from Lonsdale when she was pregnant with Trudy and said, "She had a front row seat—and that is why she is such a great musician." Oldest daughter Donna earned a degree in dance from MacPhail Center for the Arts in Minneapolis. She went on to teach dance in St. Peter for two years, which meant driving from Minneapolis to Montgomery to pick up Olive to play the piano and then going to St. Peter to spend much of each Saturday teaching.

Kathleen also loved music. Today, she lives in Auburn, Washington, and the other three children live in Minnesota within a fifty-mile radius of Olive's home. The children and their spouses have provided Olive with seven grandchildren and five great grandchildren as of our last interview.

After Ambrose received his discharge in 1946, he returned to Lexington and they bought twenty acres of land. He also went back to being a truck driver, which is what he did before going to war. After a time, they went in with another couple and bought a liquor store in the Montgomery Hotel, which they ran for about four years. Next, they bought a resort in Lexington called the Green Lantern. It included a grocery store and four cabins, and they held dances on Saturday nights. Olive said, "We worked like fools." While running the resort, Olive continued playing at church for three years. Then Ambrose bought an implement business in New Prague, thinking that it would be a good business for their son to take over since he had an interest in machinery. But Dale grew to dislike the business, and they sold it after about three or four years. The family moved on to St. Peter and bought an off-sale liquor store. Olive played the organ for the Catholic Church in St. Peter.

During the time they owned the liquor store, Ambrose suffered another serious injury. The previous owner of the store had a car parked there and they wanted him to move it. Unfortunately, it wouldn't start, and Ambrose and the owner decided to pour some gas into the carburetor. There was an explosion when they tried to start the car, and Ambrose was severely burned. Not long after the accident, he suffered a heart attack and was retired from then on.

After the war, work and family were two big components of Ambrose's and Olive's lives, but another component was added in 1946. That was when he joined the Veterans of Foreign Wars (VFW) Post 1803 in Le Center and she joined the Ladies Auxiliary. When they moved to their home in Montgomery in 1955, she transferred her membership to Auxiliary Post 5340.

Olive's membership in the VFW spans well over fifty busy years. When they moved to Montgomery, she was installed as the Auxiliary District Musician, a position she holds to this day. In 1980 Olive was awarded the title of State Musician for her excellence in music; a title she held for thirty-one straight years. Likewise, she held the title of National Musician for seven years. In addition, she held the position of second district president in 1967 and state chief of staff in 1968. She also held several state and district offices. She noted that normally a person could advance to the position of district president only by starting with guards and going through chairs and other offices first. In Olive's case, the president at the time nominated her for senior vice president and she was elected. She then went on to become president in 1967. A position she held for forty years was the co-chair for the annual Veterans Day celebration at the St. Peter State Hospital. That role included buying candy, decorating bags, and putting candy in each of the bags for the veterans. This was done for the 2nd District VFW and Auxiliary. A different Auxiliary from the district was responsible for providing talent. Olive also was involved in sending out invitations to dignitaries such as the state commander and state president of the vets organizations.

The position of National VFW Musician was not only prestigious, but also called for a lot of travel. The first time Olive was National Musician, the local Auxiliary had a testimonial dinner for her in Montgomery. She also traveled to many cities around the country including Philadelphia, Louisville, New Orleans, and two visits to Dallas. Olive noted that a highlight of her career came when she played for a VFW memorial service in 1997 which was held at the Mormon Tabernacle in Salt Lake City.

Though VFW involvement has been a constant over these many years, the other facets of Olive's musical career also have continued. She continued playing for masses at her church and other functions such as weddings and funerals. She also continued to play at other functions such as parties, banquets, dances, and pageants. If the venue did not have an organ or piano, it did not matter a bit. Olive was always able to provide her own instrument when needed. She bought a Conn Theaterette Organ and Ambrose purchased an old yellow bus that opened on the side to transport the instrument. Many times, she played past her scheduled time because the people in attendance wanted more, and she did not want to disappoint. In referring to playing past the scheduled time, she said that Ambrose would just go out to the van and sit there until she was finished.

Her mention of playing so long for events led to a cute story. She was at a convention one night, and the people were not really enjoying themselves. Well, a piano was available, and some people asked Olive to play. Of course she did, and ended up playing into the early hours of the morning. She remembered that the people ended up having a good time and she ended up with raw fingers. She said, "I played 'When Irish Eyes Are Smiling' so many times, I lost count." According to Olive, she could not remember when she ever turned down an invitation to play unless she already had an engagement for that time.

Playing at the Mormon Tabernacle may have been her greatest highlight, but it was not the only one. There was the time in the late 1960s when she played at the Cat And Fiddle Dinner Theater in New Ulm. She claimed that she got the job because she was only person who auditioned who could play both the piano and the organ. (That claim is very likely true, but it is equally likely that her quality of play helped, too.)

Her many performances as State and National Musician included playing in front of some important politicians and celebrities. Former Vice President Walter Mondale, former President Ronald Reagan, the Lennon Sisters, and Danny Thomas were among the notables for whom she performed.

Olive added the teaching of piano and organ lessons to her musical career in 1975. She often taught as many as thirty-five students in a week, and every fall, had a recital. At first, she went out to the different homes, but when winter came her husband insisted that she cut back on going out. So the students came to the Cemensky house for lessons, and poor Ambrose had to listen to a lot of children learning to play the piano and the organ. The local schools have taken on the role of giving lessons, but Olive still gives lessons to a few children each year. Past students often acknowledged Olive's mentoring by giving her remembrances and other gifts of appreciation.

She then mentioned that after retirement, she and Ambrose sometimes took trips to Arizona during the winter months. Olive even played the organ for the church they attended while staying in Arizona. She thought she played for a couple of funerals, too.

After lingering illnesses, Ambrose died in 1992, and Olive played at his funeral. Loss of a spouse of many years was difficult, but her music carried her through. She began as an organist at Holy Redeemer Catholic Church in Montgomery in 1991 and continued on after his death. She kept at it through 2003, but her heart attack caused her to cut back and she stopped playing every Sunday. She continued to play for all the funerals, though she did cut back on doing weddings. Through the years, she played many types of music, but when pressed, admitted that the popular classics from the 1940s and 1950s were her favorites.

Even though music was still a passion at the time of the interview, she had other hobbies, too. Olive did crocheting, which helped keep her fingers nimble. She crocheted afghans and covers for wooden hangers. She also did crossword puzzles, which were good for keeping her mind alert.

Besides the hobbies, Olive gave an annual Christmas party for friends and some past students. For four years she rented a room at the Montgomery American Legion for this occasion. Events include presents of hand-crocheted clothes hangers, which are given to the women guests. Olive said she hoped to continue the Christmas parties into the future.

Still, that primary passion is never far away. There are many scrapbooks filled with pictures, programs, and articles about events this talented woman played in during her career. Besides the scrapbooks, there are boxes of other remembrances of her career. Then there is her music studio with piano and organ. Olive once stated, "My ability to play music is a God-given talent." After having the privilege of listening to two musical selections, including a wonderful rendition of Alley Cat, one can only agree with her statement.

Estellene Bastyr

Estellene had good knowledge of her ancestry. She began by describing the lives of her grandparents. Her father was Frank W. Rutt and his parents were John Rutt and Mari Mracek. They both came to the United States from Czechoslovakia around 1880. According to Estellene, times were hard in Czechoslovakia. She was told many people were being killed. As a result, a large number of young people decided to seek freedom and opportunity in the United States. John and Mari were among those who made the long sea voyage and landed on American soil. Both grandparents came to this country with other family members. Mari was accompanied by her sister, while her brother remained in the homeland. John came to the United States with a brother and a sister. John and Mari met aboard the ship and were married after a romantic courtship.

He was twenty-nine and she was eighteen at the time. They had eleven children, although one died in infancy.

The grandparents from Mari's side were Frank Velishek and Katherine Parkos. Katherine's parents had also come from Czechoslovakia, making for a strong Czech connection on both sides of the family. Katherine was only fifteen years old when she married Frank. They had five children: three daughters, including her mother Mary, and two sons. Their first home was in Minneapolis, but they later moved to Kilkenny township, Minnesota. They farmed in the township a few miles west of Faribault, the same area in which Estellene's great grandparents had settled after moving from their first home in Ohio.

Estellene was born in Montgomery Township in LeSueur County on Easter Monday, March 26, 1921. She was the oldest of eleven children born to Frank and Mary Rutt. She had six sisters and four brothers. When Estellene was one year old, her family moved to Lexington Township in Le Sueur County, which was about four miles northeast of Le Center, Minnesota. This was where they worked their family farm.

Her early life was marked by illness. When she was very young, she and her brother Francis both had whooping cough. Estellene's case was especially bad. When she was six years old and ready to go to school, she stayed with her grandparents so she could attend St. Raphael's Catholic School in Montgomery. However she soon came down with scarlet fever and was very ill for quite a while. Her mother had two younger brothers to care for and she needed help, so Estellene's Aunt Anna moved in with the family to help out. Though only fifteen, Anna took good care of Estellene by giving her medicine and doing other tasks to keep her comfortable. Estellene also noted that her grandmother, with whom she had stayed, was very kind, a good nurse, and a good cook.

The illness interrupted Estellene's education, and she resumed school the next fall by again attending St. Raphael's with Francis. Her dad regularly took Estellene to stay with her grandparents during the week. They went in the family car when the roads were in good condition and used horses when the roads were bad. She noted that the roads were often bad in those days. A sleigh was attached to the horses when the snow was too deep for the car.

Model T Ford on family farm

Trips home were made on the weekends, since the children continued to stay with the grandparents during the school year. A key reason for the arrangement was the location of the school only two blocks from the grandparent Rutt's house.

During her time at her grandparent's house, Estellene helped her grandmother by grocery shopping for her. She also picked up fresh sweet buttermilk from the creamery and brought it home in a little pail. Estellene noted that the grocery store, butcher shop, and creamery were only about three blocks from her grandparents' house. Her grandmother made very good baked goods such as rye bread and kolackys on her wood burning cook stove.

Estellene added a short anecdote about the trips to her grandparents' house. She said, "One time it snowed and stormed so badly when my dad brought us to Grandma's that he had to stay overnight." Her grandparents had a barn in town where Frank put the horses. After tying them in the barn, he fed them hay and oats that he had brought along and gave them water. Meanwhile, her mother was left alone to do all the chores. Estellene added, "It must have been hard . . . that day." However, she believed her parents had hired help on the farm who may have taken some of the burden off her mother.

Estellene's brother, Joseph Edison, was the next to join her and Francis at school. Unfortunately he became very homesick while staying with his grandparents. One day, the six-and-a-half-year-old figured out where the railroad tracks went through town and followed them back home. Imagine how worried Grandma Rutt was when Joseph did not return from school. Since neither the grandparents nor parents had a telephone, there was not a quick way to communicate.

That incident helped lead to a change in schools for the children. Later, the children all attended public school in Le Sueur County District 11. Her father sometimes gave the children rides to school, but they walked most of the time. The one and a half mile route to school was along railroad tracks.

Estellene said she loved going to the one room country school house. She enjoyed reciting and especially liked the programs at Christmas time. Estellene remembered never wanting to miss school, and she always looked forward to having parts in the school plays.

Talk of school led to another related story. December of 1935 was cold and snowy, and, of course, Estellene did not want to miss school. One day, her father hitched the horses to the sleigh and tried to take the children to school. It was thirty degrees below zero and the snow drifts were very deep. Eventually

Estellene (in bonnet) with brother (in front) & schoolmates

the horses got stuck in a drift and her father had to shovel them out. She said it was so cold that he froze his fingers, and after all the shoveling, they had to turn around and go back home.

The school house was typical for the time. It was heated with wood, which was kept in a woodshed located by the school. The older children took turns carrying wood into the school entry. They also brought water for the school from the neighbors.

Students had many activities during the lunch hour and other times during the school day. In those days, the students only had lunches that they brought from home, and the lunches sometimes froze when the weather became really cold. Estellene noted when snow fell, the students rode down a hill during noon hour on toboggans and sleds.

When the snow became packed and hard, the students built igloos. In warmer weather, they played baseball and other games during recess and noon hour. In addition, they occasionally had parties at the school for events such as Halloween, Christmas, and St. Valentine's Day. She mentioned that Santa gave gifts to the students after their Christmas program. Estellene said, "I don't know how we found time to do so many things."

The school day ran from 9:00 AM to 4:00 PM, and the trek to school was sometimes difficult. Estellene noted that it was hard for her younger brother and sisters to walk to school during the winter. It was especially difficult to get through some of the snow that drifted across the school driveway after heavy snows.

Estellene also was impressed by the teachers at the country school. She said they were very kind and had a variety of custodial jobs besides teaching students in eight grades. There were usually two to four students per grade, and they almost always knew their lessons and all were able to recite whatever was required. In addition to teaching lessons, the country teacher was in charge of keeping the schoolhouse warm and clean.

From fourth grade on, she was one of the older students and became sort of a teacher's helper. Estellene mentioned that she had a younger brother who thought school was a joke and did not want to study. Still she tried hard to teach him. She graduated from eighth grade in 1936, and the graduation exercise was held at the courthouse in Le Center, Minnesota.

During this period of time, she also received two sacraments at Holy Redeemer Catholic Church in Montgomery. She received her first Holy Communion at age nine and later completed Confirmation.

In the fall of 1936, Estellene began ninth grade at Montgomery High School, which she attended until graduating in May of 1940. Like her first period of schooling, some of the time was spent at her grandmother's house. (Grandfather Rutt had died in 1930.) She also stayed with an aunt and uncle for some time and later babysat and worked for her room and board. By the time she entered eleventh grade, a school bus started taking the students to school. It picked up elementary students going to the local Catholic school as well as high school students. History, English, typing, algebra, shorthand, and home economics were among the classes she remembered taking in high school. She also went out for declaim (public speaking), but gave it up because her mother did not show interest in her work.

School meant friends, and she made a lot of friends during her school years. For people living in rural areas, friends often lived miles apart, but Estellene was willing to take those long walks to visit her friends. Going from a rural school to Montgomery High School meant making many new friends.

Then came a story about her brother, Joseph Edison, the one who did not like school. One class he did like when he was in ninth grade was music. It was probably the one thing that kept him going to school until Estellene graduated. Later he took music lessons from a special teacher, and his interest and skill led him to eventually play in bands. Next he took up mechanics at Dunwoody Institute, which fulfilled a long time interest. When he was only fourteen years old, he took apart his father's Model A Ford and laid the parts in a circle around the chassis. Obviously, his father was not very happy since it was the only vehicle he owned and therefore the only method of transportation. Whether it was skill or luck (or maybe a little of both), Joseph Edison put the car back together again, and it worked! Later in life, he worked at building homes.

Music was an important part of life for the Rutt family. Frank played in the Montgomery Kolacky Band and also played in another band with brothers Joe and Jim. That band played for wedding showers, weddings, and other local events. Estellene, her mother, and sister Dolores marched with the Kolacky Girls. Estellene marched with the group for a number of years.

Growing up also included fulfilling responsibilities such as doing farm chores. Estellene and her brother Francis had the job of moving cattle from one pasture to another. It usually worked like this: Estellene took the cattle over the railroad tracks to the second pasture. The morning process included opening two gates, getting the cattle through and closing the gates behind the cattle. Meanwhile, Francis put the bridle on the horse while it stood next to a fence. The two kids climbed up on the horse and followed the cows to the pasture. The whole process was done in reverse in the evening. She and her brother also milked cows, fed calves, and filled stalls with hay. Sometimes they mucked out the barn (took the manure out) and pitched manure onto the manure spreader to be used to fertilize the fields.

Work around the house was also among the responsibilities, and her mother was particular about having a neat house. For example, Estellene babysat her younger brothers and sisters while she was still young herself, about nine years old. Her mother liked the way Estellene ironed and had her do a lot of it. By the time she was thirteen, she helped with the canning. She said, "I canned things like peaches and cucumber pickles with my mother's help."

Estellene also remembered a time when her mother was pregnant and not able to work until after giving birth to her sister Donna Mae. As a matter of fact, her mother was away for six weeks during March and part of April. While her mother stayed at her aunt's house, Estellene had to pick up the slack. This meant baking big batches of bread, taking care of the younger children, cooking for the nine family members at home, and attending country school.

Since she also was going to school while her mother was away, others in the family also had to pitch in and do extra work. Her father helped make the meals and did the housecleaning. He also took care of Estellene's youngest sisters who were three and four and a half years old. This meant getting the farm chores done in the morning before the older children went to school, taking care of the little ones, and doing more chores when the older ones came home. Her oldest brother had to miss some school when their father needed him on the farm. Estellene also had to miss some school during those six weeks.

Her school years left Estellene with many fond memories. She especially enjoyed the time she went to St. Raphael's from her grandmother's house in Montgomery. She had several friends and enjoyed the times they played together. She noted that some of the girls had play houses, and the children spent many hours playing. She also remembered times when neighborhood children came together in the early evening hours to play games like cops and robbers and hide and seek.

During parts of the year, other jobs had to be done. For example, during haying time, Estellene drove the horses which pulled the hay rack. While her brother and father pitched the hay onto the hay rack from piles of dried hay her father had raked up in the meadow, Estellene stamped it down. During harvesting of the grain, she helped shock the grain bundles to help them dry. When her father thought the grain was dry enough, the hired hands hauled them into the farmyard where her father wanted them and stacked the straw. While one person pitched the straw onto the pile, her father worked to make the stack wider at the bottom and narrower toward the top until it came to a peak.

Eventually a threshing machine was able to come, and it was threshing time! The steam engine whistled as it came, and everything had to be ready as the big machine was parked by the stacks. The neighbors usually came to help as they did when it was time for shocking, butchering, or corn shredding. It was understood that neighbors helped each other. The women prepared a lot of good food and worked together so the threshers could get a lunch in the forenoon, a noon meal, lunch at about 4:00 PM, and a late supper, depending on how late they stayed.

Threshing from grain stacks on the family farm in the 1940s

Then she described the threshing process. Estellene said, "When threshing, someone pitched the bundles of grain from the stack into the threshing machine. The grain went into the sacks in a grain box, and the grain was hauled up to a granary. It took several men to carry sacks of grain on their backs and dump the grain into the proper bin—oats into the oat bin, barley into the barley bin, and wheat into the wheat bin." She said her mother cooked up a great meal that might typically include soup, potatoes and gravy, meat, vegetables, good pies, and cake. According to her, "It was our best meal of the year." The working men sometimes ended the day by drinking a beer or they drank water from a pail using a dipper or a cup.

In the early years from the 1920s to the late 1930s, her family had an icehouse to keep things cold. Ice was cut from a nearby lake in the winter, hauled into the icehouse, and covered with saw dust to slow melting during the heat of summer. Later the family put food products such as milk and cream into pails and hung the pails in the well to keep the products fresh.

The childhood house she most remembered was built on the farm in 1931 when she was nine years old. It was a nice house and had a wood furnace, but like many rural houses of the time, they did not have electricity, running water, or a telephone. They had a bathroom of sorts, but without running water and a toilet, an outhouse was needed. She remembered her father cutting wood to fuel the furnace in winter. She noted that her family did not get a telephone until the late 1940s. The same applied for mechanized farm equipment such as tractors, which did not become common until the 1940s.

The Rutt family farm was a busy place for all of the family members. Estellene described how the family raised chickens, ducks, and geese. Chickens were raised for laying eggs and for meat. Some of the hens were called clucks because they wanted to sit on the eggs. Her mother tended the chickens and set eggs under the cluck. While the cluck was sitting, her mother kept feed and water nearby so the cluck could easily get to it. Sometimes a cluck, after hatching eggs for the family, got out of the coop and made a new nest in a straw pile or in the hay barn. It laid a clutch of eggs and stayed on its hidden nest until it hatched the chicks, and then took care of the chicks. There also were times when Estellene's mother put goose or duck eggs under clucks.

Speaking of chickens, one of Estellene's favorite dishes was chicken soup. She described how a freshly butchered chicken became the main ingredient in the soup. During the summer, her mother added fresh onions, carrots, and celery from the garden to add flavor to the soup. In winter, she used the same ingredients, but they were dried and stored in the fruit cellar. Chicken soup was eaten most often on Sundays but also any other times her mother wanted to make it. The rest of the chicken was roasted with dressing that had onions, carrots, and potatoes added.

Although ducks were eaten often during the year, they also were butchered for Thanksgiving and Christmas, as were geese. The birds that were not kept for consumption by the family were sold at a butcher shop. This usually occurred before the holidays.

Estellene remembered her mother doing a lot of canning as she was growing up. Her mother canned fruits and vegetables and sometimes even meat. In those years, many people used salt to preserve pork, and her family also used that method for some of their pork. In winter, they made sausage from pork and beef and smoked it in a smokehouse. (Many farmers built smokehouses for that purpose.) Then they hung the sausage in the smokehouse or sometimes wrapped it and put it into a wheat grain bin which was very cold in the winter.

Another fond memory of food centered around special days like the 4th of July or someone's birthday. Her mother made delicious ice cream for these occasions. She started by putting fresh cream and other ingredients into the freezer container along with ice from their icehouse. Her parents took turns working the hand crank on the container, a job that Estellene helped with when she became old enough. The process turned out about a quart of great tasting ice cream.

Fourth of July celebrations were special for the family. Estellene's father put a flag on the front part of the hood of the car. Then they drove into town and enjoyed the annual parade.

The 1930s brought hard times. For a number of years, summers were hot and very dry, which affected crop quality and production. To make matters worse, prices also were very low for crops and livestock. She said, "When a farmer shipped a cow, he did not get enough money for it to pay the trucker." She remembered prices of many products, and they could be compared to prices today for the same products. For example, coffee was nine cents a pound, eggs were nine cents a dozen, oranges were one cent a piece, a large bag of coconut was five cents, soda was five cents a bottle, a large ice cream cone or candy bar was five cents, and beer was five cents for a large glass. According to Estellene, the family ate most of the profits from the milk her father shipped. Trips to the dentist were not affordable, and there was rarely money for new clothes.

A saving grace during the hard times of the depression was the absence of many bills that are common in today's life. The family did not have to worry about bills for electricity, heat, telephone, health insurance and the like. However, they did carry fire insurance. Estellene noted her family was lucky because everyone was healthy, meaning they did not have to face bills from doctors or hospitals.

Still, parents had to be skilled in many areas and had to work long hours. As noted above, Estellene's mother was good at canning and cooking, two tasks that took much time due to use of fresh ingredients and the lack of modern appliances. Ironing was a chore too. The irons had to be heated on a stove, with one being used while another was being heated. Estellene mentioned having to iron dresses for her sisters that her mother made from "pretty pink feed sacks." She noted her mother was so skilled at sewing that she made her own patterns rather than relying on a pattern from a store. Her mother could also make a new coat out of a larger older coat. She said, "Our clothes were prettier than bought clothes." At the same time, her father was not only a good farmer, but could cut hair like a barber. He not only cut his sons' hair but also cut his neighbor's hair, who would cut his in return. In spite of some of the difficulties, Estellene said she enjoyed living on the farm.

Times were hard and jobs were difficult to come by, and people often ended up working for room and board. But people were friendly and neighbors helped one another harvest crops, butcher livestock, and do odd jobs. When she was sixteen, Estellene was hired at Green Giant in Montgomery and worked long days for thirteen cents an hour. During what she called the corn pack (packing corn), Estellene stayed with her grandmother Rutt. She also remembered the cafeteria fare at Green Giant. Hot beef sandwiches and hamburgers were fifteen cents each. When one only made thirteen cents an hour, one did not buy cafeteria food very often. Estellene continued to work there until she was eighteen.

Her mother was sick during the summer of Estellene's sixteenth year. Since her mother could not do any work, she gave advice as Estellene took over the housework and babysitting. This was just one more example of the kinds of responsibilities she took on as she grew up.

Growing up was not all work and school, as there were many enjoyable times with the family. Estellene loved to go fishing with her father and brothers. A typical fishing venture included a picnic lunch fixed by her mother, who sat on the shore with the youngest children while Estellene, her father and older brothers fished. After fishing, the family eagerly ate the lunch. The lakes they most often fished were Clear Lake near Lexington, Shields Lake and Lake Mazasko near Shieldsville, and Greenleaf Lake south of Montgomery.

Graduation from high school meant a new stage in her journey of life. Estellene wanted to attend beauty school, but her parents were against her going to the big city. So she gave up the idea, stayed in the area, and worked as a waitress at the Alba Hotel in Montgomery. She remembered earning five dollars a week. She also stayed at another place and helped out and did babysitting for room and board.

Estellene enjoyed going to dances, and it was dancing that brought change into her life. Dances that were part of bridal showers or weddings were fun and free. But one night, she was at a dance at the Hilltop Hall in Montgomery, and that is where she met her future husband. She was seventeen at the time, and they dated for three and a half years before getting married. During that time, they went to many dances, had a lot of fun, and Estellene met many new friends.

The wedding day was October 20, 1941, a day filled with memories. Estellene Rutt and Robert Bastyr were married at Holy Redeemer Catholic Church in Montgomery. The 10 AM wedding mass was followed by a dinner for the wedding party at her house. A big wedding supper was later held at the Alba Hotel, and a dance followed at the Casina on Main Street in Montgomery. The Dick Korbel Band, which also had played at her wedding shower, played at the dance. Estellene remembered that the band played "I Love You Truly" and "The Waltz I Had With You." Their honeymoon was a car trip that included stops in Kansas City, Kansas, Kansas City, Missouri, Omaha, and Boystown, Nebraska.

The newlyweds started by living with Robert's parents. The following year a kitchen was added for them. Robert worked on the farm for his parents, and while he did not get paid in money, they received milk, meat, and butter. In addition, they had their own vegetable garden and were able to pick apples in his parents' orchard and strawberries from his parents' strawberry field.

The Bastyr's had five children. Their first was a boy, Robert Francis, born on September 7, 1942. Estellene said the second was a surprise. Joyce Ralph was born September 20, 1944. He was followed by two daughters, Cheryl Lee, born on May 20, 1948, and De Anna on January 6, 1954. The youngest was Darryl Robert, born on December 30, 1959.

Estellene followed her parents' methods when she and her husband worked their farm. She raised geese and ducks with her husband's help, and they sold some of the geese and many of the ducks. In reference to the clucks, she mentioned that ducks also made their own nests and hatched and raised as many as fifteen ducklings. She said, "The rewards were the good fresh meat."

Estellene was actively involved in her children's lives, including 4H. She had spent many years in 4H as she was involved in it while growing up and was a 4H leader and project leader while her children were members.

As the older children reached adulthood, times became more challenging. The two oldest boys were called to serve our country. Bob entered the Army and served for about three years, including a tour of duty in Vietnam . Joyce served three years in the Navy and was assigned to the USS Midway. The military duty was hard on the parents. Besides worrying about the safety of their two sons, they had to take up the slack on the farm for Bob, who had always been there to help. In addition, their youngest son became ill with cancer.

The joy of having five children was tempered by the heartache felt with the deaths of two of these children. Darryl died at the age of four years and four months from cancer, which had developed behind his eye. Visits were made to see several different specialists at many different hospitals during his illness. They even went to the Mayo Clinic in Rochester. In spite of all their efforts, including several surgeries, he passed away. Estellene described her little boy as "so lovable." Her father died not too long after Darryl in July of 1965, and her mother died in April of 1983. Then Joyce Ralph suffered a heart attack on August 30, 1990, and died suddenly. He was only forty-five, and left behind a family. The shock of that event caused Estellene to suffer a heart attack, too. She ended up being hospitalized at Abbot Northwestern Hospital in Minneapolis for twelve days. As a result, she was unable to attend the wake and funeral for her son.

The family needed money with the illness and death of Darryl, so Estellene went to work. She did some part-time waitress work and worked for Munsingwear in Montgomery in 1962. Her daughter babysat Darryl during the summer and a live-in babysitter came for the winter. Later she worked for Montgomery Wards at Southtown Center in the receiving department. She worked there until she was laid off and then found a job at Dayton's in Minneapolis. She did alterations at the department store for about three years. Then the department was transferred to the warehouse on Industrial Boulevard in Minneapolis. Getting to work from the Jordan area had always been difficult. Her son drove her to Savage on his way to work, where she picked up the first bus. Then she had to make a transfer to take a bus to Dayton's. Moving the department to Industrial Boulevard meant even more transfers, and after another year, she decided to quit. Quitting the job in Minneapolis did not mean retirement. Estellene worked at different sewing jobs in New Prague. She also did cleaning for over thirty senior citizens.

Estellene enjoyed many hobbies and activities over the years. Fishing with Robert was one of her favorite activities. Many of their vacations over the years were fishing vacations both in Minnesota and Wisconsin. She and her husband also continued to enjoy dancing, and often went dancing during their years of marriage. Although it was considered part of farm life, she also liked the tasks of working with chickens, ducks, and other farm animals.

In 1983, she and Robert decided to sell the farm near Jordan. Their son, Robert, took over the farm, and they bought a house in New Prague. They moved in on July 1, 1983, and Estellene still lives there. The farm is over a century old, and to Estellene's thinking, the housing developments nearby have spoiled the beauty of the countryside in the area.

Estellene has been a widow for the last few years because Robert died on December 9, 1997. Besides the loss of her husband, many other things changed for the family. Robert used to go to the farm and help his son, and that changed. At home, he took care of all the business, and Estellene had to take that over. He had always done all of the driving since they only had one car, so that changed her ability to get around.

She has suffered her own medical problems over the last few years. In March 1999, she received a St. Jude Heart Valve without complications. Then a tumor was removed in March 2001 and complications followed. She began to bleed internally on the day she was to go home from Abbott Northwestern Hospital. Instead, she had emergency surgery with blood transfusions. Thankfully, the surgery was successful.

She noted that gardening was an ongoing hobby: the garden included a grapevine and a pear tree. Both were usually loaded with fruit. Canning was a related activity to the gardening, and fall was a very busy time for canning fruits and vegetables. She also loved to raise flowers in her yard.

Arts and crafts are other hobbies that occupied her time over the years. The crafts included making dolls out of detergent bottles, making rag dolls, and sewing and embroidering articles, as well as many other creative crafting activities. She even sold some of these items in craft stores and through individual orders. One year she made and sold thirteen pair of Mr. and Mrs. Santa Claus, dolls, earning enough money for a vacation.

Estellene also belonged to the Minnesota Pen Pal Club and met her pen pals at the Minnesota Pen Pal Picnics which were held each year in the summer. She noted that she had many pen pals and visited many of them, and they visited her in return.

In addition, she enjoyed embroidering, sewing, and baking. She regularly exhibited at the Le Sueur County Fair and has had good results. Her embroidery work won honors for two years in the Senior Division. In addition to the blue ribbon, she won a tankful of gasoline in 2001. In 2003, she won a blue ribbon for her zucchini chocolate cake. Getting the top prize also meant receiving twenty-five pounds of free flour.

Sewing kept her very busy over the years. More recently, she did sewing for the needy, and also sewed with her church mission sewing ladies. One year she made forty-five pairs of mittens from old sweaters. Besides all this, she did a variety of other volunteer activities, including serving as vice president and president of the New Prague Senior Citizens.

This busy lady seemed to truly enjoy being active. In addition, she enjoyed and was proud of her eleven grandchildren and nine great grandchildren. She took joy in getting Christmas gifts each year for her children, their spouses, the grandchildren, the spouses of the married grandchildren, and her great grandchildren. She concluded with a concise statement, "I hope I can keep going and my health will be good."

Metropolitan Minnesota

Minneapolis

Minneapolis skyline

While Minneapolis and St. Paul are two separate cities with their own identities, they are neighbors on the banks of the upper Mississippi River and have come to be known as the Twin Cities. These two bustling medium-sized cities have a recent history of cooperation in many areas. Nevertheless, this thumbnail sketch will address each city separately. (For those interested, I found helpful information about both of these cities at the World Book Online Reference Center. Go to www.worldbookonline.com.)

Minneapolis, in the early twenty-first century, is a city rich in economic and cultural diversity. If one focuses on the Midwestern part of the United States, Minneapolis stands out as a center for finance, industry, trade, and transportation. In addition, it ranks near the top of the country in the quality of its regional theaters, music, sports, and recreation. Minneapolis is also home to the University of Minnesota (main campus), which ranks among the largest universities in the nation.

This city of 371,657, based on the 2000 census has a rich history that dates back to the 1840s. The name Minneapolis is a combination of the American Indian word "minne" and the Greek word "polis." Translated literally, Minneapolis becomes "water city," but over time, the nickname developed into "City of Lakes."

The first permanent white settlers to the area were mostly farmers and lumberjacks. The mixture of broad, flat land with rich soil, and the presence of hardwood forests, were ideal for both occupations. In addition, the location of St. Anthony Falls was ideal for providing power to run flour mills and lumber mills. Actually the original village was established in 1849 and called St. Anthony. The village, located on the east side of the Mississippi River, became a city in 1855. Settlers on the west bank of the river named their community Minneapolis in 1852, and it became a city in 1867. The two cities eventually merged in 1872 and became identified as Minneapolis.

Minneapolis was the flour-producing leader of the world for almost fifty years. From 1882 to 1930, no other city could match the production of the large mills in the city. Even though service industries such as education, finance, and retail trade are the important economic activities of today, the legacy of flour milling is still an important part of the identity of Minneapolis.

The downtown Minneapolis area is located on the west bank of the Mississippi River, and though much wider in scope, is marked by three main thoroughfares. Hennepin Avenue is where much of the city's entertainment is located. Nicollet Mall is the retail shopping area of the city, and is unique because only cabs and buses are allowed to drive on the mall. Marquette Avenue is where the financial district is located. The skyway system allows pedestrians to travel throughout the downtown area in all kinds of weather at all times of the year.

A variety of activities can be enjoyed in Minneapolis. The many city lakes and parks provide great places for recreation. Besides an abundance of high school sports, people attend athletic events at the University of Minnesota; the Hubert H. Humphrey Metrodome is home to the Minnesota Twins, Minnesota Vikings, and Minnesota Gopher football. A variety of quality regional theaters such as the Guthrie are located in and around the city, as are some fine museums. Among the most popular museums are the Minneapolis Institute of Art, the Walker Art Center, and the Weisman Art Museum on the University of Minnesota campus.

As with many cities, Minneapolis experienced some hard times from the late 1940s through the early 1960s. Urban planning brought the city back to vibrancy through urban renewal, and that vibrant atmosphere exists to this day.

St. Paul

St. Paul skyline

St. Paul is the older of the Twin Cities and is the state capital. The population of 287,151 (2000 census) makes it the second largest city in the state. It is part of a metropolitan area that has a population of 2,968,806.

As on the Minneapolis side of the river, American Indians were the only inhabitants up through the early 1800s. The military arrived in 1819 and established Fort St. Anthony. A permanent fort was built between 1820 and 1822 and was renamed Fort Snelling in 1825 after Colonel Josiah Snelling who directed the construction.

The history of the city itself goes back to 1840 when a settlement was established by Pierre Parrant along with several families. The original name of the settlement was Pig's Eye (Parrant's nickname), but it was changed to St. Paul in 1841 after a church dedicated to that saint was built.

St. Paul was incorporated as a town in 1849 and became the territorial capital for Minnesota. It became a city in 1854 and remained the capital when Minnesota became a state in 1858. The city prospered in the late 1880s under the influence of railroad tycoon James J. Hill. Besides promoting trade and transportation through his Great Northern Railway, he made many philanthropic gifts toward the development of civic, cultural, and industrial endeavors in the city

The capital city went through a downturn that began in the 1920s and lasted through the 1940s. By the 1950s efforts were started for renewing the urban area. However, urban redevelopment really went into high gear in the 1970s and after. The Landmark Center, the Capitol Centre, Excel Center, and the Ordway are just a few of the construction and rehabilitation projects that were completed, and other projects loom on the horizon.

Besides being a government center, St. Paul is known as an important distribution and transportation center. Several trucking lines are located in the metro area, and freight service is supplied by four railroads. The city has a downtown airport, and barges ply the Mississippi River bringing goods into and out from St. Paul.

The city also ranks very high in educational and cultural life. Besides being home to several colleges of the University of Minnesota, several other institutions of higher learning grace the city. The College of St. Catherine, Concordia University, Hamline University, Macalester College, Metropolitan University and the University of St. Thomas are all located in St. Paul. This is the home for the Minnesota Wild, the Ordway Center for the Performing Arts, the Minnesota Historical Society Museum, the Science Museum, as well as many other cultural attractions.

St. Paul is a place that can be enjoyed by the people of varied cultural backgrounds that live in and around the city. Besides all that has been mentioned, there are many parks and recreational areas to be enjoyed.

John Povolny

John started by describing the travels of his great grand-parents. His paternal great grandparents were from Bohemia. They traveled to Bremerhaven, Germany, and took a sailing ship to the United States in 1860. They landed in Baltimore and traveled to Chicago. While in Chicago they heard about the good farmland in Minnesota. It was that news which led to their move to Minnesota. They settled in the New Prague area about forty miles south of the Twin Cities. While John did not know how they got to St. Paul, he did know his great grand-father worked as a bookbinder for West Publishing. As an aside, John said that his great grandfather joined the military and took part in the Civil War not long after settling in Minnesota.

His grandfather took a job with the city of St. Paul writing records. It was said that his distinctive and fancy handwriting played a part in getting the job. John noted that his grandfather's job was across the street from West Publishing, his great grandfather's employer. His grandfather and grandmother were married and settled in an area of West Seventh Street in St. Paul, sometimes referred to as Little Bohemia.

The maternal side of the family had a Germanic background. John's grandfather had been trained in Germany by the Krupp Company as a machinist for the railroad. Tough economic times hit during the 1880s, and the family moved to St. Paul, Minnesota, where he worked for the Great Northern Railroad. They built a small home in the Rice Street area of St. Paul and eventually added on to the home as their family grew.

His parents lived in different St. Paul neighborhoods, but they met through mutual friends. They married and moved to a house near where Mr. Povolny worked. John's father never drove or owned a car. John's parents lived their married lives within about half a mile from their home. Mr. Povolny walked to work every day. Church also was within walking distance, as were most shopping areas and downtown St. Paul. The family included four children: Margaret was the oldest; John came next (born on January 26, 1927); Mary Jane and Jim followed.

John's father was a pharmacist. He started his career cleaning the drug store at the age of fourteen and never left the business. He worked his way up to pharmacist, which he did until retirement at the age of seventy-three. In the early years of the twentieth century, a year of drug school and a period of internship led to a license in pharmacy.

His mother took a less direct route to a career. She left school in the eighth grade to work in a laundry. Then she worked with some nuns at St. Bernard's School in the evenings to hone her abundant writing skills and cultivate her intellectual interests. She used these skills to help her children learn during their school years. She finished high school by taking night classes at Mechanic Arts High School in St. Paul. She followed that by getting a business degree through Rasmussen College just prior to marriage. Rasmussen College was a well known business school.

The family lived in the first house John remembered from about the time he was one until he was seventeen. The house had a telephone, electricity, indoor plumbing, and heat provided by a stove in the dining room. He remembered sleeping upstairs, and in the winter, the children often found frost on the bed covers forcing them to get dressed in a hurry. He was about eight or nine when a furnace was installed in the house. He called it "a marvelous invention."

The family had a shed in the back which they used to raise pigeons and chickens. The pigeons were raised for fun, and 200 to 300 chickens were raised per year for food. They bought the chicks 100 at a time for three cents a piece, so an order cost three dollars. When they were big enough, John and his mother butchered the chickens. Some were sold and the rest were canned and eaten by the family. John said that canned chicken was good. Nevertheless, he said, "It took a long time to get used to eating chicken again."

The family also had a large garden. Fresh and canned vegetables were plentiful year-round. John's mother was great at canning vegetables and fruit. In addition, the family ate about 700 to 800 pounds of potatoes a year, which were stored in the root cellar. Potatoes were the major entree at their meals and a root cellar was important in those days.

The family did not get a refrigerator until after World War II. Up to that point, they used an ice box. That meant the kids needed to take a wagon to the local store to buy blocks of ice for the ice box. He liked most of the food they had and gave much credit to the cooking and baking skills of his mother.

The chickens and garden were important during the Depression years. Many family meals came from this source of urban agriculture. The family was lucky in another sense. While wages were adjusted downward, his father always worked. John mentioned that "a number of people in the neighborhood were unemployed or marginally employed" at the time. That is not to say life was easy. He remembered walking to the grocery store looking for bargains, and getting one pair of shoes a year.

Life was busy and fun for the children in spite of the times. A playground was located across the street from the Povolny house. The children made up games or played games such as baseball, kitten ball, and kick the can. They would sometimes sneak down to the river or go to a nearby lake to fish. He remembered learning to play tennis by hitting the ball against the wall of the schoolhouse, which drove the custodian crazy. Meanwhile, hockey was popular in the winter. A particular memory was of the winter of 1936, an especially cold winter. Schools would close when it hit twenty-five degrees below zero because the heating plant was not able to keep the school warm enough. So what did the children do? They went ice skating, skiing, sledding or some other outdoor activity. There were many neighborhood activities and many friends with whom to play. There were fond memories of the pickup games that the neighborhood children played. They always had some way to play even if there were not enough children to play a regulation game.

John's education was through the Catholic school system. He started out at St. Stanislaus School which went through eighth grade. The school had two grades in each room with fifty to sixty students. Nuns were the teachers. He said the nuns were tough: "We (the students) lived in fear of them." But he also felt they were good teachers. While some students advanced more slowly than others, not many dropped out of school.

In terms of his own education, fifth and sixth grades became a turning point. By that time, he became excited about school and actually wanted to learn things. Before that it was a matter of learning because it was expected. He made another leap in seventh grade, when he became bored with the work and started doing much of the eighth grade work on his own. Remember the two classes per room? A nun strongly suggested that he skip eighth grade and go straight to high school; it was on to Cretin High School. He found mixed blessings in the experience. Being a year younger than most classmates, he found school to be a challenge socially. However, he did well academically and took a real liking to chemistry and other sciences. Graduation came in 1943. He remembered working for an uncle to help pay his way through Cretin.

Speaking of that, he felt his uncle provided some valuable learning experiences. This uncle started his own business in 1933 in the midst of the depression. The company made rubber printing plates for printing sandpaper at 3M and corrugated boxes at box companies. The plates were hand carved. John's job was to clean the shop and do other duties on Saturdays. John called his uncle a good teacher of ethics, honesty, and skills in business. In one anecdote, he related that the company also made the boxes for packing the plates for delivery. On one occasion, John was called on to make some of the boxes. The boxes turned out to be not quite as good as the ones made by his uncle. The uncle said, "You know you are going to make them over." When questioned, the uncle suggested they must be perfect. They wanted the customer to know they were getting perfect printing plates, and if the boxes did not suggest that, it would make the customer think they did not care. When the uncle finally retired, the chairman of the board of 3M paid him a complement by saying he was the best supplier 3M ever had.

Learning to drive became a bonus from working for his uncle. One day, when he was thirteen or fourteen, his uncle asked him if he knew how to drive. John replied, "I think so." In fact he had never driven. What he knew was from watching other people drive. So he began driving when given the assignment to deliver the plates. He said of his first efforts, "I didn't do very well, but it was a reasonable enough start."

His dad also helped John learn. He was soft spoken yet was very fair. John said he never heard him raise his voice and gave an example of what he meant. One day, John made the typical teen plea for more freedom by saying, "Well everyone else is going out Friday night." His dad's response was, "Well, not everyone is going out Friday night because you are not." His dad never let himself get into the position of getting into an argument.

While most of his fellow graduates went into the service after high school, John was too young to enlist or be drafted. So he decided to enroll at St. Thomas College (now the University of St. Thomas) in the fall of 1943. In the meantime, he had a part-time job with 3M as a lab person. His idea was to earn enough money to start school in the fall. Then St. Thomas decided to adjust the school program to start July 1 when a United States Navy V-12 program started. This was a wartime program that stressed math and sciences in the training of naval officers. John decided not to go to college. His dad said, "I suppose you think you can't handle it?" That comment helped John decide to enroll in school. During that time, there were 270 navy students and thirty civilian students on campus from 1943 through 1944. He completed a bit more than four semesters and majored in chemistry. Many of the classes he needed to continue on were not available, so he enlisted in the United States Navy.

When he entered the navy, he was assigned to a radar technician school. After he completed that school, he discovered they had trained enough technicians and did not need him in that area. Thus, he ended up being a storekeeper. Soon he shipped out and spent a year cruising the Pacific. Fortunately, he arrived a little late for serious action. He was assigned to the 7th fleet command, which was an amphibious fleet that participated in a number of major invasions in the Pacific. The Pacific cruise took him to Japan, China, Singapore, Hong Kong, and Korea. Upon completion of this tour in 1946, John had accumulated enough points for discharge.

The return home in the summer of 1946 included time for fishing. Then it was back to St. Thomas to finish his studies. He continued in chemistry and completed his work quickly enough to be included in the class of 1947, although the actual graduation was in January of 1948.

Many young graduates had to make up their minds—to go to grad school or to go to work. John had already received an assistantship at Michigan State University (MSU) for the coming fall. However, he needed a summer job so that he could have the funds to attend and went to work at 3M. He became involved in some of the early experiments with magnetic tape (sound recording tape). Soon it was August and John said, "I'm having too much fun here." He wrote to MSU asking for a delay of one year for the purpose of gaining industrial experience. MSU was willing to approve the request, and to make a long story short, he became so engrossed in the work at 3M that he never did attend MSU.

He felt the learning experience during those early years at 3M was fantastic. Of course being in on the ground floor during the development of magnetic tape was great. Beyond that, he was enthusiastic about the quality of the leaders and mentors with which he worked. John was certainly able to apply his knowledge of physics and chemistry to the projects.

It is an exciting time when new products are being developed and people are learning together. Uses can expand greatly as the product is developed and refined. That is what happened with the development of magnetic tape. In the summer of 1948, the ABC radio network in Chicago presented a taped program on air. They did that to accommodate the change to daylight savings time, since ABC needed to keep the programming coordinated through the country. Of course, 3M and its product were integral to this process. Another development occurred at about this time. 3M had an employee named Dr. Wetzel, who John identified as a technical expert in the area of magnetic theory. Dr. Wetzel predicted that someday television programming would be recorded. This was at a time when very few televisions were even being produced, and most people knew nothing about the medium. John was aware of a television at a local bar, but that was it. The upshot was that the comment led the other workers to talk about what would be needed to develop a tape that could record video. These ideas were being developed at the same time the company was working to improve the quality of its sound tape. All these refinements were taking place when something new was added.

In 1952 IBM came calling, and they wanted 3M to make computer tapes. The foundation was already set by earlier work on magnetic tapes, and 3M was ready to go. Dr. Wetzel's prediction of video recording became reality in 1956. AMPEX made the first video recorder that year and 3M made the tape. The tape was created without knowing a lot about the machine. Nevertheless they succeeded, with the early product being similar in concept to today's VHS systems.

John knew a good thing when he saw it. First of all, the uses of magnetic tape were exploding. Second, it was fun. People came with different skills. The skills had to fit like pieces of a puzzle for success to be realized. Management needed to be competent in order to fit the skills, encourage creativity, and channel the motivation to create a successful product. John described the experience as "fun." Growth brought in new people regularly, and new people brought new ideas. In sum, hard work and long hours led to success.

That point got John talking about company growth. John spent his entire career in the Magnetic Tape Divisions. Manufacturing was called on to produce more, and much time was spent in building and upgrading plants. To get a better handle on this, several of the plant managers met to discuss next moves. After discussions, it was found that plant construction could be delayed or shelved if production were "rationalized"—have each of the plants focus on a small group of products, become experts at those, and become much more efficient, which would avoid the pattern of continuous plant construction. Today that process is called "focused factories." This was accomplished prior to having that name. This and other experiences made it very clear that efficiencies are not all that difficult or sophisticated—mostly just common sense.

In brief, John's 3M career was an adventure. The first plant dedicated to tapes was built in Hutchinson, Minnesota, west of the Twin Cities. John went there in December of 1956 and stayed until 1961. Then he moved to New Jersey and started a new tape plant and stayed until 1966. Next it was back to Hutchinson in 1966, and he stayed there until 1970 when he moved to the headquarters in St. Paul. He went to St. Paul as director of manufacturing in charge of the domestic plants and was responsible for products in foreign plants. By 1973 he became division vice president, a position he held until retirement in 1986.

His later responsibilities called for a great deal of international travel. This meant overseeing the international plants and being involved in activities with original equipment manufacturers. He also served as chairman of the International Tape and Disc Association, a large industry group. An important point to him is that business is built on personal relationships. This is part of a philosophy that developed and grew during his thirty-eight plus years in the private sector.

Because his tenure at 3M took place during the Cold War period, he discussed some of the issues that related to the company. He noted that they had an organization in Switzerland that could sell to the Iron Curtain countries with permission of the United States government. Then he told an anecdote about 3M activities in the 1980s setting up the first company in China with total 3M ownership. The negotiations had been very difficult. 3M kept insisting that it be totally owned by them. The Chinese really wanted top level involvement. During this period, John was attending a meeting of the International Tape and Disc Association in Washington D.C., where he met a Chinese man. The man said, "Oh, you are from the 3N company." John corrected him but the man repeated it. After a second correction, the man said, "No, 3N. All they say is no, no, no." In addition, John took trips to many countries in

Eastern Europe, Southeast Asia, and the Middle East. Thus the Cold War was another issue to be dealt with in the business world.

The company also contributed to the space program, and 3M made a lot of the tapes in the 1960s that NASA used for the initial space recordings. The tapes were made at the plant in New Jersey. Tapes were even used in the early unmanned satellites. Schedules were often tight. John remembered times in which he piled the family into the car, drove to the nearby military airport, and delivered the product to an officer so it could be flown to the NASA launching point. As he discussed this incident , he pointed out the importance of giving a little extra effort here and there to make things happen and make sure you earn the opportunity to be the supplier.

During this time there was also a personal side to his life. John met his future wife at a streetcar stop one morning, and they began to talk. The Men's Club at his church was having a bingo night the next weekend, so he sold her a ticket. He was to work at the bingo night. He said, "And that's all she wrote." He was about twenty-two when he married Shirley. John and Shirley had four children. Their four children are Gregory, Kathleen, John and Thomas. As they grew up and went to college, an interesting thing happened. Kate went to St. Catherine's (St. Kate's), John went to St. John's, and Thomas went to St. Thomas. Apparently Gregory could not find a St. Gregory College so he went to St. John's. The three boys live in Minnesota and all are successful in their chosen fields. His daughter lives in Singapore. She met her husband while going to grad school at the University of Minnesota. As of 2003 he had operational responsibility for a pharmaceutical company that covered much of the globe.

John gave Shirley a lot of credit for helping the children grow to be successful individuals, since she held down the fort when he traveled. Together, they made sure to spend time with their children. In addition they taught their children the need to work for success. Each child had to earn part of their college tuition. Unfortunately, Shirley passed away suddenly in 1993. As he talked about his children and thirteen grandchildren, it was clear that he was proud of what each had accomplished in their life journeys.

Surprisingly, it was Shirley's active life that catapulted him into his second career. She had long been involved in volunteer activities, and John could not expect her to give up these activities when he retired from 3M. As a result, he decided to look for something to do himself. A man by the name of Fred Zimmerman was just starting up a program at St. Thomas in manufacturing and engineering. John came out to talk with people in the small business center at St. Thomas, and in the process, he talked with Mr. Zimmerman who encouraged him to visit companies and let them know about the manufacturing and engineering program. It was a way to see if companies were interested in a program like what was being offered at St. Thomas. John accepted and has been part of the program since.

At the time of our interview, he had been working for St. Thomas for over seventeen years. His official title is Associate Director for Graduate Programs in Engineering and Technology Management. He had long felt that more technology was not the only key to success. The issue was how to manage it. He said it was apparent that you manage through people, and the way to get the best out of people was by motivating and encouraging them. In the end, he liked the people he worked with, the work was fun, and he thought they were doing some good things for students and companies. Two St. Thomas projects that he felt good about had to do with feeding people in third world areas. For a project in Haiti, students were working on ways to preserve and create new uses for breadfruit. For a previous project in Africa, students designed practical alternative methods of grinding peanuts into peanut butter. The machines were pedal powered and had to be designed to meet cultural issues of the areas used.

In summary, John stressed seven important points about his life:

1. He was blessed with wonderful forebears, parents and siblings.

2. He grew up at a great time—early enough to see tough times and late enough to enjoy more prosperous times.

3. He had the opportunity to participate in World War II, yet to see the folly of war and the joys of peace.

4. He enjoyed a fantastic partner who was a wonderful mother, grandmother and friend.

5. He had wonderful educators and mentors that led him to great enthusiasm for learning and showed him the many opportunities available.

6. He was fortunate to choose 3M as his employer.

7. He enjoyed success in the business world with the help of all of those mentioned.

Retirement has been very fulfilling, again with the association of a great group of people dedicated to developing students eager to succeed in their personal and business lives.

Robert (Bob) Johnson

Bob has traced his ancestry back to his great grandparents who lived in Sweden and Poland. For purposes here, the story starts with his grandparents. His paternal grandfather, Alfred L. Johnson, was born in Sweden in 1858. He married Theresa Person who also was born in Sweden. They eventually immigrated to the United States and settled in Ashland, Wisconsin. Bob's father, also Alfred L. Johnson, was born in Ashland on March 24, 1898, two years before his father died. The family then moved to Wausau, Wisconsin. Alfred's mother married a man by the name of Hermanson and the blended family moved to Minneapolis.

Michael Mallack, Bob's maternal grandfather, was born in Poland in 1865. He also immigrated to the United States, settling in Silver Lake, Minnesota, a small town about fifty miles southwest of the Twin Cities. He met Francis Sworski (born in 1874) in Silver Lake. They were married and had eleven children. The family moved to Minneapolis and later back to Silver Lake where he ran a general store. The store was quite successful for several years. Unfortunately, it was pretty much wiped out by the Depression. A daughter, Mary (May) Mallack, was born while the family lived in Minneapolis. She was born on March 10, 1896, and was to be Bob's mother.

Alfred Johnson left his family at an early age and went to work as a cabin boy on steamers that plied the waters of Lake Michigan. Later he worked out west as a cowboy. Eventually he enlisted in the army at the age of seventeen and took part in World War I.

May Mallack spent most of her early years in Silver Lake. She came to Minneapolis when she was about sixteen or seventeen years old and started working for the telephone company.

Alfred and May met after the war, were married in 1920, and settled in Northeast Minneapolis. They lived on Twenty-seconc Avenue NE and Central during the early years of their marriage. Bob was born on March 17, 1922, and he remembered that first house. He noted that the house had a telephone, electricity, and indoor plumbing. These features were found in each of the houses the family lived in as Bob grew up. He did not remember much about the house itself other than it was a duplex and they were renters.

The next house was on 19th Avenue in Northeast Minneapolis and also was a duplex. The house, owned by his uncle Axel, was close to the street. Bob called the house a train house because, as you walked through the house front to back—or the opposite, you walked from one room to the next. The house was fairly narrow and lots were small so that a neighboring house might be only three feet away.

Childhood entertainment varied greatly. He remembered playing a game where each child picked a color of a car. Then they would count the cars that drove by that had the same color they had picked. His age at the time was about six or seven. He also had memories playing another game during the time they lived in this house. He and his friends played with rubber band guns. They made the guns from wood and cut strips of rubber from old inner tubes. He described it as a game of tag except they shot at each other. Down the block from the house was an ice house, and that became the neighborhood hangout. Bob also took violin lessons from about the age of seven. His parents allowed him to take the streetcar downtown to the Minneapolis College of Music for lessons. Imagine parents today allowing their children to take transportation by themselves to a downtown area! Another form of entertainment was attending vaudeville shows and movies. His mom often took him to vaudeville shows at the Pantages Theater in downtown Minneapolis. Saturdays were for attending the Arion Theater to watch western movies for a dime.

The family moved again in 1930, but stayed in the Northeast neighborhood. At first, they rented the house for fifteen dollars per month. The owners of the house were the Little Sisters of the Poor. Bob remembered being given the responsibility of paying the rent. At about age eight, he took the streetcar to the convent on Broadway Avenue. He paid the fifteen dollars and usually received a box of candy from the nuns. He then continued on the streetcar loop to downtown Minneapolis and back to his neighborhood so he would not have to use an extra token. Eventually, his parents bought the house for $1,500. Their monthly payments remained the same as the rent payments. (Bob noted that the house still existed and his son owned it.)

Certain features of the house stood out in Bob's mind. This bungalow was heated by an oil stove in the middle of the house. He talked about hopping out of bed on cold winter mornings and running to the oil stove to dress. He also noted that the house was located on a long lot (to a youngster) and had a two car garage, which was a rarity in the 1930s. The house contained a cellar which was used for storing produce from their garden, as well as other foods. He mentioned that cellars were very helpful in the days before refrigerators.

The house held a lot of memories for Bob. His brother Kenneth was born in 1932 while they were living in that house. Being ten years older, Bob babysat his brother on the rare occasions his parents went out. He also remembered playing with neighborhood friends. Baseball was a favorite summer game. They never had enough kids to field two full teams, but they adjusted and had fun anyway.

During this period of time, vendors in horse-drawn wagons came by. One example was the Bambi man who ran what amounted to a bakery on wheels. There was a Bambi Bakery in town, and people bought their bread from the Bambi man when he came by. In addition, there was the ice man. People did not have electric refrigerators, so they put how much ice they needed on a sign in their windows, and the ice man would deliver the ice for their ice boxes. Of course rag men came buy on a regular basis. These types of vendors with their horse-drawn wagons were indicative of the times, as there were not many cars on the streets yet.

Speaking of cars, Bob remembered his own experiences behind the wheel. When he was quite young, a friend of his father had a Model T. This was before the Johnson family had their own car. This friend, Harry Benson, let Bob sit in the car and pretend that he was driving. After a time, he did learn to drive from his father. First it only involved steering the car, and later he learned the other controls. He said it came pretty easy for him.

Alfred Johnson worked as a motorman for the Twin Cities streetcar company. May was a housewife. Alfred had steady work throughout the Depression, but pay was rather low, as he made only about five dollars and fifty cents a week. Bob was expected to contribute to the family.

When he was about twelve, Bob took a job selling newspapers. An early goal was to use the money he could keep to buy a baseball glove. The newspaper job was the beginning of a working career that went without interruption through the time of the interview. He eventually bought his first glove for two dollars and fifty cents. The glove was in a shoemaker's shop and had been restitched but never claimed. The glove had great sentimental value, and he was able to keep it for many years. At any rate, he took over his own route by age fourteen and worked at it for about another two years.

At about the same time, he took another job. He filled shelves and carried out goods at a local grocery store called Thomas Grocery which was located at 19th Avenue NE and Central. He worked for the store for several years.

Another of his early jobs during the Great Depression was caddying at Midland Hills Golf Course. His parents let him drive the family Essex to the golf course. However, he was not allowed to drive alone. His mother went with and sat in the car while he caddied. He made up to seventy-five cents for an eighteen hole round plus tips. He said, "A twenty-five cent tip was a big deal." He often stopped to get bread and milk on the way home. He was able to keep the change for himself.

He also learned a valuable lesson on the golf course. He met a young black person one day who was a football player. Bob asked him, "Are there other niggers on the team?" The black person looked at him and explained that black people did not like being called niggers. This had really been Bob's first encounter with a person of color, and he said the message was one he would never forget. He noted that the young man was nice and educated him on how to deal with other minorities.

The Great Depression meant the family had to work together. While Alfred was able to keep his job as a motorman, he lost his regular route and became an extra. He had to stay around and wait for someone to get sick, and he would take the person's place. As noted earlier, Bob was expected to use his wages to help the family out.

Still, the family always had a roof over their heads and had enough to eat. Meals commonly included pot roast and vegetables, round steak, and stews. His least favorite foods were cooked spinach and rutabagas.

He noted that his grandmother Hermanson was the best cook that he had seen. She made great ginger beer (similar to ginger ale), sodas, Swedish sausage, and rolls that would melt in your mouth. She made egg coffee and was responsible for making him a coffee drinker when he was five.

They used to charge their groceries, and Bob paid at the end of the week. The bill was usually in the four to five dollar range, and the grocer gave him a bag of fruit for paying in cash. That bag would cost quite a bit of money today.

In addition, they did not have a car through much of this period, which made walking the most common method of transportation. New cars were never purchased. They were always used, and his father took care of the car by changing the oil, grinding valves and such himself.

Speaking of cars, Bob related another anecdote. When he got a job in 1940, the family bought a car. The monthly payments were twenty-five dollars per month. Bob paid fifteen dollars and his father paid ten dollars, yet the car was Alfred's. Bob had to ask permission to use it and had to be home by eleven PM. It was not even an issue to be argued.

Bob then talked about another aspect of the family. His parents were from different religions. His father was a Protestant and his mother a Roman Catholic. In-laws from both parents were not very tolerant of the religion of the other parent. His father did not practice his religion, and Bob was raised as a Catholic. Though Alfred was not religious, Bob called him "the most honest man" he has ever met in his life. Alfred also was a tough man. He was concerned about muggings and always carried a blackjack on the streetcars.

Education took place in the Minneapolis Public School District. Bob's school career started at Whitney School, which included kindergarten through fourth grade. It was located on 19th Street and Lincoln in Northeast. He had good memories of those years. He noted that he played his violin in a jazz orchestra at the school, and the instructor was paid through the WPA.

Next he went to Prescott School located on Lowry Avenue and Taylor Street. It went from fourth through eighth grade. The fun times included playing ball in the school yard. One memorable incident related to a teacher who was a distant relative. Bob had been a school patrol captain. One day, he told her that he did not want to be captain anymore because he wanted to play ball. She was very disappointed in him, but it was another indication of his love for playing ball.

This led Bob to recount an anecdote about playing basketball while he was going to Prescott. His team went to Pillsbury School for a game which had a gym that was small with a very low ceiling. He said the ceiling was so low that you could not even arch the ball. The game stood out in his mind because he was the high point man. The score was 11 to 10 and Bob had 3 points. Talk about high scoring!

After Prescott, it was on to Edison. One thing that made the transition to high school memorable was that he graduated from knickers to long pants. Although Bob's high school experience was pretty good, he wished he had taken greater advantage of the situation. He felt he did not study as hard as he could have. He did study for the classes he liked, but let some of the other classes slide a bit. Favorite classes were machine shop, drafting, math (through algebra and geometry), chemistry (but did not study as hard as he should have), history, and civics. English was the main area that was neglected. He enjoyed playing the violin, and played through high school. He was also on the music council. In addition, he played a variety of sports, so one could conclude that he was quite active.

Graduation came in 1940, and as he neared graduation, his advisor basically told him to get a job. It also was during the early part of World War II, and enlistment was something else to consider. His academic efforts and athleticism more or less guided his career path.

While talking about his high school experiences, Bob re-counted an anecdote about an injury he had while playing high school hockey. Edison was playing against North. (Games were played on outside rinks in those days.) He was hit in the side and suffered a broken collar bone. His coach sent him home, because trainers and doctors were not on hand in those days. His mother gave him a token so he could take the streetcar to see the doctor downtown. Without taking X-rays, the doctor concluded that the collar bone was broken. He taped Bob up (without shaving him first) to hold the shoulders back and prevent movement. Then he sent Bob on his way. It was a sign of the times.

Bob thought about taking more schooling, but did not think in terms of college. At any rate, graduation took place on a Thursday, and he was working on the following Monday. He went to work at Northwestern Drug for twenty-eight dollars per week, which he thought was pretty good pay. It was a job his Grandmother Hermanson helped him get. The first day on the job, he did not know how to dress, and he found himself a bit overdressed to be working in the basement of a drug company loading boxes. Bob always believed in doing the best he could at a job. This attitude helped him progress up the ladder. Soon he was working upstairs as an order filler. He also swept the floor and did so well at this level, he was offered a job in sales. This reinforced his belief in the idea that a person can elevate himself/herself through hard work.

Working after graduation allowed Bob to continue helping the family. Helping pay for a car was noted earlier. He also bought the family its first refrigerator. This was because he was willing to take on debt, something his father was loathe to do.

While Bob was working at the drug wholesaler, his mother noticed that the University of Minnesota was offering a program in engineering drafting. The class was sponsored by the federal government. She felt this would meet his interest and skills from high school drafting, machine shop, and math. She also felt it would keep him out of the war. Bob worked for Northwestern Drug during the day and went to class at the University at night, five nights a week. The courses were all paid for by the government. He learned additional skills in designing mechanical parts and in math. This program and his achievement led to several job offers.

At this time, a young man lived across the street from the Johnsons, and his father worked at Honeywell. The father knew about Bob's education and interests. This man offered Bob a job in tool design, which marked the beginning of a long career at the company. He felt a major reason for getting the job may have been his name. Although half Polish, the name Johnson gave him a Swedish identity. At the time, it seemed that being Swedish (or having a Swedish name) or being a member of an organization such as the Shriners helped people in the area get ahead economically. Ethnic and religious bias was part of the culture.

Bob remembered his first job—copying an angling fixture that was to go into a system in an airplane. He felt he had made so many mistakes that he would not last a week. However, it all worked out. He worked for Honeywell for about nine months and continued to take classes at the University of Minnesota.

While working for Honeywell in 1942, he decided to enlist in the military. He joined the Naval Air Corps. His action was precipitated by the feeling of patriotism and the fact that he did not want to be a foot soldier. He barely qualified physically. His height and weight were at the maximum allowable because the pilots had to fit into the cockpits of the planes. The first phase of training took place at St. Olaf College in Northfield, Minnesota, in 1943. (Northfield is about forty miles south of the Twin Cities.) The program was called the Pre Preflight School and was mainly a classroom program but did include physical activity.

Bob did have one problem that needed to be corrected. He did not know how to swim. It became one of the reasons he was sent to Mankato State Teachers College (Now known as Minnesota State University). Mankato had a swimming pool and also was the place where the students started flying planes. It was at Mankato where he learned to fly a cub and flew solo for the first time. He became squadron leader while at Mankato, and said leadership positions such as this would continue not only during his time in the Navy but also in private business afterward. He said he did not ask for the leadership position in the Navy, but liked doing it. The time at Mankato was memorable for a variety of reasons. The people at Mankato treated the servicemen well. The men even took part in a 4th of July holiday parade with support of the town's citizens.

After spending three months at Mankato, he was sent to the University of Iowa, which did not include flying. For the first time, the cadets received their full array of uniforms. The program was very scholastically and physically rigorous. He had many memories of rigorous athletic activity such as calisthenics, running obstacle courses in addition to required participation in sports such as football, boxing, wrestling and the like. Swimming also was emphasized. Cadets had to swim four laps of the college pool using the breaststroke, backstroke, sidestroke, and the crawl. A person was stationed by the side of the pool armed with a boxing glove on the end of a long pole. If any cadet tried to go to the side of the pool to rest, the person would hit him on the head with the boxing glove. Bob said, "You got to hate those guys." The cadets also had to jump off a huge tower, take your clothes off, blow up your shirt for buoyancy and stay afloat for thirty minutes. Then there were trainer lessons in which a mock-up cockpit was shot into the water and the cadet had to get out. Overall, the training at Iowa lasted six months. He rose to battalion commander at Iowa and ended up graduating in the top five percent out of 300 cadets.

There was one break in the middle of the training. It was memorable because of an incident that occurred when he was on a date. Bob had a dinner date with a young lady from New

York who was going to school to become a writer. Suddenly, she had a seizure during dinner. Here he was, twenty years old with limited experience, and just did not know how to help her. He kept talking to her and she eventually recovered. It helped him realize how people learn through life experiences.

Being among the top five percent of graduates at Iowa meant that Bob could pick where he wanted to go next. For some reason, he chose Olathe, Kansas. It was here where he learned to fly the "yellow peril," a biplane that was yellow in color. He called it "tough flying" which was made even more treacherous because it involved night flying. He did say it was a plane that "you could do anything to it without wrecking it." Flight instructors created all sorts of testing situations for the cadets. He had a reputation for being a safe pilot. However, he was not above doing some crazy things while in Kansas. He had been dating a college girl in Kansas, and on one occasion, he flew over the college town's water tower— upside down at about 500 feet.

From Olathe, he went to Corpus Christi for six months. Again, training was a combination of academics, flying, and physical fitness courses. Bob felt it was a growing up period for him. He had taken his first drink in Kansas City when he was a cadet in nearby Olathe. Now, at the age of twenty-two, he was drinking beer. Flying was taken to new levels during the time in Corpus Christi, as the cadets flew more sophisticated planes. They also simulated dog fights in the air. Graduation came in August 1944, and he was commissioned as an Ensign.

The next step was to specialize. Choices were to be a multiengine pilot, a fighter pilot, a dive bomber pilot, or a torpedo bomber pilot. Bob chose to be a multiengine pilot. Thinking ahead, he felt it might help him get a job with an airline such as Northwest once the war was over. As luck would have it, he was assigned to become a dive bomber pilot. This required a move to DeLand, Florida, about twenty miles west- southwest of Daytona Beach. They flew in real operating squadrons and in fully armed Navy aircraft. They also had to learn the fundamentals of landing on an aircraft carrier. Carrier landing required that the pilot be in a near stall condition with the tail hitting the deck first so it could be grabbed by the hook wire. To practice this type of landing on the ground was harder than on a carrier because it lacked the relative motion, and crashes were common. This type of landing had to be practiced both during the day and at night. It was a memorable time because he met many of his lifelong friends while stationed in DeLand.

Actual carrier landing practice took place on Lake Michigan. They landed on a ship called the Wolverine which had been refitted with a deck for landing. Bob made ten to twelve landings on this ship and became a carrier pilot.

Another skill learned at DeLand was dive bombing. Pilots were taught to go into a seventy degree dive. It was steep enough to create the sensation that the pilot was headed straight down. The pilot knew he was at the correct angle when the seat of his pants came off the parachute under him. The release point for the bomb was 3,500 feet. Everything was built around that angle of descent. Once the bomb was released, the pull out point was 1,500 feet. That altitude was set for a safety factor. A pilot could get mesmerized during the dive and be unable to pull out. The angle of pulling out of the dive created such a G force that red (blood) would flood the eyes and there would be a momentary black out. The pilots flew planes called SBDs (scout bombers built by Douglas). They were equipped with superchargers. During his first ride, Bob was practicing a bombing run and as his dive hit about 8,000 feet, the engine started smoking and choking. He got on the intercom and announced he had a problem and pulled out at about 5,000 feet. Then he realized that he had forgotten to pull back on the supercharger and it was getting too much air. The choking engine made him feel certain that they were going to go down.

This experience at DeLand was heightened by his father coming down to visit for a week. One evening, Alfred had dinner with the commander of the squadron. The commander told him that Bob was not necessarily the best pilot, but was the safest pilot on the base. When the commander said he wanted Bob on his wing, it made Alfred feel good.

After a short leave, Bob was sent to San Diego where he waited for orders. He and the other pilots with him finally received orders to take a seaplane tender (a ship about the size of a destroyer) to Hawaii. When they got to the base the ship was gone, so they went to the commodore's house, and they were offered use of the admiral's gig (a long, light ship's boat, often with a sail) to get to the ship. Then they took the ship to Hawaii for what turned out to be a short stay.

Soon Bob received orders to go to Tarawa. The job of his squadron was to look for enemy subs and surface ships and to keep shipping lanes open for American ships. The pilots flew a mission every day. On one two-plane mission, Bob flew to the island of Abemama, the site of a Japanese base. He and his mates brought food provisions to a Brit who lived among the native people. Then they started back, but a large storm forced them to return. They ended up back at the hut where the Brit lived and ate some of the food they had brought earlier. That night, they went to an abandoned Japanese barracks to get some sleep. Unfortunately the barracks were full of rats that kept running over the men's bodies, so they decided to go back to the planes to sleep. Matters did not improve in the morning. The ignition to Bob's plane was accidentally hit during the night, and the battery was dead, so the plane would not start. Luckily, one of the radiomen cut down some Japanese telephone wires, connected the wires from one plane to the other, and jump-started the engine of the dead plane. Generally, there was not much action near Tarawa by the time they arrived. A key activity at the time was to escort some ships out to sea.

The squadron was moved north to Majuro in the Marshall Islands. Majuro was in good condition compared to Tarawa, which was pulverized by the time they arrived. The Japanese-held islands of Jaluit, Wotje, and Maloelap were all nearby. The squad went out on two-plane sorties. They carried a variety of bombs and had a target to hit. Bob remembered a mission in which they all peeled off, went in to bomb, and he took flak.

On another occasion, they were flying a two-plane sortie over Wotje. The leader said they had to go back for another look because he thought the Japanese were firing at them. They were flying at about 500 feet. When they went back, the leader's plane was hit. It turned upside down and came apart when it hit the water. Bob radioed the base to tell them what happened and was told to circle the area. They sent up twenty Marine F4Us (a Corsair fighter) and a large seaplane to look for survivors. Bob did not see any survivors and was low on gas, so he could not stay long. With bad weather moving in, he had to fly back just above the water. He called the incident very traumatic; it was shocking to see a friend shot down and die. Everything seemed to go fast. At the same time, the surviving pilot had to keep his wits about him in order to give accurate information back to the base—something that was very hard to do.

While the squadron was still at Majuro, it received new airplanes. They went from the SBD to the SB2C Curtis Hell Diver (a scout bomber). This plane was nicknamed the "flying coffin," and Bob felt it was a frightening airplane to fly. But, it was supposed to be an upgrade, so they flew it. According to Bob, the SBD and SB2C Curtis Hell Diver both had the same mission, to scout and dive bomb. Both were designed for carrier landings. The 2C was supposed to be an improvement over the SBD (which had been the workhorse for the Navy in the early years of the war). It didn't turn out that way. He felt the SB2C was a poor design and believed to be an unfriendly, unsafe airplane to fly, while the SBD was like motherhood to fly. It was safe, and well built.

Majuro was their base for the rest of the war. After the atom bombs were dropped and the Japanese announced they would surrender, a new task was given to Bob and the skipper. They did not know if the Japanese on the outpost islands were aware that the war was over. So they flew over two of the islands they had been patrolling, Wotje and Maloelap, and dropped surrender leaflets. Fearing that they might encounter firing, they flew low and fast.

After the war, Bob and others started ferrying planes to a place called Roy. While there, he was tested and checked out on every fighter plane the Navy had, including the F6 Hellcat and the F4U Corsair. Then he returned to the United States on the carrier Hornet.

Back in the states, Bob was assigned to be an instructor at Ottumwa, Iowa. However there weren't any students, so he was given a new assignment—to lead a group of pilots to Camden, South Carolina, which is a town about twenty miles northeast of Columbia. The planes they flew were the "yellow perils." These biplanes were very basic. They had a compass and running lights, but they did not have any means of communication. Pilots followed an aerial roadmap. He made seven landings on the way. Except for being forced to land in Nashville because of a snowstorm, the rest of the landings were planned. He made one landing near Knoxville to get gas and a cup of coffee. Then he started the engine to let it warm up and got out. Suddenly, the engine started idling faster and faster, and the plane started going down the runway. Bob had to chase down the plane, jump into the cockpit, and swerve the plane so it would not go into a ditch. Another time they could not find the airfield and had to land in a corn field. Luckily, it was after the corn had been harvested. That was Bob's last assignment in the Navy. He was discharged in December of 1945.

The willingness to take on debt also led him to make some land purchases while in the Navy. While home on leave, his mother encouraged him to buy some property, and he took her advice. Some of the property he purchased was lake property. Meanwhile, some new homes were being built in Northeast Minneapolis. According to Bob, each "had an attached garage, a fireplace, the whole bit." One of the houses could have been purchased for $3,500, yet his dad refused. He was unwilling to take on new debt in order to upgrade his home. This was an example of the thinking of the day. People did not want to buy an item if they could not pay the full amount. It applied to Alfred and many others who grew up in the same era.

After his separation from the Navy, Bob returned to work at Honeywell and took more classes at the University of Minnesota. He continued to take extension courses at the University for about nine years.

This was also about the time that he met Dorothy Gormley. According to Bob, there was a local Northeast hangout called Danielson's Drugstore which had a soda fountain in the back room. One day, Dorothy and her sister were sitting in a booth with a male friend. After the friend introduced them, Dorothy and Bob had a coke and he walked her home. One day Bob asked her out. On the day of the date, he was playing basketball and sprained his ankle. He picked her up while on crutches and took her to a Minnesota - Wisconsin basketball game. They dated casually for a while.

One day he called her up and asked her out for the coming Friday. She said she had a date. Then he asked for Saturday. Again, she said she had a date, but she added that she was free on Sunday. His response was, "I have a date." Even though he did not really have a date, he felt that she was just too busy for him. He did not see her for a year after that. He was working at Honeywell and she was working at North American Life Insurance Company, so they did not have much opportunity for casual contact. `

Then one day he was driving home from work and she was going to catch a bus. He stopped and asked her if she wanted a ride home and the relationship developed from there. They were married on June 26, 1948.

It was time for the new couple to get settled. Remember the car that Bob and his father paid for? It was a 1940 Pontiac four door coach, and Bob bought it from Alfred. They built a house on old Highway 8, which was based on a home design they had seen in Better Homes and Gardens magazine. Bob said it was a mistake, because the house looked "like an old chicken coop." But two of their children, Michael and Steve, were born in that house.

Two other sons followed, Jeffrey and Tim. They all grew up and went on to successful careers. Mike and Jeff are lawyers, Steve is a nurse, and Tim became a research scientist for General Mills. Bob mentioned an important part of his child rearing philosophy. He made sure each of his children knew how to swim by the age of five. He did not want them to learn like he had to when he went into the Navy. He did not want someone with a boxing glove on a pole bopping them on the head.

Dorothy's married career was as a homemaker. Bob seemed to really appreciate her role in raising the children and the labor of love she put into helping the grandchildren. Up to the time of the interview, she was gladly putting in time driving grandchildren to their various activities.

Bob also had some nice thoughts about his parents. He pointed out a typical difference between mothers and fathers. He thought his father was in the doghouse for the entire time Bob was in the war for signing the form allowing Bob to enlist. His mother's instinct was protection. But she was a doer. When Alfred became ill and went to a nursing home, Mary started running the candy cart. She ended up doing that for eight years. His dad lived to the age of eighty and his mother lived to age ninety-three.

Next we got back to his career. Bob went back to tool design when he returned to Honeywell. By his admission, he was not very good at it, but it was a stepping stone. Then he went into production engineering at Honeywell. He felt the work was interesting and he wanted to broaden himself. He also was pretty good at putting things together and wanted to get into the basic manufacture techniques of making components and parts. His boss discouraged him. A previous boss heard about his desires and brought Bob to his plant where he became the lead engineer for an assembly department. Then he was made assistant supervisor, which put him in charge of three floors of engineers.

At that point, Bob remembered an event that greatly shaped his career. When he was still in tool design, he joined the American Society of Tool Engineers (ASTE). The organization had monthly meetings, and at one of the meetings, Bob was asked to be the assistant program chairperson. About three months later, the chairperson quit and Bob moved up to that position. All of a sudden, he was planning many programs for engineers throughout the state of Minnesota. He quickly moved through the various chair positions, and by 1955 he became the chair of the ASTE chapter of the state of Minnesota.

Bob was involved in the organization at the national/international level at the same time. He had become the area membership chair. Meanwhile the name was changed to the American Society of Tool and Manufacturing Engineers (ASTME). Then he went on to become the membership chair for the whole organization of 40,000 plus members. The new position meant travel to various cities in the Midwest to establish new chapters. Eventually, he attained the membership chair of the ASTME and became known on an international basis. In 1962, he was elected to the board of directors. Then in 1964 he was at the annual meeting in Cleveland and was asked to run for vice president of ASTME. Bob protested that he was not qualified and did not know if Honeywell would give him the time off. The people who asked him debunked his supposed lack of qualifications. When he called Honeywell, they encouraged him to go for it. He did and was elected. He became president in 1968, and the name of the organization changed again. The name became the Society of Manufacturing Engineers (SME). Overall, Bob's rise in the SME was a boon for Honeywell (in the form of sales, and so on) and himself.

He told an anecdote about one of his experiences as SME president that related to World War II. On one of his international trips, he visited a Honeywell plant in Japan. The director of the plant invited Bob to his house for dinner. The director asked him what he did during the war, and Bob answered that he was a Navy pilot. The director replied that he had worked in an airplane manufacturing plant. Bob felt that such an exchange was not uncommon. There was a natural curiosity to find out what a member of the other side did during the time of conflict. His conclusion about the Japanese was that they were pretty good people.

Getting back to his work at Honeywell, Bob did recount a setback. He contracted polio in 1953. Though he did not develop paralysis, he did have to undergo therapy at a Twin City health care facility called the Sister Kenny Institute. While going through therapy, he tried to keep up with his work. He maintained a position of supervision of about twenty-five engineers, which was quite a responsibility.

In 1954, Bob expanded his horizon even more. While still working at Honeywell, he decided to start a company with his brother-in-law called R and R Sales. The company sold a variety of products from carpets to appliances. They sold the merchandise for ten percent over cost. Although they sold $100,000 worth of merchandise in a year, the profit margin was very low. He worked with the company on the side and stayed with the business for over two years. Unfortunately, his brother-in-law developed cancer and died. Bob tried to keep the business going himself but gave it up after a few months.

At Honeywell, Bob was a supervisor and had moved from the main plant in Minneapolis to a plant in suburban Golden Valley. The person who had hired him for that position had moved on to another division and wanted Bob to manage the arsenal plant. It involved supervising 700 people in a plant doing ten million dollars worth of business a year. Bob took the job without hesitating, and what was especially interesting was what came next. Bob was pumped up after accepting a very important position. When he told his dad, the first question Alfred asked was, "Is it a steady job?" It was a classic example of the depression mentality. Job security had top priority for many people from the Depression. At any rate, Bob stayed in the arsenal division for about the next five years.

This was a time when the Vietnam War was at its height and the arsenal division was expanding. A new operation was set up in a very modern plant in the suburb of St. Louis Park. The director of the plant left for another job, and Bob was asked to take over. Now he was supervising 5,000 people and doing $500 million worth of business per year. Avionics manufacturing took place at the plant, which was an area that Bob knew and enjoyed. He ran the plant from 1969 to 1981, a time of rapid growth and large profits.

Then the company decided to break up the manufacturing in the plant to create more growth. The transition led to almost zero profits within about two years. The transition led to more management people being hired. This made division top heavy in management and led Bob to change positions. He became director of productivity and director of the management development school. The whole change took its toll on him.

Bob finally moved back into ordinance. He took a position as Director of Advanced Manufacturing Technology, which he kept until he retired in 1987. However, he did continue to work as a consultant for Honeywell, as well as other companies, for two more years.

The association with SME not only helped Bob at Honeywell, it helped him become involved in the engineering department at the University of St. Thomas. SME also contributed laboratory equipment, scholarships, and grants to the college. His actual involvement with St. Thomas began with Fred Zimmerman, who was an entrepreneur and started the engineering management program at St. Thomas. He asked Bob to teach. Although Bob questioned his qualifications for such a position, Fred was able to convince him that he could do it. Bob started this "new" career in 1988 and has been doing it since. He teaches a course in the summer called Automated Systems in the United States and Overseas.

He was never one to be idle. Along with the work for St. Thomas, he worked on several other endeavors. Many of these began around 1995 or later. He was on the board of directors and did consulting for Brown Photo, which eventually became Ritz Photo. He also consulted for a medical firm on automation for a period of seven years. In 1999, he was asked to be on the board of directors for Provis, a fault chip simulator company; the company develops logic systems for testing chips.

He also talked about running a golf tournament for the last thirty years. It is for the people who grew up and/or live by Silver Lake (the neighborhood lake). Over the years, the tournament has been held at several different courses around the state.

Looking back over the last ten years and more, Bob mentioned that appreciation for family became more important to him—he basically meant the grandchildren. He talked about taking his oldest grandchild downhill skiing. This was similar to what they did with their own kids. Bob and Dorothy were also active in attending the events of their grandchildren.

Overall, Bob felt that home and family meant a lot to him. While he had prestigious positions at Honeywell, he would not disrupt his family to take jobs offering even more prestige and money than he was earning in Minnesota. To illustrate, he spoke of an opportunity to move to New York to work for Smith-Corona. The job would have doubled his salary, and it included perks such as a country club membership. It was definitely high-level management, but he turned it down. Though he admitted to wanting more money and more prestige, he did not think it was worth sacrificing the family lifestyle. The roots in Minnesota were deep and important to Bob. He knew he could not duplicate what he had if he had taken any one of the opportunities to move up the ladder in a different location. That story clearly defined Bob.

Matthew Little

This story began in the state of North Carolina. Matthew was born and raised in the coastal town of Washington, which is located at the mouth of the Pamlico River off Pamlico Sound. To the east of Pamlico Sound is the Outer Bank area. Matthew guessed the present population to be about 8,000. He said, "The only thing it had to boast about was that it was the first town in the country to be named after George Washington." Apparently, Washington had stopped by the area while on a trip during the time the town was being developed, and they named the town after him.

Matthew's parents were Arthur and Bessie (Parmley) Little. Back in those days, being a housewife was a fulltime job. Consider these facts. The house did not have running water (indoor plumbing) or electricity. The family included eight children.

Chores took a long time. Washing clothes, for example, was done by hand. A tub had to be hand filled with hot water. Clothes were scrubbed on a washboard and wrung out and hung up by hand. Water was brought in from the pump on the back porch. It was then heated on the wood burning stove for washing the clothes, taking baths and the like. Matthew and his brothers were responsible for cutting wood for the stove. Obviously, cooking and cleaning also took longer without the modern conveniences of today.

Arthur was the "breadwinner" working as a miller. He worked for the same company for his entire career. His father was in charge of grinding up the wheat and other grains that came in from nearby farms. He described his father as being very "proficient" at his job. Besides being Arthur's lifelong work it had been the occupation of Arthur's father. An advantage to being a miller meant that the family had a good supply of flour. This meant that they had plenty of bread, and it helped meet Arthur's demand for fresh biscuits three times a day. This was part of his father's desire to have three hot meals a day. Matthew has often wondered how his mother kept up with all the work seven days a week. Since the family lived on the edge of the small town, they did own some land behind their house. They farmed this land for food and to sell the produce.

Among the children, Matthew was second in line. He pointed out that there had actually been ten children. Two died before he came along. One died of tuberculosis and the other of whooping cough. The eight surviving children are as follows: Bertha, Matthew (born August 21, 1921), James, Doris, Robert, Arthur Jr., Martha, and Malcolm.

Keeping the farm going required a lot of work. The children had regular farm chores. Milking three cows before school and feeding the cows and chickens were among the chores assigned to him. In addition, the family sometimes hired outside help to work the farm. In spite of this time-consuming labor, his father instilled in his children the importance of education. Nothing could come in the way of their education. How this paid off for Matthew will be described later.

When asked about diet, Matthew said they basically ate whatever they were given. However, there were some favorite foods. Collard greens was one favorite (and still is). He loved apples too. He ate apples whenever he could, even if it meant stealing one on occasion. This led to an anecdote. One day his mother decided to teach him a lesson. She gave him a full bucket of apples. She sent him to his room and instructed him not to come out until he had eaten every apple in the bucket. Her idea was that the episode would make him sick of apples. In fact, this was heaven for Matthew. He said, "It was like Brer Rabbit in the briar patch." He gladly stayed in his room and ate every last one—and continued to eat apples whenever he could.

Matthew pointed out that this was still during the time of segregation. He lived under these conditions into his early adulthood. He described the system as "dehumanizing to African Americans." As he thought back to that time, he said he "bore no bitterness at the time because that's the way it was." It was the only system he knew. As Matthew was growing up, he felt that whites were superior and African Americans just had to live with the indignities.

He went on to give examples: Matthew said that you could tell where the African American neighborhood began because that was where the pavement ended. The dust and sand were a constant. They also did not have the benefit of conveniences like electricity and running water as noted above. He did not get to experience these conveniences until he went away to college.

His father was enterprising. By combining prudent living with income from the milling job and selling farm products, he was able to accumulate some material wealth. Now this was a time when he could not even let on to his boss, Mr. Moss, that he owned tillable land. Such material wealth would have made his boss suspicious of his honesty and could have led to his firing or worse. At one point, the family's size meant the need for a larger house, so Arthur had one built. Yet he could not let Mr. Moss know it was his since he would not think Arthur could afford a house larger than his own. Arthur claimed that the house was owned by a neighbor "who was principal of the colored school across the street."

The same thing was true when his father bought a car, a 1933 Chevrolet. He could not drive the car to work for fear that the mill owner would question how he could afford it. Arthur left a bicycle at his brother's barbershop in town because the shop was near the mill. He drove to the barbershop, picked up the bike, and rode that the rest of the way to and from work. These and many other incidents were things that Matthew thought were normal.

Of course the schools were segregated. He went to a small town school that housed grades kindergarten through twelfth. The school was called Washington Colored Public High School. In spite of the fact that the school was supposed to educate African American children from most of the county, there were no busses. The school building itself was not as nice as the ones for the white students. In addition, most of the school supplies were hand me downs from the white schools. Their school even had to have the same nickname (the Yellow Jackets) as the white high school because the uniforms came from the white school. Being the only school for African Americans, several grades were taught in the same classroom. An added indignity for these students was the fact that the city dump was right behind the school. Remember this was before environmental enlightenment. Garbage was not covered so things blew around, flies were always present and the smell was ever present. This was all part of his environment, and he did not think it was out of place.

Education came in spite of these shortcomings. Matthew talked about having inspiring teachers. He gave an example of one such teacher, Mrs. Wittington. Since the books were from the white schools, the students did not have a way to read about black history. But this fifth grade teacher brought in her own books and taught the students well. With teachers such as Mrs. Wittington and Matthew's parents preaching that education was the future, he did persevere.

Another aspect of segregation dealt with how an African American related to whites. Matthew told about how his dad taught him to address white people, even the children. Arthur always addressed the white kids he came in contact with, "Yes, ma'am," and "No, ma'am" or "Yes, sir" and "No, sir." This was especially true when talking to the boss's daughter. On one occasion Matthew responded to her with a simple "Yes." His father really took him to task for not saying, "Yes, ma'am." This type of thing was tolerated as a way of life.

The Ku Klux Klan was very active during the years of Matthew's boyhood. He knew of the Klan and heard the whisperings of Klan activity. He described an occasion in which an African American blacksmith was insulted by a white man. In his anger, the blacksmith picked up an ax and was going to hit the insulter. Even though he did not carry out the threat, the blacksmith was in danger. Matthew's father and his friends decided that they had to get the blacksmith out of town. Arthur Little had heard whites talking about "burning the blacksmith's place that night and taking care of him." So they collected some money and helped the man leave town. In another instance, a boy in the same grade as Matthew's younger sister was accused of having an affair with a white. Matthew knew they had to get him out of town immediately. They could not let him be arrested, for it was likely a mob would come, get him out of jail, and lynch him. In spite of these kinds of incidents, Matthew did not feel frightened or bitter at the time. Nevertheless, these incidents indicate an advantage of total and complete segregation. It created a closer knit black community. Within a few minutes of an incident, word would spread throughout the community, allowing rapid response to incidents such as these.

There was an upside for the family during this period of time. The 1930s were the Depression years. Many people had suffered. Luckily for the Littles, Arthur was able to keep his job during the whole time. In addition, he often used a hired hand to help on the farm. He was able to pay the help eight dollars and fifty cents per week. Matthew noted the knowledge of the salary was because of his father's effort to instill the sense of economics within him. These lessons started at an early age. Arthur gave his son the responsibility of paying practically all of the bills related to farming. He added, "Needless to say, I had to account for every penny on paper."

The topic turned back to education. The question was what motivated Matthew not only to graduate from high school, but to get a college degree. As before, he credited his parents with motivating him. His parents lacked education themselves, but they knew education could lead to a better life for their children. Their urgings helped him to develop his own curiosity over time. (This must have worked because all eight children ended up with at least some college education.)

After graduating from high school, it was time to go to college. There were not many black colleges in the area. He chose North Carolina A&T College in Greensboro. Today it is known as A & T State University and is now integrated. Some influential black people such as Jesse Jackson and Ronald McNair attended A & T. Mr. McNair was killed when the Challenger Shuttle exploded in 1986. Being an agricultural and technological school, it had a good reputation in both areas. Beyond that, the college is noted for the four students who started the lunch counter sit-in movement of the Civil Rights movement. As a matter of fact, one of the youngsters was the son of a classmate and a good friend of Matthew's—Ezell Blair.

College was an exciting thought, but Matthew had to find how to pay his way through. Tuition at the time (1938) was fifty dollars per quarter. Room and board was twenty-five dollars per month. Arthur Little tried his best to help his son. He gave Matthew enough money to cover early costs such as his entrance fee.

Matthew remembered having to get a variety of part-time jobs to pay his way. This was not an easy task. He went down to the employment office every day, and every day he was told there were no jobs. Finally the lady who was in charge told him, "I'm going to find you something." First she gave him a job as a waiter in her house. He received very little pay but made an impression. She found other work for him—part-time jobs such as cleaning other peoples' houses. Matthew became a favorite of hers. She pulled out and saved the best jobs for him.

Eventually he worked his way to being a bellhop at a hotel. There was no salary for the job. The money he received was from tips and the tips were good. The job paid so well that Matthew did not have to ask his father for any money. That, in turn, made his father suspicious. Arthur was worried that his son might be doing something illegal if he was making so much money. Arthur sent a younger son to the college to check up on Matthew. His brother discovered that Matthew was working at a major hotel for tips. But that is not all. The hotel was located in a "dry" county. When Matthew asked the customers if they wanted anything, they often requested liquor. The bellhops bought the liquor from the bell captain and then sold it to the customers for a profit.

Matthew's college major was in biological science with a minor in chemistry. He also completed prerequisites for entering medical school. His plan was to go on for a medical degree but the events of history got in the way.

He found out that he was likely to be drafted soon. But he also discovered that if he joined the enlisted reserves, he could be deferred. He felt he saved himself from a year of military service by being in the reserves and joined up in 1942. Nevertheless, the demands of war meant that his whole unit was to be called up. At this time, Matthew was a senior and close to graduation. Graduation was to take place in June of 1943, but the unit was being called up in May. With the patriot fervor of the time, the school forgave the reservists the time they were to miss and conferred degrees on them in May. He ended up spending three and a half years in the military.

A black serving in a segregated army is a story of its own. There were many incidents of humiliation and degradation. At one point the recruits were sent to Camp Croft in Spartanburg, South Carolina, for basic training. There were several black newspapers on the east coast at the time (his favorite was the Norfolk Journal and Guide, but he did not know if it was still in existence). At any rate, during the early stages of the war all of the black papers were strongly advocating integration of the services. The governor of the state issued an executive order prohibiting the distribution of black papers on the base. His justification was that they were unpatriotic and subversive. He claimed they were detrimental to the morale of the black troops. Another incident occurred after basic training. Matthew had been assigned to a permanent unit, the 364th Infantry Regiment. At the time, most blacks were assigned to service units (quartermaster, engineering, and so on). At the time, there were two all-black infantry regiments left from World War I. They were the 92nd and 93rd. But there were very few independent infantry regiments. They had been assigned to the 3rd Army and were on maneuvers, training in the Louisiana swamps when the unit managed a "breakthrough" in the simulated maneuvers. The commanding general was observing the maneuvers. For the first time he became aware of the fact that a black infantry regiment was attached to his 3rd Army. The very next day they were detached and orders came down for the unit to be deployed to Seattle, Washington. They were sent from there to the Aleutian Islands to do guard duty.

In the meantime, Matthew had applied to medical school at Howard University. At first, he was conditionally accepted. He was told that his time in the military would require taking some premed courses again. He completed his course work and reapplied. Unfortunately there were many returning GIs at the time. The school turned to different methods to limit enrollment. For example, it gave priority to students who had connections, such as having a father who had graduated from the school. As a result, Matthew was not accepted to medical school

This event made him very frustrated. He felt everything he had worked for had gone down the drain. He left Howard with the idea of getting lost, and that is how he ended up in Minneapolis. He did not know where he was going to go. Two places stuck in his mind: Denver and Minneapolis. He did not know his destination even when he arrived at the train station. He had to decide before he could buy a ticket. So he flipped a coin. Heads meant Minneapolis and tails meant Denver. Of course it came up heads.

The train dropped him off in Minneapolis in February 1948 and he stayed. But it was not an easy transition. He was an African American in a strange town. There were no family members or friends living in Minneapolis. He stayed at the downtown YMCA for four days. He used that time to walk around the city. He said, "I felt so out of place because I did not see another black person for the whole four days." Finally he asked a cop where the black people lived. The policeman directed him to a bar owned by a black. Matthew went there and it was full of blacks. One of the first things he asked was, "Where could a person find a place to stay?" He was directed to a barbershop where he was told they could tell him where to go. Sure enough, he went to the barbershop and was told to go to a house owned by a Mrs. Smith who took in renters. This was his introduction to Minneapolis, Minnesota.

Then it was time to get a job. Matthew sent out many resumes without luck. He decided to go back to something he had done before and did well—waiting tables. He was able to get a job at one of the better hotels at the time, the Curtis Hotel. He worked on the dinner shift only. Later he got a job serving lunch at the Dykeman Hotel. He made connections while doing these jobs but was still unable to get a job in which he could use his degree. The experience made him quickly realize that not only was there job discrimination in Minnesota, but in many ways it was more pernicious than in North Carolina, for it was more illusive. In the segregated South, the job pattern, like everything else, was clearly separated. There were "black jobs" and "white jobs." A black person knew that he could only apply for a black job regardless of his qualifications, and a white could not apply for a black job, even if so inclined. The separation was distinct and ironclad. In the North, it was all de facto. One could apply for any job, but getting hired was another matter. He remembered picketing Dayton's in the early 1950s to get them to hire black store clerks.

At that point, he remembered the seminal event in his life. He said the event had a greater impact on him than all the segregation he had been subjected to in the South. It had to do with his attempt to get a job as a fireman. He was told about some openings in the Minneapolis fire department. He looked into it and noticed that the pay scale was pretty good. He decided to try for it. He knew he was in good physical shape. He had boxed and run track in college. In addition, he was not long removed from the military. He was certain he could handle the physical part of the job. There were over 200 applicants, and each applicant was given a number. The number was used for identification rather than the name. The test included three parts: a physical section, a written section, and an oral interview. To qualify for the department, the applicant had to achieve a score of seventy-five or above in each of the three parts. Matthew excelled in the physical part. He also did well in the written part. It came down to the interview. For the first time, he would not be a mere number but a specific person. Three retired fire captains asked him questions. He was asked: "Why do you want to be a fireman? Why do you want to leave the job you have now? Does your wife know you want to be a fireman?" He felt he answered the questions truthfully. His score for the interview was seventy-four plus. It was not the required seventy-five so he did not qualify for the department.

Matthew was so disgusted that he decided to pursue the matter. He called the civil service office to find out why he did not qualify. He was told they had nothing to do with the testing that was done by the fire department. They could not do anything about it. Nevertheless he did not give up. Finally, a woman in the civil service office gave him the name of one of the retired fire captains who interviewed him. He looked up the address of the individual and on a Sunday morning he went to the man's house. The man said one thing that is important in firefighting is the buddy system. You have to live with each other, eat with each other, and fight fires with each other. You have to take the other person on as your brother. The man said he just did not think it would work if the fire department was integrated. This amounted to an acknowledgment of discrimination based on skin color.

This event convinced Matthew to get involved in the fight for civil rights and led to his long involvement in the NAACP. He went on to become head of the NAACP. This position would eventually lead to his position as a chairman of the Minnesota delegation for the 1963 March on Washington. Ironically, years after his own efforts to become a fireman, a case was brought by the NAACP, then headed by Matthew. The NAACP filed federal suit on behalf of an African American who tried to become a fireman and felt he had been discriminated against. The national office and general council of the NAACP gave their support. Matthew became a key witness because he had carefully documented the particulars of his own efforts to join the fire department. The NAACP won the suit. The settlement did not only lead to the hiring of the African American who brought the complaint, but the fire department also had to hire about twenty qualified black applicants before they could complete the rest of their hiring. This was the beginning that made the Minneapolis fire department one of the most diverse by the end of the twentieth century. Matthew later received a plaque for the part he played in ending discrimination in the Minneapolis fire department. The plaque was given by the local branch of the Black Fire Fighters Association. Maybe his greatest satisfaction came from righting a wrong that he had personally experienced.

The vast majority of people who worked for the local or regional branches of the NAACP did their work voluntarily. In spite of his tireless efforts, Matthew still had to have a career. He finally became a postal employee. He eventually rose to the position of station superintendent. The station had about sixty-five carriers. He retired from that position in 1977 and started his own landscape and garden center. This was something that he had been doing part-time while he still worked for the postal service. The business was called C and L Landscape Center. He ran the garden center until 1992 when he sold it. From then on he worked full time for the NAACP.

The path of his career was in itself ironic. Here was a man who tried and tried, but was not given the opportunity to practice his area of expertise as earned in college. Years later, people came to him when he was head of the NAACP. Company heads came to him asking how to find qualified blacks for positions in their companies. Of course, this was after the gains made during the civil rights movement, and it became "fashionable" to give minorities more economic opportunities. Matthew was happy to refer these company leaders to people he knew and to black colleges. He pointed out that the Honeywell Corporation actually hired a recruiter to scour black colleges for people qualified for jobs in the company.

While career and avocation made up important parts of Matthew's life, he did have a personal side. He met a young lady named Sylvia who was from South Dakota. She had recently graduated from high school and was working for the Internal Revenue Service when they met. They were married in Sioux Falls, South Dakota, in 1949. They ended up having five children. When we had our interview the total included eleven grandchildren and four great grandchildren. The marriage ended in divorce after twenty-seven years. Matthew remarried in 1996. He married Lucille on a tennis court because they both enjoy playing tennis and they had met playing tennis. Lucille retired as a teacher the year they were married.

One of the high points of his work in civil rights was the March on Washington in 1963. Matthew was the organizer in Minnesota along with Marge Wynn. He was first contacted in the fall of 1962 and told that a national committee was thinking about a march, but they were not certain of the date. At first it was to be in the spring of 1963. He credited A. Philip Randolph as being the most responsible for the march of 1963. Mr. Randolph had threatened a march in 1941 to protest segregation in the defense industry. His threat led to President Roosevelt (through the urging of Eleanor Roosevelt) to issue Executive Order 8806, which opened the way for integration in the defense industries. The order also headed off the march. However, Mr. Randolph was not ready to take this victory and fade away. The Montgomery Bus Boycott and the emergence of the Reverend Martin Luther King in the mid 1950s made him more determined to organize a new march. He and Bayard Rustin set the foundation for the 1963 march. The Reverend King was the one who pulled together the different factions within the civil rights movement which made the march so successful.

The local planning for the march began in the spring of 1963. Matthew set up a committee. They were told by the national group to get a diverse economic, ethnic and religious delegation. The local committee was reminded that the march was for freedom and jobs. John Lewis, one of the march leaders, came to Minnesota to make sure the delegation knew the expectations. Among the expectations was to be nonviolent, and each delegate was required to sign an oath to that effect.

Once goals and expectations were set, they needed to recruit delegates and collect funds to finance the trip. They called on churches and some political people to help them with the funding. He credited then Mayor Arthur Naftalin for helping out by calling a news conference to publicize the effort. The system was set up to ask the participants to pay what they could. Any unemployed participant did not have to pay. They even used a house-to-house collection effort to get some of the money.

They had the money and the delegates. Next it was time to take a chartered plane to Washington D.C. to show support for ending discrimination. The event itself turned out to be very uplifting and unifying. The delegation was ecstatic on the way back. Matthew made an important point when he told the delegation, "If we know anything, we know this is not the end. We have got to continue." As a matter of fact, the March on Washington Committee did continue and supported future actions. It became supportive to other civil rights actions such as the Mississippi Summer Freedom Project in 1964 by sending a bus with a Minnesota delegation to Mississippi for the voter registration project. It also contributed money to SNCC, which ran the project.

Matthew pointed out that the successes of the civil rights movement led to other movements for equality. He talked about senior citizens speaking out as members of the Gray Panthers. He also talked about the renewal of the women's rights movement and movements for the environment. He said the civil rights movement "made us, in a lot of ways, a kinder and gentler society with consideration for all people."

From this point, Matthew focused his attention more on local issues. The Twin Cities did not have a meaningful civil rights commission at the time. He worked to get a strong commission established. It helped that Mayor Naftalin helped push the issue through the Minneapolis City Council. Once the commission was established, Matthew became one of the first appointees. As a matter of fact, the commission started out to be very strong. Unfortunately, the next elected mayor, Charles Stenvig, worked on changes that diluted the commission.

He had many accomplishments over his thirty plus years with the NAACP. Some of those have been chronicled previously. One of his disappointments, however, was what he called the "fruitless fight for desegregated schools." The segregation he was fighting was de facto segregation. This was segregation created by the racial and ethnic residential patterns in a city. Schools in areas heavily populated by African Americans and other minorities reflected that population. Schools in areas with mainly whites reflected that population. Integrated schools have always been important to the NAACP.

An important case went back to 1971. That year they had won a federal segregation suit. The plan that resulted from the case was to use transportation to achieve integration. Judge Larson was in charge of putting the new plan into force and for supervising the plan over a ten-year period. Matthew felt the federal plan should stay in effect regardless of the migration to and concentration of African Americans in specific areas. Nevertheless, Judge Larson discharged the supervision of the plan to the State of Minnesota after the ten-year period. The action was taken on the promise by the state to maintain the desegregation policy. However, the promise was not carried out. Matthew fought the state on this issue claiming that the state had violated the federal order. The state maintained the growth in the African American neighborhoods was so great that they could not integrate according to the standards of the federal order. Matthew responded by suggesting boundary crossovers. Students from the Minneapolis district should be able to attend school in a nearby suburb. It would be a form of school consolidation. Eventually a compromise was worked out in which neighboring suburbs agreed to take some students for a certain time period.

In another area, he worked behind the scenes to achieve change. In the 1980s Grand Metropolitan, a British company bought Pillsbury. After the purchase, management fired the executive director of affirmative action at Pillsbury. The woman who was fired called in the NAACP. Matthew arranged a one-on-one meeting with Metropolitan manager, Ian Martin. He proceeded to give Mr. Martin a lesson in the history of affirmative action and how his competitors were profiting from affirmative action. After several sessions, Mr. Martin not only decided to keep the department, but also expanded it and gave the executive director more power. Mr. Martin became a supporter of the NAACP and later sent Matthew a present when he retired from his position in the NAACP. Matthew felt very good about the outcome of this situation.

At the time of the interview, he reflected back on the system. He identified two elements in the power structure. They are political and economic power. He felt both elements reside in the suburbs. When people are isolated in pockets, they will never get to share the power. He said people must be vigilant. They must not let their guard down in order to keep the rights that have been won and to prevent backsliding.

Matthew has moved on. As of 2003 he chaired the board of a music academy. He also was on the board of a tennis academy which worked to teach about 2,500 inner city youngsters. He worked for Citizens For A Safer Minnesota, and he maintained ties to the NAACP as a lifetime member. Finally one of his proudest moments occurred on a sunny day in May 2002. At graduation ceremonies that day, University of Minnesota President Mark Yudof presented Matthew with an honorary Doctor of Laws degree for life service. How appropriate!

Robert (Bob) Samples

Bob started by talking about his parents. He said that his father was born in South Carolina, and his family moved to Chicago. His mother's family came from Mississippi and eventually settled in Iowa. Bob was named Robert H. Samples after his father. His mother's name was Nettie Dye.

He said that he always tells people he was "born in Champaign, Illinois, and diluted in Waterloo, Iowa." An only child, Bob was born on October 18, 1920. He was born in his great uncle Phil's house in Champaign. However, he and his mother moved when he was six months old and was raised in Waterloo. His father stayed in the Chicago area and was not a major factor in Bob's upbringing.

Nettie was a singer in an orchestra for a while. She was on the road quite a bit during that time. As a result, Bob lived with his grandmother, Irene Dye, for about the first seven years of his life and saw little of his mother. They finally got back together when he was seven and a half years old. Nettie became a maid and worked as such pretty much the rest of her life. He described her work schedule as "long and hard." She worked twelve hours a day on weekdays and six hours on Sunday for eight dollars a week.

Bob did not remember his childhood as being out of the ordinary. One of the things he most enjoyed doing was going to the movies. He started going to movies during the mid 1920s, a fun activity during his early years. When Bob was about six, he was given fifty cents a week (a princely sum for the time), and he spent it all at the movies. He said he was "practically raised at the movies."

Bob was back with his mother when the 1929 "Crash" occurred. He described his home as a "little old shack that a guy had hand made." He said it was sufficient, and the rent was right for someone who made eight dollars a week. The house had electricity, but no indoor plumbing. Bob said, "We were in a ghetto." However, he did say there were some whites scattered through the neighborhood. He described the neighborhood kids' gang as the reverse of the Our Gang Comedy. The community was mainly populated by blacks with just a few whites.

Even though pay was low, Nettie was able to keep her job through the Great Depression. That helped keep food on the table. Another thing Bob remembered was sometimes taking his little red wagon to the welfare office to get groceries. He also remembered going around the neighborhood with his grandmother picking dandelion greens. He was not picky about eating. He said, "I ate myself silly." It probably helped that his mother was a good cook. There were two foods that he did not like—oysters and okra. He loved some of the traditional southern food such as black eyed peas, corn bread, and chili.

Since the family moved quite a bit, Bob ended up going to several different schools in the Waterloo area. This fact had some impact on his education. He did have a good ability to read. He also had an exceptional ability in math. These strengths helped him minimize the bad effects of switching schools. Switching meant losing time in the classroom. For example, he might have spent most of a year in second grade and then switched to another school in the spring. The next school put him in third grade. Nevertheless, he read many books and remembered reading books such as Heidi to the rest of the class in fourth grade. The school he went to the longest was Grant School. Unlike most of the schools he attended, it was pretty well balanced racially. He experienced success in grade school.

Things changed when he went to junior high school. His mother was working. He did not receive any direction or intellectual inspiration from any males. Bob had two years in his life that he was lucky to get through. He said he was "a 135-pound punk." He said his "mind was working but it was working in the wrong direction." Bob classified himself as an inspirer. If guys were talking on the street corner, he would walk up and say, "What the hell are you talking about? Let's go and do something." Then he would do something like throw a rock at the porch of a house and then laugh as the rest of the neighborhood guys ran away. This type of behavior continued all the way through junior high.

Things changed when he was a sophomore in high school. He had a teacher—Mr. Starr. He called Mr. Starr a "saint." Here was a kid who was just there, but was not productive. Then one day Mr. Starr said something. During a lesson, Mr. Starr explained something by saying "it was like a nigger in a wood pile." This angered Bob. He and the other two blacks in class looked at each other and nodded in agreement that they would get Mr. Starr after class. When class ended, Bob ran up toward Mr. Starr. But when he looked around, the other two students were leaving the room. It was too late, for Bob was in Mr. Starr's face. So he told Mr. Starr that he did not like what he had said. To Bob's surprise, Mr. Starr apologized for the comment. The following day, he called Bob up after class and tried to explain the comment away. More important, he started talking to Bob after that incident. Mr. Starr (possibly without realizing it) was making Bob feel like a real person. Here was an adult willing to spend time outside of school just talking to Bob. He was making Bob into a new person.

Bob's lifestyle changed dramatically from this relationship. Instead of being on the streets and staying up until 1 AM, he started going to bed around 9:30 PM. He started reading again. His grades rose from D's to B's and A's. He took part in gymnastics and football, and made the first team for football. And then he shocked his mother by telling her that he wanted to go to college. All of these things happened without Bob realizing that the transformation came because a teacher took time to care about him as a human being.

An event in high school also had an influence on Bob that helped shape his life. He was asked to try out for a school play. The role was a stereotypical black role for the time. It was like a Stepin Fetchit character—kind of slow witted and shiftless. The play was to be performed in a competition in Des Moines. There happened to be a big white guy by the name of Art, a student, who liked plays. He also was pretty well off in that he owned a car. Art befriended Bob and made him part of the gang. While in Des Moines, the guys went to a very nice cafeteria and they were served. The next day they went to a hamburger place and ordered about twenty hamburgers. This time the management refused to serve Bob, and Art got angry. He told the cafe people to take their hamburgers and stuff them. Then the young men walked out, leaving a lot of hamburgers uneaten.

The incident showed the type of segregation that existed in the North as opposed to the South. In the South, it was a matter of law. In the north, it varied from place to place, and one did not often know which places would not hire, serve, or admit blacks.

Meanwhile Bob's desire to attend college did not go unchallenged. His grandmother reflected her attitudes from living in a racist society. Her position was, "Why get the education, you won't get the job anyway." This led her to argue with Bob's mother about letting him go to college. Irene thought Nettie would lose control of him and he would not do anything except be a "smart ass" anyway. But Bob was not swayed. College was in his future.

Bob went on to relate the influence of a radio show, One Man's Family, on his hopes and dreams. The radio show was about a functional family that seemed to deal with problems efficiently. It was a stable family, something Bob had lacked but yearned for. He remembered bugging his mother and her husband to buy a house. It would be a step up from the rooming house in which they were living. The family finally did rent a house. Bob responded by painting rooms and even planting a rose bush in the yard.

During his senior year in high school, something else happened that helped shape his life. A few of the young men in the area were activists. They formed a club called the Comrade Club. The founders invited a few young people they thought were concerned to join. One of the first things the club did was to clean up the neighborhood. In 1939, the Catholic Daughters engaged Marion Anderson to come to Waterloo to sing. Bob gave her a dozen roses during the intermission. This was a time when the people of the neighborhood began identifying who they were and began working together to improve their community lives.

At about the same time, a second event happened. Bob was walking down the street one day when an influential woman, Mrs. Hackett, stopped him. She asked him to start a local youth council for the NAACP. This was a time when the youth council of the Detroit NAACP was making news for its activism. Bob wanted the authority to decide what kinds of things the council would do. Mrs. Hackett did not promise anything, but said she would see what she could do.

One of Bob's first targets was a white grocery store owner in the neighborhood named George. The grocer was selling third-rate products for first rate prices. In addition, he was not always honest in matters of money. Many of his black customers would cash their payroll checks in his store. Some of the people could not read or write. He did not always give them the full value of their checks. At the time, a young lady from the council in Detroit was visiting. Bob thought she would be a big help, so he acted to form a boycott of the grocery store. He took his plans to the senior members of the NAACP. They listened and set up guidelines for the youth council to follow. The guidelines included getting the backing of the local churches. The churches supported the boycott as long as the council did not take any action until after it was mentioned in the pulpit. Bob thought everything was set. Unfortunately, Marie Wilson, the young lady from Detroit, went into the grocery story on a Saturday and told the grocer, "We're going to get you on Monday." It pretty much killed the boycott. However, he related that they eventually got what they wanted.

A friend of Bob's and the friend's uncle then opened a grocery store about two blocks from George's store. Bob and his friends thought this would be real progress because a black-owned grocery store was finally being opened. Wrong! They did not know how to run or maintain a grocery store. Meat and produce spoiled and rats were seen running around. It certainly was not progress.

These two events pushed Bob into an active life to better the conditions of people. He described his attitude at the time like this: "When I walked downtown, it was like walking out from under the blanket. When I walked back to my neighborhood, it was like walking back under the blanket."

However, college would take a good part of his attention in the early 1940s. Bob enrolled at the University of Iowa. He majored in and eventually graduated with a bachelor of science degree in commerce. Bob was active at the University of Iowa. He started out as a business major. He had the thought of going on and becoming a business lawyer. He also became a member of Kappa Alpha Psi, a black fraternity. He joined an organization called the Negro Forum. The main objective of the Forum was to bring black people of esteem and prominence to the university to speak to them. He went on to become president of the organization. So college would prove to be a busy time.

Unfortunately, problems even arose in and around the campus in Iowa City. Blacks were not allowed to eat at certain restaurants, and housing was limited. One of the reasons for joining a black fraternity was for the members to pool their resources for housing. Luckily some of the black residents of Iowa City owned large homes for the purpose of renting rooms. It was a way for them to earn a living. Bob went on to tell an anecdote that typified the situation. He had a roommate named Paul who was from the east. His parents were pretty well off. He was in Iowa because no other school would take him. At any rate, one day Paul said to Bob, "No offense, but you guys make too much noise and my parents are paying too much money for me to learn, and I just cannot study with all that noise going on." Paul decided to ask the dean if he could live at the quadrangle (student housing on campus.) He returned with a sad look on his face. Even though he could afford to pay for the housing, Paul was turned down. The dean said, "We don't mind the whites mingling with the colored, we just don't want the colored mingling with the whites." It was the attitude of the times.

A racial policy of the times also was illustrated in Missouri. If there was a bright black student who deserved a college education, he would not be allowed into the University of Missouri. If the student enrolled in another college, the University of Missouri paid the tuition. So a good friend of Bob's from Missouri went to Iowa.

Another anecdote related to restaurant policy. One night, Bob and his date, a black woman, went into a restaurant and ordered a couple of sodas, and they were served. The very next day, Sammy Caanan, a friend of Bob's, went to the same restaurant with a white friend. The difference on that day was that the manager was there. The manager walked up to the table and told them that the restaurant did not serve colored people. As the story went, the white student jumped on the table and said, "This restaurant refuses to serve colored students. Are you still going to eat here?" According to Sammy, about half the people walked out of the restaurant. The story quickly got around the campus. One of the people who reacted was a visiting professor who happened to be an acknowledged communist. She organized actions such as arranging for pairs of white people to separately go into restaurants in Iowa City. They were to observe what was going on. Then a black student would go in. Restaurants that did not serve blacks were put on a list that was distributed throughout the city. The situation finally came down to the finest hotel and restaurant in Iowa City. Jim Walker, a star football player for Iowa, was chosen to go to the restaurant and attempt to be served. For whatever reason, he backed out at the last minute. Guess who replaced him? Bob would not go in by himself, so another young man came with him. To his utter surprise, a waitress came over to serve them. Bob became the first black person to be served in that exclusive restaurant. Thus, while Bob was at Iowa, the blacks were able to break the color line in restaurants. They did not succeed in housing.

Bob then made an interesting comment. He said that whenever he had a negative experience, it was accompanied by a positive experience. He also noted that he seemed to gravitate toward those activities related to human events. Some examples of these observations have already been discussed, and others will follow.

Then there were the economic issues. During the summer he worked at a packing plant to earn money to continue his education. Bob felt he was on an even level intellectually and academically with most white students at the school. He was first hired as an unskilled laborer on the hog-killing floor. However, there was concern about his age because he was not yet twenty-one. So he became a janitor's assistant. The company refused to give him an office job. Company policy prevented blacks from being hired for office jobs at that time.

In 1942, when he was a senior in college, his life took another turn. He became the first person from his chapter of Kappa Alpha Psi to be drafted. He came back to the fraternity one day, and his fellow brothers were standing around the table that held the draft letter. Bob entered the army knowing nothing about military life. His first stop was at Fort Leonard Wood for basic training. By this time, his wife-to-be, Mary Jane Saunders, was a student at nearby Lincoln University. They had met and started dating while going to high school in Waterloo. He was a little ahead of her in school. They stayed in touch when he went to college and later got back together while he was at Fort Leonard Wood.

The military was still segregated during World War II. Basic training was three hard months. Bob became a squad leader. Then one day the master sergeant called out his name and told him that his test scores qualified him for OCS (officers candidate school). Bob was asked if he would go. He said yes even though he did not know what OCS was. A Lieutenant Brevard talked to him one day. He told Bob that he was too young and inexperienced to go to OCS. That sounded reasonable to Bob, so he asked the Lieutenant what he should do. Lieutenant Brevard said he would take his name off the list and Bob could stay at the camp for more training.

Meanwhile, a new general came to the post. He stated that too much favoritism was going on. He then said everyone had to go out and do their duty. Bob did not realize the order also applied to him. The day came when they called out the names of people to be shipped out the next day. Bob sat unconcerned in the mess hall eating spaghetti. Suddenly an enlisted man burst in and told him his name was called. Bob did not believe it at first, but sure enough he was going to be shipped to another camp. Was he angry! He felt a promise had been broken. Since they were shipping out, their gear had to be put out for inspection. A lieutenant came into the barracks to make the inspection. When he saw Bob's gear, he spoke to Bob. He apologized and explained that the new general had issued the order. This effort by an officer who did not even know Bob made an impression on him. That the lieutenant went through the pains to talk to him made Bob feel that the lieutenant cared.

Then came the train ride to the next base. The one fear that Bob had was that he would be sent to a base in the South. After the train started, Bob noticed that it was heading south. His spirits sank. Then he noticed that the position of the sun had shifted and the train was headed west. He ended up at Luke Field Air Base in Arizona where he was stationed for two and a half years. Wherever they were, the blacks were placed in Squadron F.

He arrived at the base in 1943. Bob had several short anecdotes about racial issues in the area. For instance, he had just missed a race riot among soldiers. He never found out what started it, but saw and heard about the damage that took place. Phoenix was the city nearest the base. It was much like Iowa cities as far as blacks were concerned. One had to get used to the base and the town. For example, in the movie theater, the blacks were to sit in the balcony. Also, the southern white soldiers felt free to use the term nigger. This was a dangerous practice around blacks from the north. They did not like the term and were not willing to put up with it. On off days in the city, buses would take the men back to the base. If a soldier missed the last bus, there was a little "cowboy" bus to take him back to the base. The soldier needed to know where it was parked. On one occasion, a white soldier got on the bus and said, "Hey, it's technicolor in here." Then he heard clicks of weapons. He crept to the front of the bus and told Bob he did not mean it. Bob told him to "Sit down and shut up."

Meanwhile, the adaptation to the segregated army continued. The blacks could use the base swimming pool only one day a week. Bob was assigned to be the lifeguard and ended up saving three lives during his time as lifeguard. As noted, the movie theater was segregated. One night Bob asked a friend named Owen, "What would happen if we sat outside the reserved section?" His friend said he did not know. Bob replied, "Are you game to find out?" Finally they sat one row into the white section. Then all the other blacks moved into the section too. They did not receive disciplinary action.

Life in the army had other challenges. For example, Bob started out as a clerk in the orderly room. Then he was assigned by Lieutenant Reichle, his squadron commander, to help run the orientation program on the base. Captain James Burnie had asked Lieutenant Reichle to run the program. Reichle said he would only do it if someone from Squadron F was assigned to help. He asked Captain Burnie for the most competent man he could find, and Captain Burnie sent Bob over.

The Lieutenant had been a speech professor at the University of Notre Dame and was a rebel in the army. He was very progressive for the time. He got along well with Bob, but because his progressive ideas irritated the other officers, he was transferred. He was followed by a Lieutenant Reeves from Texas. Lieutenant Reeves made slips of paper listing the duties for the enlisted men. He changed Bob's assignment to cleaning floors, windows, and furniture. Bob questioned the orders, and Reeves confirmed that they were right. Bob then went to his commanding officer, Captain Burnie from North Carolina. The captain was upset over the change in assignment and ordered Bob back to his squadron on base. Bob went back to the base as ordered.

During his stay in Arizona, a change took place in his personal life. He had been engaged to Mary Jane at the time. Then he met a young lady by the name of Ruth Wade. They had a lot in common and he became very smitten. Yet he thought of his commitment to Mary Jane. Bob and Mary Jane were married and she moved down to Arizona. They ended up staying in a room of a house off base in Phoenix. Previously, she had transferred to the University of Iowa where she earned a degree in journalism, but chose not to use it at that point.

Since he lived in Phoenix, Bob often had to hitch rides to the base. Many times officers picked him up on the road and drove him to the base. Not long after the incident with Lieutenant Reeves, Bob received a surprise. The officer who gave him a ride that day informed Bob that Lieutenant Reeves was on his way out.

Eventually new orders came for Bob. He was assigned to a base in Florida. Bob was in transit in August of 1945 and was driving his wife back to Iowa before heading down to Florida. The news of an atomic bomb being dropped on Japan occurred during the drive. It was quite a shock.

Once in Florida, Bob's job was to brief the soldiers on their rights upon returning home. He took real advantage of this. He told the soldiers to get involved when they got back home. Soon he found a couple of officers coming to his sessions to find out what he was saying.

Discharge from the army meant a return to the University of Iowa to complete his degree. He only had about one semester left and earned his bachelor of science degree in commerce. Upon graduation, he had to decide what to do. One choice was to continue in college and get a law degree. The other choice was to go out and look for a job.

Being married and wanting children pushed Bob to look for a job. Remember, this was a time when blacks were not encouraged to go to college because they often could not get jobs in which they could use their degrees. Bob had not received any counseling about getting a job in his field so he really did not know what to do. At about that time, the college newspaper came out with an article that said the United States Government was looking for college graduates to go to Japan, Korea, Austria, and Germany. Bob said to Mary Jane, "Wouldn't it be interesting if our first years of marriage were overseas somewhere?" He did not say any more about it. Days later, Mary Jane asked if he had applied for the job overseas yet. When he said that he had not, she encouraged him to go ahead and apply. He applied for the job and even sent a picture, based on the advice of a friend of Mary Jane. He did not hear anything for a month. So he wrote a letter to the War Department and asked about the status of his application. Two weeks later, he received a letter telling him he was hired.

The assignment sent him to Germany. The idea was that they were going to be trained to help run Germany for the next fifty years. Secretary of the Treasury Henry Morganthau was a good friend of President Roosevelt. Bob was told that Morganthau had convinced Roosevelt that since Germany was the aggressor in the two World Wars, it should be reduced to an agricultural state. This policy was then started when Harry Truman became president. The policy did not come close to being completed because it was not workable in theory or practice. Bob was placed in the export - import branch in the Office of the United States Military Government. New personnel were coming in at regular intervals. Bob was among the early arrivals. Orientation included a tour of the Spandau concentration camp. They learned how to administer the program. They also attended a meeting involving the big four countries (the United States, Great Britain, France, and the Union of Soviet Socialist Republics) in Berlin regarding the administration of Germany and its capital city. Most of the workers concluded that they were only going to stay for two or three years.

About seven months later, Mary Jane and their first child Bobby joined Bob in Germany. Bob ended up staying for three years and three months. In 1949, Bob was the clerical administrator for the import branch of the department. He was responsible for all the paperwork related to imports to Germany. There also were negotiators who were involved in determining prices of the goods. One day, Bob saw three negotiators, two American and one British, arguing with a woman. She was in the personnel department and was responsible for making recommendations for appointments. In this case, the negotiators were arguing for making Bob a negotiator. The woman, who was from Virginia, refused. Bob did not understand why he was not even consulted about the position. Though not happy, he continued in his position.

Eventually the State Department took over the governing of the United States sector of Germany. Bob and his family made the decision in 1951 to return to the United States. Interestingly, a Catholic priest stopped him one day before they left Germany and advised Bob to stay in the job. He warned Bob that he would have a very difficult time finding a job fitting his qualifications in the United States. Bob agreed that it was possible, but he had to try.

The encounter with the priest was followed by a meeting with one of Bob's supervisors in Germany. This man had been a sheriff in Wyoming. He had connections with people in Denver and wrote a highly complementary letter of recommendation for Bob. The friend assured Bob that he could get a good job in Denver. However, Bob wanted to go to Minneapolis. They chose Minneapolis because it was fairly close to Bob's and Mary Jane's relatives in Iowa, but far enough away to give them independence. They thought Denver was too far away.

First they went to Waterloo to see what was available. The year was 1951. Bob went back to the packing plant that he had worked at previously. One of his old high school classmates worked there. He came down and told Bob that the company did not hire Negroes for office jobs. The policy from his college days had not changed.

Then came the move to Minneapolis. He went to all kinds of companies in the city. On one occasion he went to a company in north Minneapolis. It was a small parts company that was just up his alley. The work fit nicely with what he had learned while working in Germany. One of the managers seemed ready to hire him. However, his partner, who was married to the boss's daughter, was against having a black work in the office, and Bob did not get hired.

At this time, Bob was acquainted with a man by the name of Frank Faeger. Frank was the office manager of the mayor's fair employment office. His assistant, Eunice Brown, was a personal friend of Bob and Mary Jane. Frank tried to direct Bob to places where he might have a chance to be hired. At the same time, an organization of faculty wives from the University of Minnesota joined with nurses to pressure businesses to hire qualified blacks in office jobs.

With this as a background, Frank sent Bob to some banks that had openings. The Federal Reserve Bank was one more place that turned him down. Bob was no longer surprised to hear rejections. He had applied to more than twenty-five businesses without receiving one offer that met with his qualifications. The only type of employment offered to him was janitorial work. Then he called the First National Bank and asked for an interview. He talked to a man by the name of Jack Ewing, who told him to come in the next morning. When Bob walked in for the scheduled interview, Jack Ewing said, "You are just the man we are looking for." Bob got the job. Bob did not know it at the time but felt the job offer came because of the pressure put on by the women. Apparently, the bank president called a meeting after a visit from the women's organization. He told his staff that they were going to hire one black person. To the credit of management, the bank actually hired two black women before hiring Bob. The job was as a clerk in the accounting department.

During the time of his job hunt, Mary Jane and their two children stayed in Iowa. Bob notified her when the job offer came. At that point, she and the children moved to Minneapolis, and the family set out to find a house. Eunice Brown was aware that they were looking. Eunice was also friends with a family that went to the same church as her. When she mentioned to this family that the Samples were looking for a place to stay, she received a surprising response. They asked Eunice if the Samples were friends. When she answered yes, the family said they were about to leave for a vacation in New York and were looking for someone to live in their house while they were gone. This was a very generous offer to come from a white family in the early 1950s. Thus, the Samples moved into the house for a one-week period.

Now they had one week to find a permanent place to live. Of course that was not a very long time, but Bob and Mary Jane added another hurdle for themselves. They decided that they would not move into a ghetto area. To top it off, they even had trouble getting a real estate agent to help them. Finally a freelance agent contacted them with just two days left to find a house. The agent found a suitable house in Richfield. The house needed some work, which Bob and Mary Jane were willing to do. In addition, the owner was anxious to sell. A deal was struck. Bob had the money for a down payment, and his bank was willing to give him a mortgage. They moved into the house on July 3, 1951.

Settling into the neighborhood was not easy. July fourth was a holiday, and many people were away. On July fifth, Bob went down to the hardware store to buy tools so he could start fixing up the house. Now people of the neighborhood had an opportunity to see who had moved into the area. Later the same day, Bob was pulling a wagon down the street. He was going to buy some ice for their ice box. Along came a garbage hauler. After asking Bob if he lived in the house, he advised Bob to sell the house because the people in the neighborhood would not like it. When Bob replied that he wouldn't sell, the garbage hauler said, "We'll see about that." When he was returning with the ice, the garbage hauler's assistant came up to him and warned him that he should take the garbage hauler's advice. He said the garbage hauler was mean. Bob's reply was that he was mean, too. More was to come.

That evening, Bob was outside mowing his lawn. He noticed a stream of cars driving by his house. The cars were bumper-to-bumper, very unusual for a residential street. His wife and mother-in-law also saw the parade of cars. The next day, the tension escalated. After work, Bob noticed cars streaming by his house again, but this time they were headed for a meeting called by the garbage hauler at a local tavern. Bob wanted to telephone Frank Faeger to let him know what was happening. Unfortunately their telephone had not yet been installed in their new home. Bob had to walk to a pay phone. His path was taking him past the tavern. Luckily, as he was nearing a gas station, Bob heard a "beep" behind him. The sound nearly frightened him to death, but it turned out to be Frank Faeger. Talk about good fortune! Bob told him what was going on. Frank left and came back with a minister. They talked about what to do in case a mob showed up. At that moment, a knock was heard at the door. The visitor introduced himself as George Rice and said that he lived in the neighborhood. He volunteered to go to the tavern and report back what was happening. George Rice turned out to be a part-time reporter for the Minneapolis Star newspaper. Later, a rather large policeman came to the door. He informed Bob that they had a squad car nearby and they were watching for any trouble that might come along.

George came back with a report. Before the meeting, Bob said George reported that small children were standing outside the bar. They were asking some of the adults why they did not want black people living in the neighborhood. During the meeting, one guy who had a British accent rose and asked if it was an open meeting. When told that it was, he said he was against everything the garbage hauler was saying. Suggestions at the meeting included whether to buy out the Samples, kill them, burn them out, or do nothing. In the end, the people from the area did nothing.

Bob wanted to make the point that such attitudes were not isolated. He told an anecdote to illustrate. A black man was hired as a bus driver in the Chicago area. He searched for a home near his bus route, which was in Cicero. He rented an apartment and furnished it with new furniture. Neighborhood people broke into the apartment, threw the furniture out, and ransacked the apartment. Bob said that police were at the scene but refused to act. This event took place at about the same time Bob and his family were facing the difficulty accounted above.

It was still July 1951, and Bob did not have to go back to work until July fifteenth. He had a few more days to get the house organized. Bobby, the oldest son, was four years old. He had a tricycle, and in the spirit of adventure, wanted to ride down the street to play with the other children. When he asked Bob, he was told no. Bobby was persistent and kept asking for the next two days without success. Finally, he decided to sneak down the street. Bob saw what he was up to and realized that he had to let his son go sometime. He noticed his son sneak his tricycle over a small bank down to the street. Bob pretended that he did not notice. Soon his son was pedaling down the street. But he did not find any children outside. Their mothers made them come in. Bobby came back puzzled about why the children went in. It was an incident that really stressed out Bob and Mary Jane.

In another vein, the Sample family became parishioners in a new Roman Catholic Church in the area. They started a new liturgy at the church and much of the mass was in English. This was before the second Vatican Council, so it was ahead of the times. Bob sang in the choir and was active in the Men's Club. His family did not have a car at the time, so people often picked them up as they walked to church. That was how Bob's family was able to know other families in the church.

However, even among church members, acceptance was not automatic. Bob was involved with a group that played volleyball once a week. Bob routinely walked to the church gymnasium with a friend who lived a couple blocks away. This friend had a cute daughter about the age of Bobby, and they were in kindergarten together. Bobby really liked the little girl and was very protective of her. One night, while walking to volleyball, the friend said he had something to tell Bob. He said they were moving because his wife did not approve of interracial marriage. She was already worrying about that issue when her daughter was only five years old!

One of the reasons why they did not have a car was because of the low pay at the bank. Bob said that banks were notorious for paying low salaries. Finally Bob went to see his boss, Jack Ewing. He told Ewing that his pay was so low that he just could not make ends meet. Bob mentioned that he was going to have to get a second job. Ewing said that bank policy discouraged employees from working a second job. However, he would try to help Bob by getting him overtime. As luck would have it, the bank soon changed accounting methods—from hand to machine. The change allowed Bob to pick up a lot of overtime.

A decent income was very important as the family grew at a constant pace. Bob and Mary Jane had eight children. One died at two days old, but the others are still living. The children's names from oldest to youngest are Robert, Frank, Peggy, Christopher, Deborah, Randall, and Jennifer. All of the children lived in the Twin Cities area.

Money came in handy as all seven of their children ended up going to St. Richard's Catholic School. One would expect that tolerance would be more prevalent at a parochial school than at a public school. Although Bob did not learn about it until after the fact, the children had racial fights with other students almost every afternoon on the way home from school. They did not tell their parents and possibly did not tell anyone else either. This was just another piece of life that left a bad taste in his mouth.

Yet another incident was tied to this. Bob and his wife collaborated on a play for the church called *The Twig Is Bent*. One day a parent of one of the boys Bobby frequently fought with approached Bob. The parent offered to organize a stage crew for the play. Bob thought it was great. Then came the dress rehearsal. The parent brought the crew, but they stayed in the back of the gym and did nothing. Luckily, some Franciscan seminarians jumped in and helped out while the crew stood in the back and laughed. The play was given on a Friday and Saturday, and the seminarians' work helped make it a success.

Racial attitudes proved to be persistent whether in the neighborhood community or the church community. Bob heard over and over again that the Samples were okay, but people did not want more blacks coming into their community. This type of attitude spurred Bob and Mary Jane to become more active. Mary Jane joined the League of Women Voters. Bob joined a church group called the Catholic Interracial Council. A panel discussion on housing was to be held at the College of St. Catherine's in St. Paul. Bob was asked to be one of the panelists. That event was what led to Bob's involvement in the council. He went on to be elected president twice.

As a side note, research showed that the FBI was involved in monitoring the activities of Bob. At least one person whom Bob thought was a friend, and treated him as a friend, was in fact working for the FBI. This was apparently part of a nationwide effort on the part of the FBI to gather information on civil rights activists for the purpose of finding something damaging so the activists could be neutralized.

It was during a term as president of the Catholic Interracial Council when the March on Washington took place in 1963. Upon their return, Bob and others had several requests to travel the state and speak about the experience. One day, Jack Ewing called him into his office at the bank. Instead of reprimanding Bob for going here and there, Ewing offered him the use of the company car—a very selfless act.

The main purpose of the Catholic Interracial Council was to change the racial attitudes and policies of the Church. For example, the council wanted to get rid of the "missionary" churches. If you were black, you belonged to a missionary church. Where you lived did not matter, it was a segregated system. The effort was not successful. But Bob and his family never did follow that policy. However, James Luger from the Catholic Interracial Council was able to spearhead the effort at getting equal housing legislation passed at the state level.

The early 1960s became a period of turmoil for Bob. There was the work for the Catholic Interracial Council. The March on Washington took place at this time. It was followed by the speaking engagements throughout greater Minnesota. These and other factors put a lot of stress on the marriage between Bob and Mary Jane. They finally separated and then divorced. Mary Jane eventually went on to write for the St. Paul Pioneer Press.

Bob continued working for the bank until 1966. He had achieved his own desk and supervisory duties. However, he was also aware of the fact that he had hit the glass ceiling. But the lure of local activism was still pulling him. He still had the desire to improve the conditions of the people in the community.

Personal circumstances led Bob to move to south Minneapolis. It was at this point that he became acquainted with Reverend Stanley King, a Baptist minister and activist in the Twin Cities. It was also a time when Bob was still working with the Interracial Council and in a program to help kids stay in school and realize their potential. Then a program developed called the Twin Cities Opportunities Industrialization Center (TCOIC). The purpose of the program was to train disadvantaged people so they could get jobs. Bob began to support the TCOIC. First National Bank let them use the Marquette building as a training center. Bob was one of the first people to enter the building and start cleaning it up.

Looking back at the program, Bob concluded that they were trying to train people who were untrainable. He felt it was too late for many of the trainees. He said they were too set in their ways. When the TCOIC was able to get jobs for the trainees, most of them did not know how to handle it. Also, most did not know how to get along with other people. The experience taught Bob that people should not be placed in situations they could not handle. They needed more than just job training.

Bob described himself as just drifting along with the program. He was a special promoter for the program and often helped stage events in the Twin Cities. For example, he arranged a musical program featuring Della Reese and others. He also organized a parade for Martin Luther King.

Then came a change. A man named Roy Lockett was placed into his office at the TCOIC. Lockett had started an arts program for gifted children. He had persuaded some talented people to leave their jobs and work with the children. Unfortunately, he developed some serious administrative problems which brought the program to a halt. Bob concluded that Roy Lockett was like many artists in that they had great creativity but lacked good managerial skills. Yet the idea was fascinating to Bob and he offered to get involved. A couple of meetings were held to see how they could get the program off the ground. No investors were interested at first. Bob went to Russ Ewald, one of the major forces in the city at the time. Russ flatly turned Bob down at first, but after some persuasion agreed to put money into the program. Bob took over the program, but instead of limiting the program to gifted children, he wanted any child to be able to participate. It was agreed upon. Then the Reverend Emmanuel Johnson, pastor of Messiah Lutheran Church, offered the second floor of the church's community building as a site for the center. The job running the center meant that Bob would no longer be working for the TCOIC.

A fellow TCOIC worker, Tom Tipton, questioned the move. He asked Bob what made him think kids would be interested in the arts if they did not have enough food to eat? Bob replied that no one had asked youngsters yet and it would be worth finding out.

At about this time, Bob remarried. He and Pat met in 1968, and according to Bob, both were coming off situations and were looking for support and security. She was a writer and twenty-five years his junior. They came from very different backgrounds.

Bob referred to himself as "a ghetto boy." Pat came from a conservative North Dakota background. They married in 1969 and had one boy named André. They were married until 1992, when the marriage ended in divorce.

The Metropolitan Cultural Arts Center was opened in May 1969. The main purpose of the program was to train children's minds so they could reason on their own and to foster curiosity. Yet not much advertising had been done. His wife Pat Samples was a partner in the MCAC. She and a friend went out into the neighborhood to recruit children for the program and resulted in Pat becoming a key contributor to the MCAC. Then came time for the opening. It was a beautiful day to be outside. Bob did not expect many children to spend a whole day in school and then come over to the arts center. Instead he said the kids "almost knocked me over trying to get into the building." He said that kids started drawing, and some waited to start learning how to play instruments such as the piano. This was still a period of turmoil for the civil rights movement. He felt gratified to see such enthusiasm for the program under the circumstances.

Since the kids were not charged anything, money had to come from somewhere. The program had a board. Bob Schmidt of the Schmidt Music Company joined the board and helped obtain financial support. However several other organizations were operating at the same time. They included the Hospitality House, the Plymouth Youth Center, The Way, and the Phyllis Wheatley House. They discovered that the groups were working at cross purposes to each other. Because of the overlap of services, money was hard to come by. That situation led to the establishment of the North Side Agencies. It was a cooperative effort by the different North Side organizations and Bob became the first president.

Eventually a drama group was started as a part of the MCAC. Bob was so interested in this that he joined the classes. The group started out doing things like improvisations. Then they did a play called *In White America*. The play was presented at various locales such as the Newman Center at the University of Minnesota, the Old Log Theater in Excelsior, Minnesota, and at Mankato State University. Eventually, the Reverend Johnson from Messiah Lutheran Church came by. He was pastor of a sister church, St. Thomas. The church had an old church building that was not being used. Reverend Johnson suggested talking to the church council to see if they could use it for a theater. The council said yes; the MCAC board of directors approved the project and named the theater the Shoestring Playhouse. They went on to produce successful plays for a period of eight years.

Then the Lutheran Church sold the community building that the arts center was using to another church organization. At the same time, the Minneapolis Library Board closed a library in north Minneapolis. Bob went to the Minneapolis Preservation Commission, which had placed the building on the social registry. He asked for and received permission to use the building for the Minneapolis Cultural Arts Center. The upshot was that Bob was persuaded to become a member of the commission.

As time went on, Bob became somewhat disillusioned. He did not think that giving people free things all the time was the best way to help people improve their lives. He thought more emphasis should be placed on encouraging people to establish values. So in 1982, Bob asked at a board meeting of the Minneapolis Cultural Arts Center to consider charging a token fee for the classes. (He pointed out that there was not one person on the board from north Minneapolis—the area being served.) The board did not agree and Bob quit.

After the breakup of his marriage, Bob moved to Hopkins and entered the next phase of his life. He started the Shoestring Players in 2001. This is a regional theater group located in Hopkins. At the time of our interview his position was president of the board, and the company was putting on a production.

Bob concluded that his training and experience geared him toward activism at the local level. He did not see himself as a politician. As a matter of fact, a local Minneapolis politician asked him to run for the city council. However he turned down the opportunity. As of 2003, Bob still saw the prejudices in society. He related cases of lip service from people who expressed friendship toward him, but never socialized or invited him into their homes. He spoke of his hope that the type of work he has done and is still doing would lead to more acceptance between people. He did not lay all the blame on the majority. He went so far as to say that many whites did not always realize their prejudices. At the same time, he said blacks had problems of their own and should not use blackness as a crutch. Bob is certainly an uncommon man.

Sally Ozwoeld

Sally's parents, Benjamin and Clara (nee Kunkin) Shaich, came from Russia around 1912. She was not sure of the specifics, but thought they came to the United States to better their lives. Benjamin and Clara had one child at the time of their immigration, Eva, who was born on May 3, 1909. Sally was the second child, born on April 23, 1914. She was followed by brother David on October 20, 1916.

Her childhood was adventuresome, marked by many family moves. Benjamin had a bit of wanderlust, causing him to change jobs often, looking for something new. One of his first jobs was working in a meat-packing plant. Many of the moves were in the western states, but the family also spent time in Minnesota and Connecticut. Sally was born in Omaha, Nebraska. The family moved to Cheyenne, Wyoming, when she was about four years old. During their stay her father worked on a railroad, and after a short time he was given a half section of farmland by the railroad. He did not farm the land but did rent it out for a while. The land is still owned by the family. Then Benjamin, who had a brother in Minneapolis, formed a business partnership. That partnership did not last and he moved to Scobey, Montana, after establishing another business partnership. The rest of the family stayed in Minneapolis for a time, but later joined Benjamin in Montana. The stay in Scobey, a town of about 1,200 people at the time, lasted about eight years. The stay was interrupted for a year when the family moved to East Haven, Connecticut. Her father opened a fish and fruit market in a brand new building. However, they only stayed a year, apparently because he did not like it, and they returned to the west.

Clara was not eager to move around. She wanted to settle in the east and establish roots, whereas he wanted to live in the west. At one point, she put the children in a children's home and went back west to try to bring him back to Minneapolis. Though he did come back, it did not work out. Clara was greatly stressed by Benjamin's lifestyle and suffered emotionally. She died in 1926, and Benjamin ended up marrying her sister. After that, family life became more stable.

Talking about the time in the children's home brought back memories for Sally. First of all, her older sister Eva was placed with a family, rather than being sent to the children's home. When she returned to her family, she had lice. For her part, Sally went to kindergarten while at the home. She remembered standing on a chair in school and singing, so it would appear that her interest in this activity started early. She also remembered being clothed in starched dresses every morning—something she really liked.

Frequent moves probably strengthened the bonds between the Shaich children. Sally did not mention the kinds of activities that kept the children amused when they were young, but she did have two great interests during her teen years. She loved to dance, saying that her motto was, "I would rather dance than eat." As noted earlier, she also loved to sing, and compiled a songbook with all the words of the popular songs of the time. She still sings today—and still has the songbook.

Sally went through high school in Scobey and said, "Those were my happiest days." She went to school in the town—a school that went from kindergarten through twelfth grade. The family lived five blocks away from the school, so the children walked home for lunch. She graduated from the high school in 1933.

Her father taught her how to drive while the family was living in Scobey. She had to drive to and from school because she needed to take the family typewriter to school for a class since the school did not have any. She also mentioned an incident in which she was driving her father's panel truck along an icy highway. She wanted him to get a little rest, but he was so scared that he wouldn't shut his eyes. It was a scary ride!

The family often had big meals at noon. Meals were often of the meat and potatoes variety. Her favorite food growing up was strawberries and cream. While Sally did not mention any foods she did not like, she told an anecdote about one meal. She was eating a bowl of chicken soup one day when she found a tiny red feather from a chicken. She was so disgusted by this discovery that she went outside and sat on the curb and waited to go back to school.

Sally did not waste any time after graduating from high school. The very next day, she and her sister joined a trucker as he traveled to Minneapolis. She spent the summer, June through September, going to business school in the city. She ended up with certification as a private secretary. Unfortunately the country was in the depths of the Great Depression and jobs were hard to find. She ended up getting a job in a bakery for four dollars per week. She noted that even with that low pay, she saved one dollar a week. When winter came, Sally gave up the bakery job and returned home to Scobey. She returned to Minneapolis the following spring. She again had to look for a job and eventually landed a position with the Shedlov Oil Burner Company answering phones and doing clerical work. She mentioned that Mrs. Shedlov was still living and was noted for wearing a coachman's hat.

Her father sold his store and the family house in Montana, and her parents returned to Minneapolis in 1935. Her father bought a grocery store in town in order to set Sally and David up with jobs. In the meantime, brother and sister had signed up with the city civil service. So they left the grocery business to work in civil service. Sally worked at keeping records, first at General Hospital (now Hennepin County Medical Center), and later at Lymonhurst (which became known as the Sister Kenny Institute). She finally worked for the health department. This type of work took up most of her early career years.

While discussing the years of the Depression, Sally talked about how it affected her in different ways. For instance, she did not have money to buy clothes. So her father gave her a letter to Butler Brothers (a wholesale clothing company that her father dealt with). She was able to get clothes from them. She mentioned that they also saved money by walking rather than riding the street cars, although they did wear out their shoes more quickly. In addition, it was harder to get some foods, like meat.

Another important event took place in 1935 when Sally met Victor Ozwoeld. They met in a car in which six people were riding. She found herself on Victor's lap. He gave her a ring on her birthday, and they were married two years later on July 25, 1937.

Their honeymoon turned out to be quite a surprise for Sally. She left the planning up to her new husband, and he told her they were going to Chicago. When the train stopped at its destination, they were in Duluth! The reason Victor chose Duluth was because he had an uncle living there, and they stayed with the uncle. She said, "That's the first time he pulled the wool over my eyes." She also said, "I was burned up by the whole thing, because he fooled me."

Speaking of that incident made her say that was only one incident that made her angry. She went on to give an account of another incident after they had their first child. It was a Sunday, and she was waiting for him to come home and take them up to the northside of Minneapolis to visit her parents. Well, she waited and waited and he did not come, so she took the baby and walked down to his store. She found him chatting away and never looking at the clock. She also did not like to go grocery shopping with him. Being in the fruit and vegetable business made him picky. Sally would throw a head of lettuce in the cart and Victor would take it out and replace it because it was not good enough. Nevertheless, they had a good, loving relationship. She described him as "a good, honest man, and he was crazy about his children."

Victor had a variety of jobs during their marriage. First he had a small store in Minneapolis selling fruits and vegetables. When World War II began, he did not pass the military physical but became a welder during those years. When the war ended, he took over her father's business in dealing with second hand boxes. He had a route that took him to various stores like Kresge's and Woolworth's, picking up discarded cartons. He then sold these boxes and cartons for two to three cents each. He often worked until 11 PM, but as Sally said, "he made a living." Some of the boxes had broken merchandise in them like vases, ornaments and such. When all the pieces were found, Sally glued them together. When she had enough items, she took them to a rummage store to sell. One could say she was resourceful and an environmentalist at the same time. Her husband later went to work for his brother-in-law in the fruit and vegetable business as the produce buyer.

Acquisitions came gradually. The Ozwoeld's did not have a car when they were first married. Meanwhile, the Ozwoeld's first home was an apartment in a duplex in north Minneapolis. It was a made-over duplex and she felt it did not offer the kind of privacy that they would have liked. The first home they bought also was a duplex. They purchased the home in

1946, lived in the upper level and rented out the lower level. The Ozwoeld's charged twenty-eight dollars rent per month, and that was used to pay off the mortgage. They had two bedrooms and a den and were quite comfortable. However, the locks were very poor. Sally mentioned that when they were moving, they left some canned goods and an ironing board with the intention of picking them up later. When they came back, everything was gone. Sally and Victor eventually moved into a single family home in north Minneapolis. They lived there for eight years and then moved to a house in Golden Valley where they lived for twenty-two years.

During World War II, the family felt the effects of rationing. Sally told a story about rationed meat. Because meat was hard to get, she put a roast in the freezer and saved it for a special occasion. One day, a boyfriend of a friend recommended that they visit her. Even though she did not know the person, she took out that roast, cooked it, and served it to them. She had to serve her precious roast to someone she didn't even know!

The family grew over the years. The Ozwoeld's added four children. Carol Jean was born in 1939. She was followed by Lois in 1944, Bob in 1946, and Pamela in 1956. All of the children are married and doing well. Sally's children have given her twelve grandchildren and two great grandchildren. A major health crisis developed when Lois contracted polio at the age of two. The virus was centered in her back and throat areas. While there was some paralysis for a time, Lois made a complete recovery. By coincidence, Sally worked for the Sister Kenny Institute prior to the illness.

Through the 1950s and 1960s, Sally continued to work at least part-time. She became a supermarket cashier. Her brother-in-law had a store and sent her to get training; she worked in his store for a time. She also worked at Dayton's (Marshall Field's) for a while. She worked in the credit department and also often worked as a cashier during the sales.

All of her children work in the health care fields. Sally remarked that the children were able to combine work, help from parents, and scholarships to further their education. In 2003 Carol Jean lived in Salt Lake City and worked as a dental hygienist. Bob lived in Eugene, Oregon, and was a clinical psychologist. Lois and Pamela lived in the Twin Cities metro area. Lois worked as a medical technologist, and Pamela was a dental hygienist. All their families were doing well.

She added that her son came back to Minnesota for a liver transplant in February, 2003 and was still recovering from the surgery at the time of this interview. He had suffered from Crohn's Disease for many years, and it eventually affected his liver. The liver problem was diagnosed in June 2002, and his health steadily declined over the months. He finally came back to Minnesota and was put on the liver transplant list. Luckily, a match was found, and he was able to have the transplant.

All the travel that Sally did as a child did not dampen her desire to travel later in life. She recounted a trip back to Scobey for a reunion in which they had to describe their worst experience during a trip. She said her experience came on a train trip. First, the train left late—it was supposed to leave at midnight but did not leave until 2 AM. Then, when she got to her seat, a rather large lady came, sat next to her, fell asleep and spread herself out so that Sally could not get out of her seat. She said, "I was a captive in there." Her favorite travels with her husband were to Hawaii. They had been to Hawaii sixteen times! At first, they toured several of the islands, and later they spent their vacation time on the island of Oahu.

Sally continued to live in her home for two years after the death of her husband. Then she decided to move into a St. Louis Park apartment. In talking about the move, she noted that it was like starting over. She furnished the apartment with new furniture so she kept very little of what they had in their house.

Much time has been devoted to volunteer work and other activities over the last several years. She first did clerical work for Mt. Sinai Hospital, and then did the same type of work for the senior clinic at Abbot Hospital. She amassed 1,250 hours at Abbot.

She had been attending activities at the Jewish Community Center in St. Louis Park for about ten years. She regularly sang with the choir on Wednesdays and took part in the exercise program on Thursdays. The center had a piano player come in, and Judy Dworsky managed the choir. Sally said that it was a good way to spend the day. At times she even performed in singing shows at the Jewish Community Center as part of the Senior Choir under the direction of Mark Bloom. She enjoyed the exercise teacher because she not only had good workouts, but also used humor, danced around, and told stories while they exercised. Last but not least, she attended the Yiddish Vinkl at the Jewish Community Center and spoke fluent Yiddish. That was quite an accomplishment!

Sally experienced a varied lifestyle through the years. Her early years were somewhat unsettled, but she seemed to have learned some good lessons about life. She and her husband worked well as a team and certainly earned their trips to Hawaii. Age has not slowed her much, and she has continued to remain active.

Trudy Rappaport

Many people who recount the history of their lives speak of many ups and downs. It is rare for these high points and low points to be extremely intensive or long lasting. Few people could describe an event or point in their life that could be called miraculous. This is not one of those histories. This is about a person who experienced unspeakable terror over several years, and her survival was miraculous.

Trudy's parents were born and raised in Germany. Her father, Julius Gumberich, was a traveling salesman who sold dowries. Her mother, Erna, was a homemaker. The Gumberich's had two children—Lotte (born April 6, 1915) and Trudy (born February 21, 1918). The family lived in a two-bed-room apartment in Stuttgart, Germany. The apartment had all the amenities like a telephone, electricity, and modern plumbing.

Her formative years seemed quite happy until 1933. She loved listening to good music on the radio. Trudy also enjoyed playing games such as marbles with neighborhood children. She attended a German public school and also attended Hebrew classes twice a week. She thought school was okay until Hitler came to power in 1933.

Trudy told an anecdote about how life changed after Hitler became dictator. She had a girlfriend who lived just around the corner from them. Trudy described her as her best girlfriend. They were together day and night. They often slept over at one another's apartment. They even celebrated each other's holidays together. Suddenly, the young friend became distant, something that Trudy did not understand. The friend finally admitted that she could no longer be friends with Trudy because her father, who worked at a radio station, said if the station personnel found out that his daughter was friends with a Jew, he would lose his job. Trudy said, "So that was that." A friendship that started when she was six years old was over. Trudy was not yet fifteen.

Restrictions upon Jewish life became common with the passage of the Nuremberg Laws in 1935. The laws stripped the Jews of their citizenship and essentially legalized discrimination of the Jewish community in Germany. Trudy was most affected by restrictions on free movement. For example, Jewish people could no longer go to movie theaters, nor could they not go into some restaurants. She remembered going into a cafe with a friend one day and the owner recognized them as Jewish. He came up to them and said he was sorry but they would have to leave, so they did. Trudy then said, "This was just the beginning; it got much worse later."

Since the Great Depression was essentially worldwide, the German people also had to deal with it. For a time, things went fairly well for Julius, since he was able to keep his job and earn a living for the family. So economically, they were getting by.

Trudy said, "Then it got very bad in 1938—the moment we had the Kristallnacht" (the night of the broken glass). During the nights of November 9 and 10, mobs in Germany and the newly acquired territories of Austria and the Sudetenland went on a rampage. Jews were attacked indiscriminately; about 2,000 synagogues were burned, almost 7,500 Jewish businesses were destroyed, and much vandalism took place in such areas as cemeteries. In addition, 30,000 Jews were arrested and sent to concentration camps. Many consider this event the actual beginning of the Holocaust.

The impact of Kristallnacht was felt by Trudy. She was working in a Jewish owned factory at the time. She picked up her story the day after the Kristallnacht occurrence. She and all the other Jewish employees were told they had to leave and that they could no longer work there. The Jewish owners had to sell the factory and gentiles bought it. The new owners did not want Jewish people working for them. The same day, as she was walking to work, she passed by her synagogue, which was engulfed in flames. The fire department was there—to protect only the buildings next to the synagogue. It was a crushing day for her, but things got worse.

The next day, the Gestapo came to the family home and arrested Julius. He maintained his innocence and asked why he was being arrested. The Gestapo agents never gave him an answer. Erna was quite upset and cried as the scene unfolded, but her husband reassured the family that he would be back soon. It was not to be; instead, he was shipped to Sachsenhausen, a concentration camp close to Berlin. Trudy's mother did not even know where he was taken at first. It took her a while to find out where he was. He ended up spending nine months in the prison.

In the meantime, older sister Lotte tried to get out of Germany, knowing that staying in Germany was extremely dangerous. Finally, in the beginning of 1939, she obtained a permit to go to Amsterdam, the Netherlands. She moved to the Netherlands and was able to gain employment as a household maid.

There also was a Jewish Family & Children's Service in Stuttgart that was trying to help Jewish people leave Germany. The Gumberichs told the service about Julius, who was among the thousands imprisoned at the time. The service told them it would try to help and eventually came up with emigration papers for him to go to La Paz, Bolivia. The papers helped get Julius out of the prison. Trudy said that when they picked him up, "He was just half the man (he had been) when he left." Trudy said the treatment at the prison was "terrible," that the prisoners "dropped like flies" from slave labor, starvation rations, and executions.

Julius asked about Lotte as soon as he returned home, and was told that she had escaped and she hoped to bring the rest of the family to Amsterdam. Then the family found out that the emigration papers were false, that they had been made up just to get him out of the concentration camp. Her father had to report to the Gestapo each week about the status of his emigration. He was finally given an ultimatum that directed him to leave the country by a certain date or he would be arrested and sent back to the concentration camp. This was, of course, shocking for the whole family. Her parents had already sent for passports because they had thought the papers to Bolivia were legitimate. At the time, a request for a passport was not made for Trudy because the emigration papers only applied to her parents. The passports for the parents came through, and were soon followed by some good news. A transport ship was leaving for Shanghai in two weeks, and there was room aboard for Trudy and her parents. She applied for her passport at once, but it had to be sent to different countries to be put into a visa to give her a right to pass through those countries. The day before the transport left, Julius gave Trudy the bad news that her passport had not come through and that she would not be able to go to Shanghai with them. After experiencing the grief of this situation, they received some good news; a second transport ship would leave for Shanghai in two weeks. They thought Trudy would certainly be able to take that one.

Her world turned completely over during those two weeks. The German invasion of Poland took place and World War II started. Trudy had lost the opportunity to leave Germany. Her parents made it to Shanghai and returned to the port to meet their daughter when the second transport ship came in. To their dismay, she was not on board.

At the time, Trudy was still free, but needed a job, and few jobs were available for Jews. She could only get a job as a maid for a Jewish family. She eventually met a nice family who hired her as a live-in maid. The family treated her like their own. The wife was not Jewish and that allowed them to stay in Germany. Eventually the couple left for America, and Trudy had to find another job. That lasted a while and then she was out looking again. With little money to spend, she eventually rented a room and lived by herself.

During this time, her sister kept writing to her and tried to find her a job in the Netherlands, but she was unsuccessful. Nevertheless, she regularly sent packages of food and other goods. The packages were important because the Jews living in Germany had limited access to food. The Jews had only one grocery store to go to in their area and there was not much to buy. People had to wait in long lines to get into the store, and when they did, the shelves were mostly bare. It was ironic that Lotte ended up being arrested when the Nazis took over the Netherlands. She was sent to Auschwitz, where she died.

Trudy's own arrest took place on November 27, 1941. An aunt and uncle living in Stuttgart were also arrested. Their son had accompanied the Gumberichs to Shanghai—another irony. Trudy was notified beforehand that she would be arrested.

The letter notified her of the date for the arrest. It also specified that she could take what would fit into one suitcase and a little food. Many of her belongings had to be left behind. Reasons for the arrest were not given, but she knew. Then on the appointed day, two Gestapo agents in civilian clothes came and picked her up like she was a common criminal—like a killer.

She was taken to a gathering place in Stuttgart where they stayed for three days. The people were fed three times a day and slept on the floor. Then they were taken to the train station and loaded on a passenger train without knowing the destination. The train trip took three days and three nights. The Nazis treated them very well the first two days—the train was heated. Things changed on the third day. The heat was turned off, resulting in the windows frosting over so the people could not see out. Obviously, it became freezing cold in the cars. When the train finally stopped and the doors were open, the people were met by S.S. (blackshirts) and S.R. (military) troops with dogs. The people were ordered out of the train quickly.

Right away, one man was shot dead; Trudy said she did not know why, but that was the beginning of the terror that would follow. The people were forced to pick up their bags and walk. She did not know how long they had to walk, but they ended up at Jungfernhof, a former farm near Riga, Latvia.

Thus began her first period of imprisonment. The people were forced to stay in a barn that had been made over. It contained three levels of beds, and the beds were not individual, but laid out in long rows and people had to sleep right next to each other. The young people had to sleep on the top tier. Since it was winter and the barn was not insulated, it was cold. Trudy remembered waking up in the morning and being covered with snow that had come in through openings in the roof and through open windows. She had only one pair of shoes and they were not waterproof. The wet conditions and bitter cold led to painful frostbite. Trudy said the pain was so bad she did not think she would be able to walk again. Time was spent sitting around or standing in line for food and according to her words, "freezing, and freezing, and freezing." Most people still had a little food from home, but it ran out fast. She spent about three or four weeks at that camp.

Then one day, the guards took all the older people away on trucks—including her aunt and uncle. They were driven into the forest and shot. Trudy had two girlfriends who insisted on going with their parents on the truck. At first the guards would not let them go; then they gave in and Trudy heard the guards say that the girls would be very sorry. At first the survivors did not realize that people were being killed en masse, but the trucks would go out with a full load, come back empty, load up and go out again. Conclusions were made. About two weeks later, everyone between twenty and twenty-five years old was told to get ready to leave on a specific day.

On the specified day, the prisoners were told to gather their things. They were forced to walk to the ghetto of Riga. Trudy and five friends were put in a large room of a big house. The room had three beds, so two girls slept in each bed. There was no running water inside, which meant that it had to be carried in from outside. There was a small cooking stove in the room, but they had little to eat. For example, they were sometimes given fish heads to eat—nothing else. One day it was her turn to get the water from outside, and she got a pail and went out. Suddenly, she heard a noise and looked up. A window pane came loose and fell from the third story, smashing into her face. She received an especially deep cut above her upper lip and had lacerations all over her face. Ghetto people came to her aid with a white towel to place on her face and called a Jewish doctor. By the time he came, the towel was soaked in blood. He sewed the worst cuts together without being able to give her anesthetic because he did not have any. Trudy said three people held her while he sewed. The scar above the lip is still clearly visible.

The Riga ghetto actually had two parts with an electric fence around it. One part was populated by people who had been brought in from all parts of Germany and other areas. The other part of the ghetto was populated by Jewish citizens of Riga. By the time Trudy arrived in the ghetto, all the women and children from the Latvian ghetto area were gone—killed. It was said that blood was flowing in the streets. At that point, Trudy hesitated and then said it was so horrible she could not believe it herself now.

One day, they were taken to the part of the ghetto where the Latvian Jews lived. They were ordered not to take anything—just clean up. When they went inside the houses, they found food on the stoves and dining tables set for meals, many filled with food. It was apparent that the Nazis came into these places, picked up the people while they were eating, took them away, and killed them. They found frozen potatoes that they took back with them and the guards did not stop them. They cooked up the potatoes once they were back in their own ghetto area. Trudy said they didn't taste very good, but it was food. Trudy lived in this ghetto for three years. Life was hard; the people labored every day doing heavy work like sweeping the streets, carrying boards for construction across the frozen river, and pushing heavy stones up a hill with wheelbarrows.

During part of her time in Latvia, Trudy was sent to Libau to work in a sugar factory. The factory had large kettles for cooking up the sugar beets. Often, these kettles boiled over, sending the sticky substance flowing onto the floor. Her job was to clean the floor. She did this work for a few weeks.

Later, she was sent to the Strassenhof Camp. Trudy and the other prisoners were given the job of repairing communications cables at this slave labor camp. The prisoners had to repair the cables, check them, and then attach their names and numbers to the repaired cables. Trudy noted that the Nazis would sometimes sabotage repaired cables by cutting them and blame the prisoner responsible for the repair. The prisoner was then taken away and killed. Over thirty prisoners met this fate during the time she was there. Trudy felt that since the prisoners' lives depended on fixing the cables properly, it was not possible for them to make inadequate repairs.

One time in the ghetto they were ordered to stand in line with their blankets for delousing. After standing in line for a long time, they were told that they could go home, and it was only later they learned that they were to be killed. The story that spread around the community was that the mayor put a stop to the killings. Trudy did not believe that story, because when the Nazis took over the town, the mayor lost his power and did not have a say. All she knew was that the Nazis called it off. What made an impact on her was that the Nazis did this type of thing all the time.

There was another time when Trudy was sent outside the ghetto to another slave labor camp, near a small town in Latvia. The prisoners were forced to dig peat to be used for fuel. The process included setting the peat out to dry.

Later, the ghetto was liquidated. Liquidation meant that people who were considered to be too weak, too ill, or too old to be of help to the Nazi war cause were killed. The rest of the people were moved to slave labor camps. Trudy was among those sent to the Kaiserwald concentration camp.

Trudy then talked about the last camp she was in before leaving Latvia in 1944. It was a slave labor camp, like others she had been in. One Sunday, the prisoners were told to go to a specific area and wait. Everybody who was over thirty years old was taken away in trucks to be killed. She said, "I was lucky again, because I was only twenty-six." She noted that a few hid, but the Nazis looked for them and found them. They suffered even more. She remembered one woman who was found and beaten so badly that "one breast was hanging on by a thread." She was almost dead when they put her on the truck to be taken away. In another instance, a man who had hidden was being chased by the Nazis, and Trudy witnessed the man jump out of a third floor window of the building. He landed on a ledge and was seriously injured but not dead, so the guards fired and killed him.

At this point, reflection was given to what kept her alive through the long ordeal. She said that she did not know, she only knew that she survived. However, Trudy told an anecdote which may at least partly explain her survival. She said people were dying all the time—from executions, starvation, and sickness. She recounted how she was in the hospital herself with a severe bladder infection. One day, a nurse came by her bed and told her that an inspection was going to be made the next day. This kind nurse told her that she had to leave. Though she was still sick, Trudy took the nurse's advice and left the hospital. The next day, the inspection took place and all the patients were removed from the hospital and killed. Trudy said these kinds of incidents went on all the time, and she attributed her survival to "plain dumb luck."

The removal of prisoners who were over thirty years old dropped the camp population from about 2,000 to 300 to 400. At that point, the prisoners were given the typical blue and gray striped clothes, a dress, one pair of underpants and socks, a dish, and a spoon. The Nazis walked the remaining prisoners to a shipping port. After a few hours, they were put aboard a ship and were taken to Danzig (Gdansk). The prisoners were assigned three to a bunk bed, so they had to take turns sleeping in one to two hour shifts. In addition, they were fed very low quality food. Maybe the most humiliating aspect of the trip was not having bathrooms to use. Then Trudy talked about something that happened to her and may have happened to others. The life as a prisoner under the Nazi regime meant hard labor and a starvation diet. As a result, women stopped menstruating. Unfortunately, she started menstruating on the first night on the ship and had no way to deal with it. She did not even have access to water to clean up.

The prisoners were put on another ship from Danzig to Stutthof, another concentration camp. She said they were packed in the ship like herring. Once they landed and were put into barracks in the camp, they just stood around. She said, "We just deloused ourselves." The prisoners had all sorts of infestations including lice, bedbugs, and fleas. Hygiene was difficult because necessities like toothbrushes, toothpaste, and soap were not often available. They used their fingers and cold water to brush their teeth. Only cold water was available for washing. Sometimes they had the luxury of soap, but then the water was turned off after they soaped up. Obviously, there was no way to rinse.

Trudy remembered laying in the dirt without hope. Trudy also remembered one day when they were ordered out of the barracks. A guard stood at the door with a stick and gave her a whack on the back as she went by. Though it hurt quite a bit, she was not severely injured. Another time, the Nazis announced that they were going to do selections. The prisoners had to take off their clothes and parade naked in front of the officers. Then the officers sorted them to the right and to the left. Those that looked fit enough to work were sent to the right, the others to the left to be killed. Trudy was sent to the right and her hand was stamped to show that she was designated for work.

Soon, those designated for work were herded onto a train and transported to another concentration camp—Russoshin. The camp was small, housing about 150 to 200 women. Again, they were forced to do slave labor, doing work on the railroad. It was now the winter of 1944. One day at work, she sprained her ankle going down a steep hill. The pain and swelling was bad enough that the Nazis held her out of work and let her spend a couple of days resting at the camp. Trudy knew that she would live only as long as she could work and be useful to the Nazis' cause. If she did not get well, they would kill her. So even though she could barely walk, she went back to work. Some of her friends literally helped support her during the work day. She said, "Sometimes we said we would like it if they (the Nazis) would throw a bomb in our place (barracks) and kill us all." They were thinking about how good it would be to end their miserable lives, but for many it did not happen.

Eventually the prisoners were moved to another camp, Strellentin, in Pommern, Germany, where they had nothing to do. Then it was off to yet another camp, Chinow, a death camp.

Conditions were very bad in the camp, and the cold weather made things worse. Then in March 1945, in the middle of the night, the guards came in and told them they had to go right away. They could hear shooting in the distance. Meanwhile the prisoners were trying to gather whatever possessions they had in the dark. To make matters worse for Trudy, she was suffering from diarrhea and was very weak. She felt so weak that she said she could not go, but her prisoner friends insisted and helped her. The prisoners walked all night and something changed. Usually during such marches, a lot of people would go off to the sides because they were too sick and or weak to continue. In the past, those prisoners were shot on the spot. (Trudy recounted a ten-day "death march" in which this type of thing happened. People were suffering from starvation, injuries, and illness. Whenever a prisoner became too weak and lagged behind or went to the side of the road to rest or just collapse, the prisoner was killed. This time, the guards were leaving them. They were in a big hurry and did not even want to take time to shoot the stragglers. Some of the guards were women, and the guards said, "If the Russians come and get us, they will kill us all." Trudy said the prisoner knew the Russians would probably kill the Nazis, but not the prisoners.

All of a sudden, out of the darkness, they came to a big barn. The prisoners thought the barn was empty, but it was full of women lying on the floor. As Trudy and her fellow prisoners were forced into the barn, they started stepping on the women who were already there. Suddenly, the relative quiet was broken by women yelling, "Don't step on us." The new prisoners had to feel their way through the darkness to find places to sit down. Trudy said, "It was terrible." Once things settled down, the first group of women said they had been kept in the barn for four weeks and conditions had been awful. They did not get any water; black coffee and boiled potatoes were given as rations in the mornings. They received nothing else. Women were dying in that barn every day from typhoid fever. A mass grave was kept open in an area across from the barn, and as the women died their bodies were tossed in the grave. Trudy sat next to a woman that night who had typhoid and was groaning from the pain, and saying she wished she was dead. All Trudy could say to her was, "Don't worry, you will be okay."

When daylight came, there was a change. No guards came in the barn, and when they looked outside, they did not see any guards. Finally a few women walked out toward the main road about 500 yards away. Those women came back yelling, "We are free! We are free!" Trudy said, "It was a moment you cannot imagine!" The women laughed, cried, and hugged one another. Then they started thinking about their families and where to go. The did not know what to do, but the women who had gone out to the main road had some information. They had met some Russian soldiers and tanks on the road who told them to go in the direction the soldiers were coming from, for that territory had been taken from the Nazis and would provide safety. At that point, Trudy had an additional problem. Since German was the only language she could speak, the Russians might identify her as a Nazi enemy rather than a Jewish prisoner. This made some of the other women prisoners caution her not to speak in the presence of Russian soldiers.

As the women walked out on the main road, they saw the signs of war along the way. They saw dead German soldiers, dead horses, and overturned wagons. Some of the wagons had all kinds of food that belonged to German farmers fleeing the oncoming Russians. Trudy remembered finding a piece of smoked meat. She carried it with her for a while, but she was so weak and it felt so heavy, that she threw it away. That night the prisoners came to a small German village that had been abandoned. Trudy and her friends went into one of the houses for the night. They found a lot of food like eggs, goose meat, and schmaltz. She was not feeling well and did not eat, but cooked for the others. The next morning, the women started walking again. They eventually came to another small village and spent the night. They ended up walking for about four days.

Finally they came to a bigger town called Lauenburg. The Russians had been through the town, and much of it was burned. Surviving houses were torn apart. Still, Trudy and her friends found a house in which to stay. She was still sick and could not eat. Her symptoms included a fever that returned every evening. At this point, typhoid was epidemic among the Jewish prisoners.

Eventually Russian soldiers came through the town and picked up the sick people, including Trudy. She was taken to a German hospital that was under the control of the Russians. German doctors and nurses were still allowed to work there under the supervision of the Russians. She had typhoid and said, "I had the highest fever you can have for three days." The disease seemed to cause the most discomfort in her head, while most people had it centered in their stomachs and had diarrhea. She described her pain as having a machine in her head with great noise day and night. In addition, the hospital was so crowded that the patients slept two to a bed. Nevertheless, she said the Russians gave them good medications and took good care of them, and she survived.

During her stay, the medical personnel shaved her head. She was told if they did not shave her head, her hair would not grow back. It took Trudy about seven weeks to recover, and then she had to spend two more weeks under quarantine. She spent that time taking care of the other sick people in the hospital, most of whom had typhoid.

She felt terrible over the irony of it all. Here were people who had survived years of imprisonment under unspeakable conditions and survived only to die shortly after being freed.

The war in Europe ended while Trudy was in the hospital. She talked about how the Russian soldiers drank vodka, danced, and sang in celebration. The prisoners were happy too, but they did not know what to do or where to go. Trudy decided to return to her hometown of Stuttgart.

The ravages of war pretty much disrupted the transportation system. Schedules no longer existed and passenger trains were rare. She ended up taking a freight train back home, and the trip took a few days. She had accumulated two suitcases of clothes taken from houses the prisoners stayed at after leaving the last camp. She arrived in Berlin, got off the train, put the suitcases down, looked around, and before she knew it, one of the suitcases was gone. She laughed about it, saying it did not bother her, but it did say something about the situation in postwar Germany—the chaos reduced people to do whatever they could to survive.

She took another train from Berlin to Stuttgart. At that point, Trudy mentioned a couple of interesting things. Because freed prisoners did not have money, they did not pay for the train transportation. They just explained they had been in the concentration camps. She also noted that the Germans they talked to denied being Nazis. She smiled and said she knew better, saying, "If you did not belong to the Nazi Party, they (the Nazis) would send you away." She finally arrived in Stuttgart and from there went to a D.P. (displaced persons) camp.

The stay at the displaced persons camp lasted a few weeks, and it was there she met her future husband. Abe Rappaport was from Poland. He was a soldier in the Polish army when the war began. After Poland was overrun, he was "drafted" into the Russian army, but he ran away from the army and they caught him. He was tried and sentenced to seven years in prison. After a year in prison, his health had declined dramatically. He was so sick and weak that he was let out of prison and sent on his way. The Russian authorities thought he would die anyway, but he did not die. He found out that his parents, sister, aunts, uncles, and grandparents were all gone. The Nazis had come to the town, taken all the Jews to the marketplace, and shot them. When he found no one left, he did not want to stay there either. Eventually he was advised to go to the American sector in Germany, and that is how he made his way to Stuttgart. He arrived at the D.P. camp about two weeks after

Trudy. They had about a six-month courtship and were married.

At about this time, Trudy wanted to find out about her own family. Of course she had not had any contact with them for years and did not have any idea about what had happened to them. She did not have an address or anything. She did have an uncle living in New York, but did not have an address for him either. Luckily, she found relatives in Stuttgart who knew the address of the uncle. She wrote to him, and he wrote back notifying her that her parents were alive and still living in Shanghai. To say the least, they felt great joy in receiving that first letter from her. Trudy said her mother baked a cake and invited all her friends over for cake and coffee to celebrate her survival.

The family happiness was tempered when they inquired about Lotte. The Red Cross informed them that she died in Auschwitz. She had been twenty-six years old. The family also found out that she was married while living in the Netherlands, and that she and her husband of six months were both arrested. Of course, he too was killed.

Trudy and Abe decided they wanted to emigrate to the United States. Her uncle assisted them by sending the papers for them. They were able to come to the United States in January of 1947. They were met in New York by her aunt and uncle with whom they stayed for four weeks. The couple only had seven dollars when they arrived, so her uncle helped by giving them twenty dollars. She said one of the first things they did was to ride the subway system. They looked at all the different stores and the "wonderful food." Trudy saw food that she had not seen in years! The Jews experienced lack of food even before the mass arrests started taking place. Then there were the starvation diets in the ghettos and concentration camps during the war. Even after the war, the destruction and chaos in Germany meant little food was available. Thus the abundant food they found in New York was quite a treat. Unfortunately, twenty dollars did not go far, even in the late 1940s.

After a few weeks in New York, Abe said he did not want to stay there any more. He felt New York was just too big. Since he was a furrier by profession, they wanted to find out where they could go to have a good chance at finding work. So they asked around and were told to come to the Minneapolis/St. Paul area. People figured that Minnesota was a cold state, and a lot of people would want fur coats in the winter. Trudy and Abe did not know anyone in Minnesota and knew nothing about the state, so they used the "eenie, meenie, miney, mo" method and chose Minneapolis. Her relatives were not happy about the prospect of Trudy leaving, and to be honest, she said she liked New York. Yet she knew that her husband wanted to move and she was willing to follow.

A twenty-four hour train ride brought the couple to the Twin Cities. They had a room waiting when they arrived. A cab took them to the address that they had been given. Then the Jewish Family & Children's Service stepped in to help. They took the couple shopping and bought a whole outfit for each of them. The service gave them advice on places to eat and shop. At this point, Abe could not speak English, but Trudy could since she had taken four years of English when she was in school. Language was still an obstacle, but her background allowed them to get by. Since the couple arrived in Minneapolis with almost nothing, the service also gave them $100.

A break came after three days, when Abe found a job with Rockler Fur. Even though he could not speak English, the fur company had a Polish foreman who was able to communicate with Abe. He earned seventy-five cents per hour. Trudy found a job in an overcoat factory four weeks later and also made seventy-five cents an hour. Their salaries did not amount to a lot, but they still managed to save money. Within a year, they were finally able to use their savings for a new bedroom set.

More changes took place after they had been in Minneapolis for about a year. For one thing, Trudy became pregnant and quit her job. They had been staying in a single room, so they had to go out and look for an apartment. They found a small one bedroom apartment with a very small kitchen and living room. The bathroom was shared with another family. Trudy noted that it was hard to find an apartment in the late 1940s. Many GIs had returned home and needed housing too, which created a short supply.

Trudy had been corresponding with her parents during this time. She wanted to have her parents move to the United States and worked for a year to accomplish it— they came in 1948. Trudy and Abe rented an apartment for her parents right around the corner from their own. Her parents' arrival resulted in quite a reunion.

Although the reunion was like a miracle, not all was well. Every immigrant to the United States had to go through a physical exam. The doctor discovered that Julius had a bad heart condition and predicted that his heart could go at any time. That was upsetting news after having been apart for nine years. Yet, it turned out that he lived another six years.

Trudy's first child, Irvin, was born on December 4, 1948. He was followed by Rose Linda on January 9, 1950, and later Julie on August 10, 1956. All of the children still live in Minnesota and are doing well. Irving lives in the Twin Cities. The two girls are married and have their own families. Rose Linda has two children and four grandchildren. She and her family live in Farmington. Julie has two teenage daughters and lives in the Twin Cities area.

Abe was progressing nicely in his line of work from this time on. In 1950, he started his own furrier business. Since his business was going well, Trudy became a "stay at home" mother. As their economic situation improved, they were able to move into a house. They borrowed $2,000 and bought a fourplex on the northside of Minneapolis. They were able to use the rent to pay the mortgage. They stayed in that house until after Julie was born, and then moved into a single family home also on the northside. They lived there until 1968, and then bought a house in St. Louis Park. Trudy and Abe lived together in that house until he died from emphysema in 1997.

Trudy continued to live there for another two and a half years before selling and moving into an apartment in St. Louis Park. She said moving was a very hard decision, but she liked living in the apartment. At the time of the interview, Trudy said she was relatively healthy, although she did have a pacemaker and suffered daily aches and pains.

At the time of our interview, Trudy still had a busy life. She went to the Jewish Community Center in St. Louis Park twice a week and participated in a singing group. She also played cards every night with friends in her apartment building. Every Sunday, her daughter and son-in-law visited from Farmington. Her son visited every Saturday night and took her out, and her youngest daughter, Julie, made it a point to call daily. Meanwhile, the Jewish Family & Children's Service provided a person to take Trudy shopping every two weeks. While she paid for the service, she said it did not cost very much. A young lady volunteer that Trudy called "a wonderful person" came to take her out every other Saturday. The visits and outings helped very much. Trudy never learned to drive and said she would be lost without such activities.

Trudy did not know how or why she survived the holocaust but was very thankful. Her survival allowed her to meet and marry a wonderful man, get reunited with her parents, have three children that she loved dearly, along with the grandchildren and great grandchildren. She has lived a truly remarkable life.

Hazel Melander

Hazel is a very straight forward and dynamic person who presented her life history in a very direct manner, starting with her parents. Her father, Austin Jonah, was from Canada, but moved here and became a United States citizen. Her mother, Serena, was born and raised in Minneapolis. Her father worked first as a printer and later as a yard man for the Great Northern Railroad. She described her father as a good worker and a quiet man. Her mother was a homemaker, and Hazel described her as being "gracious" and "full of fun."

Austin and Serena had six children, three boys and three girls. Hazel was born on December 17, 1921. Growing up in the Twin Cities was a happy time for her. Her mother made people feel welcome in their home, so it seemed as though it was always filled with friends. Hazel was somewhat of a tomboy from a young age. She liked all sports. She remembered swinging on a rope from a tree over the Mississippi River and she did not even know how to swim. She just did not consider the danger. She, her siblings, and friends did other potentially dangerous activities, but the fun of the activity itself outweighed the possible dangers. Competitiveness may have been a big part of what drove her. She and her mother also loved football, and she remembered listening to Minnesota Gopher games on Saturdays, cheering on the home team while her mother baked or cooked. Gopher teams were very good during the 1930s, so they had a lot to cheer about.

The family did not suffer a lot during the Great Depression. Austin was able to work throughout the Depression, so there was always a source of income. He was not one to take many chances, which lent a sense of stability during those years. Serena was a good cook and always had plenty of food on the table. Hazel's favorites were spaghetti with bacon in the tomato sauce topped with onions. Devil's food cake was her favorite dessert. However, she was not particularly fond of vegetables. The family was not rich, but it certainly got by.

Hazel did not have too many memories of school. She earned average grades in school and felt that her two sisters were the brains. She said she "graduated from high school just to get a graduation ring." Graduating was not a big deal.

But then she added something that was more revealing. She said she was kind of different in that big events to most people were not big to her. For example, Hazel said having her first child was not a big deal—any woman could do it. (That does not take away the love she had for each of her children.) She also said she did not know if she loved her husband when they were married; it was something she wanted to try. (Of course she and her husband did have a loving relationship that lasted many years.) The point seemed to be that Hazel had a need to experience life in many ways, and the need to do and experience is what drove her.

Roller skating became a favorite activity for Hazel during her teens. She loved it so much that she and her friends skated five times a week at a roller rink in St. Paul. She added, "Sometimes we would have to hitchhike because we didn't have a way to get there." It was likely that her parents did not know about the hitchhiking, as they probably would not have approved.

Hazel did okay in school, labeling herself an average student. She understood the value of education and graduated in January of 1940, but school was not the center of her life. An event occurred during her senior year of high school that shaped her early years of adulthood—the Roller Derby came to Minneapolis. Her heart was set on trying to join the Derby.

After graduating from high school, Hazel worked as a waitress, a cafeteria worker, and did other jobs. When she and her friends heard that the Roller Derby was coming to town, they had their own races in the streets. They raced at 5:00 or 6:00 AM when there were not many cars in the streets. Sometimes they raced at tennis courts in a nearby park. Eventually Hazel went down to the Minneapolis Auditorium to practice with some of the skaters and try out. She said, "When they asked me to join, I was really excited." Joining the Derby did not mean becoming a star skater right away. She had to train every day until she became good enough to skate with the team.

In those days, the Roller Derby was made up of a troupe of skaters—ten to a team. As they traveled around the country, one team was always designated as the home team and it was the "good team." Another team represented a distant city and was the "bad team." For example, if they skated in Minneapolis, that was the home team and St. Paul would be the visiting team. The show was entertainment rather than sport but still required athletic skills, endurance, and toughness.

As noted, a Roller Derby team consisted of ten skaters—five men and five women. A skater's equipment consisted of a numbered jersey, shorts worn over tights, shin guards, knee pads, hip pads, and a helmet. Helmets were not originally used, but were required after a skater died of head injuries. The skaters did not wear elbow pads, something Hazel remembered because she suffered a bruised elbow that swelled up like a baseball. The track was torn down at the end of a run in one city and transported to the next city to be set up for the next matches.

Life in the Roller Derby was a new experience for Hazel. It involved a lot of travel, which was a big change for someone who had not been away from home very much. The teams traveled by train from one city to the next, and they would stay in a town for up to three weeks. Hazel loved skating in front of thousands of people, but it was not all pleasant. She skated on the "bad team," and of course the hometown fans did not like them. The fans booed and threw things at the team members. One time in Fort Worth, Texas, the skaters needed a police escort to get back to their hotel. She said, "It was scary, but also exciting when you are young."

Hazel met her husband, Henry, while skating for the Roller Derby, as he too was a skater. Among the lows of Roller Derby life was when Hazel and her husband both suffered broken collar bones. Hers was broken on the right side, his on the left. They ended up marrying on April 18, 1941, in Indianapolis.

She told three anecdotes about close calls while traveling during their days in the Roller Derby. On one occasion, they became stuck in a terrible snowstorm and had to stay overnight in their car on the side of a road. Luckily, help came in the morning. On another occasion, they were driving in the mountains of California and must have somehow driven onto an area used by the military. At any rate, no one warned them that they were entering a dangerous area. A tank came around a curve in the road, hit their car, and kept going. Their car could have been knocked down the side of the mountain. The third event came when they were going home during a break in the Roller Derby schedule. They took a wrong turn and drove onto a road being inundated by a flash flood. Hazel was swept out of the car, and the current carried her downstream. She was able to grab onto a fence and eventually made it back to dry land.

The December 7, 1941, attack on Pearl Harbor changed their lives completely. Rumors spread soon after the attack that the Japanese were going to bomb California. A few of the skaters, including Hazel and her husband, decided to leave the Derby and they moved to San Francisco. Henry took a job in the shipyards; Hazel started working for Western Electric and later at a Standard Oil service station, doing all sorts of jobs like washing and waxing cars and lubricating cars.

After a time, Henry decided to follow a goal of owning his own business. They leased a gas station across from Golden Gate Park. Hazel helped wash cars and waited on customers. She said, "The work was hard, but I loved it."

In talking about World War II, she remembered rationing of goods such as gas, sugar, and nylons. But she noted that you could always get things if you knew someone important, and indicated that it is not any different today.

The family started to grow during the time they were running the gas station. Their first son, Dan, was born on September 24, 1943. He was followed by Bruce on September 21, 1944. Day care was not available in those days, and they did not have any relatives to fall back on for babysitting, so the children went to the gas station with Hazel.

Even though she was very active, she never got her driver's license. Henry tried to teach her one day, and two of her friends were in the back seat. The car was parked by a restaurant; her husband told her to put the car into reverse, and she hit the building. After getting it straightened out, he gave her the same direction with the same result. By that time, her friends were laughing hysterically and he told her to get out of the car. After another disastrous try later, she gave up and never drove again.

As the war wound down, they decided to move to Chicago, Henry's home town. They first settled in a suburban area and for a short time leased a roller rink in Mundeline, Illinois. Hazel ran the rink and her husband commuted to Chicago for his job. The commute to Chicago was fifty miles—a long drive indeed! She noted that it was "a really fun time." Unfortunately it was not to last, since the landlord raised the rent and they had to give up the rink.

The job situation continued to change. Henry worked at a couple of different jobs for a while. Hazel worked at the Sears Department Store for a time and then worked in downtown Chicago as a long distance operator. However, her husband never gave up on running his own business and the next effort involved renting a store. They lived in the back, partitioned off by nothing more than thick brown paper. Needless to say, there was not much privacy, and Hazel called it "a rough time." Nevertheless, they persevered and reached the point of having two stores at one time. The main store was like a neighborhood grocery, similar to a convenience store today. They sold staples such as milk, coffee, eggs, sugar, butter and some canned goods. They also sold soda, ice cream, and a lot of candy. Half a block away was the second store that Hazel called the school store. They sold hot dogs, malts, candy, and school supplies to the students.

Running two stores created a hectic schedule for Hazel. She opened the main store at 6:00 AM and ran it until students would be arriving in the area. Then she closed the main store and ran to the school store and sold to the students until the school day started. Next it was back to the main store, which she kept open until the school's lunch time, when the whole process was repeated. She noted that she had some help at the stores but not much.

This was a time of racial tension in the Chicago area, and events of the time directly affected them. Some black people bought the building that contained the school store, and this led to threats to bomb the store. The result was that they had police protection at the store all the time. This was a sad time for Hazel since some of her best friends were black.

More change came near the end of 1945 and early 1946. A daughter, Sharon, was born on December 21. Hazel suggested to Henry that they move to her home town of Minneapolis. Her husband had loved the fishing from previous visits to the state, so he agreed to the move.

Once back in Minneapolis, they had to get established. Her husband took a job at the Minneapolis Courthouse, and Hazel returned to a type of work she had done before—as a long distance operator for the telephone company. Accommodations were made to care for the three children. Hazel and her husband worked different shifts so someone was always home for the children. A good friend came up from Chicago to live with them, and that helped quite a bit.

Hazel mentioned that she had always been a person who was active. A sedentary job like being a telephone operator was just not active enough for her, so she quit and took a cleaning job at Augsburg College. At this time, she made a point that she would repeat. Admittedly, she had held several different jobs, but said, "I never had a job I didn't like."

A physical outlet for Hazel and Henry in Minneapolis was roller skating. They developed different styles, with Hazel wanting to do more of the power type of skating similar to what was required for the Roller Derby. Her husband was more interested in intricate steps which included dancing. He continued recreational skating after Hazel stopped, but he also quit eventually .

After a time, they bought a house that was quite a distance from the college. She had to quit the college job, but received a very good recommendation. She was able to get another job cleaning (it was the type of job she liked the best), this time at a nursing home.

During this time, three more children were added to the family in quick succession. Ed was first, born on June 21, 1955. He was followed by Rick on December 17, 1956, and Pat on December 6, 1957.

However, not all things in life go smoothly. Hazel and her husband began drinking during their time in the Roller Derby, and the drinking gradually increased year by year. When both parents drink, there is likely to be a substantial effect on the family.

That is what happened with the Melanders. By the early 1970s, challenges to the family were great, and moments of happiness were few. First, the Roller Derby was having a big reunion in 1972. The reunion was to be in Chicago, and Henry really wanted to go. Unfortunately, he was suffering the effects of long term heavy drinking—cirrhosis of the liver. His doctor had warned him that if he continued drinking he would soon be dead. Apparently, he could not or would not quit because the habit continued. They attended the reunion in June and he died in January of 1973. Hazel said she quit drinking soon after and joined Alcoholics Anonymous.

If the death of Henry was not enough, other family problems were raging. The three youngest children were all teenagers and having difficulties. All were drinking and doing some drugs. Hazel said, "Being that I was an alcoholic, I guess I did not notice." The older children tried to help as much as possible, and Hazel related one telling example that occurred before the death of her husband. One son, Rick, who was on drugs, was involved in a high speed police chase. Apparently the police really worked him over when they finally stopped him. Hazel said, "At first I was angry at the police; then I realized my son could have killed some people on the highway going 100 miles per hour." Because of some difficulties between Rick and his father, the oldest son, Danny, stepped in after the chase incident and took the younger boy to live with him in Iowa.

Even before Henry died, the older sons tried to help them change. The sons tried to tell their parents about Christ. Hazel and her husband wouldn't listen, saying, "Hell is on earth." She added, "When you drink it is." However, all the turmoil and preaching did not go to waste. Hazel said she realized she would lose her family and her house if she kept drinking. She and her daughter joined AA, and Hazel gave AA a lot of credit for bringing about the changes in her life.

At about this time, what she called "a miracle" took place. She said, "One by one, all of my children turned their lives over to Christ." She noted that the older ones already "knew" Christ and the younger ones gradually followed. Hazel said that she was the second to last family member to give her life to Christ and added, "What a difference it made in our lives."

Once clean and having Christ in her life, Hazel was able to resist the temptations of drugs. She refused opportunities to use or sell. In 1976, she and her daughter Pat cleaned homes for the wealthy. On one occasion, some owners actually asked her to sell drugs, but she would not.

Besides the issue of drugs, cleaning homes included some other bizarre incidents. Hazel and Pat were cleaning a rather strangely furnished house one day. The bedroom was all mirrors and the house had strange serpents all over with a devil statue in the hall. While cleaning in the kitchen, Pat noticed something about an owl in the corner of the room. She asked Hazel to look at the owl and asked, "Tell me, what do you see?" Hazel said, "Its eyes are following me." They finished their work and got out of there. They did not work at that house again.

Four of the children went to a missionary school in Texas to learn Spanish. They had to complete a four year course in nine months, and Hazel decided that she needed to join them and also learn the language. She was in her sixties at the time, and being away from school for so many years made the coursework hard. She did graduate in May of 1988, but said her work skills were better than her language skills.

Some time later, one of her older sons and the three youngest went to Mexico as missionaries. They spent two to three years there. Hazel visited her children while they were in Mexico and often stayed for weeks at a time. They walked through jungles and up into the hill country to talk to the people about Jesus. The Mexican people fed them whatever they could afford, which according to Hazel, "was not much." She noted that it was hard to eat some of the food they were given, but prayers helped her do it. Animals were part of everyday life. When they held a prayer meeting or songfest, pigs, turkeys, chickens and so on came right into the meeting places. Yet the events went on without a hitch. One of the hardest things for Hazel was dealing with all the bugs. It also was difficult seeing rats lying dead in the sewers in the marketplace. In spite of those difficulties, she felt the Mexican people were wonderful.

Then the youngest son, Rick, went to Lyon, France, for another three years. Hazel went to France to stay with her son and his family for a time. He and his wife had two children with a third on the way. Hazel went to help out the family. The time in France was followed by visits to Spain, and Tangier and Casablanca in Morocco. They had to be careful about talking about Christ in Morocco because it was not allowed.

A missionary school in southern Texas asked her to join the school as a house cleaner and later as a second cook. She accepted. She moved to Texas, where she worked from Tuesdays through Saturdays with Sundays and Mondays off. Hazel noted that nearby Padre Island was a "special place to go to relax." She ended up working at the school for nine years and called them the best years of her life.

By the late 1990s, Hazel had to make a decision about where to live. Her children were all back in Minnesota. The older children were doing pretty well. Dan, the oldest , became a court reporter. Dave, the second son, became a teacher, and Sharon joined the Navy. Getting older, she felt the pull to be closer to her children. After much prayer, she made the decision to return to Minnesota. An apartment was made ready before the return, and in 1997 she moved to Coon Rapids. In spite of being near family, she missed her friends in Texas as she adjusted to the move.

Never one to just sit around, Hazel helped her children by cooking and cleaning and doing odd jobs for them. But even that was not enough; something was missing— she just did not feel fulfilled. Then one day, a friend asked her out to lunch at the Coon Rapids Senior Center. Hazel used the opportunity to ask Darlene, the person in charge, if any help was needed. The answer was positive, since volunteers are always needed there. She worked Mondays, Tuesdays, Thursdays, and Fridays. (Wednesdays were reserved for a seven-year bible study program that she completed in 2003.) She was trained and paid to take over the kitchen if the Volunteers of America could not get anyone for that day. She agreed to do it on a volunteer basis and did it a few times to help out in an emergency when the V.O.A. could not get anyone.

At the time of the interview, Hazel seemed to truly enjoy her life. She was thankful that her health was good, and she enjoyed her time at the senior center. Further, she made many good friends at the senior center and at her apartment building. In addition, her four sons and one daughter lived nearby, and she saw one or more of them almost every other Saturday. Playing croquet, or darts, or watching movies were among their usual activities. One daughter lived in Lebanon, Indiana, but they still talked on the telephone at least once a week. She said that her children, their spouses, and the grandchildren were a great part of her life. Then she made a very telling point. She said that when a person gets older and lives alone, adjusting to a life with less social interaction can be difficult. Even though her children saw and talked to her often, she recommended staying busy. She said doing volunteer work and doing random acts of kindness for people living nearby can help keep away the feelings of loneliness. She loves to cook and will bring zucchini bread or cakes to the senior center or bake pies and other goods for the people in her building. Hazel ended by commenting about feeling bad for older people who do not have children or who have children that only visit on holidays. In comparison, she was quite blessed.

Physically, Hazel feels she is slowing down. She has trouble with sciatica and has trouble with her knees, especially after a recent fall. So she moves slower and more carefully than she used to. Yet she certainly demonstrates the toughness that she must have had during the days in the Roller Derby. As with the rest of her life, when she talks about her physical condition, she feels she has nothing to complain about.

Hazel did a very good job of putting the story of her life in perspective. She said, "I know there are probably many things left out that could have been important to my children. . . like delivering newspapers at 4:30 AM with Rick and then stopping to pick up glazed doughnuts on the way. Helping Pat, my youngest to deliver and stack newspapers. . . collecting money for the papers on a very cold night and being told to come back another time. I guess I can look back on my life, and I believe the good outweighs the bad."

Arthur (Art) Holter

Art's Minnesota roots go back to his grandparents. Both were born and raised in Norway, immigrated to the United States, and settled in Cook, Minnesota, a small town in the far north woods. They homesteaded near Cook and raised their family on the farm.

His father, Peter, was born and raised in Cook. The homestead was not big enough to split up among the seven children, so they went off on their own. Peter went to a town in the far southeast corner of Minnesota called Caledonia and bought an eighty acre farm. His mother, Evina, also was born in Minnesota, and joined her husband on the farm. Peter and Evina ended up raising nine children. Art was the seventh, born on February 1, 1910. Of his five brothers and three sisters, one sister was still living.

The farm was typical for the day in that they had a variety of animals and raised a variety of crops. The farm animals included cows, pigs, chickens, and of course, horses, since they were the source of power. Art said they did not know what a tractor was in those days. They plowed with a team of two horses, then they had to drag the plowed land with a team of four horses. Besides plowing, Art did several other jobs on the farm. He milked cows by the light of a kerosene lantern, cleaned manure out of the stalls, and cleaned up chicken droppings—his least favorite job. He also noted that at first, only forty acres were arable. He and his dad had to cut down twenty acres of trees, remove them and the stumps, and plow up the land to make it suitable for planting. Preparing the land was one of the necessary chores for the original farmers in an area.

Something more enjoyable was learning to drive around the farm when he was somewhere between nine and eleven years old. He said he learned in the family car, an old Ford.

The first farmhouse was what Art described as a "small shack." However, as the family grew, a bigger house was needed. They bought a house from a German family that lived nearby, put it on skids, and moved it to their property. Then they took the original house and made a summer kitchen out of it. The new house had two floors with two bedrooms downstairs and three bedrooms upstairs. At first they did not have furnace heat, indoor plumbing, electricity, or a telephone. Before the days of a furnace, most farm houses had a round pot bellied stove in the middle of the parlor and the kids used to stand around it to stay warm. He noted that they were the first family in the area to get a furnace. They also dug out a root cellar in the basement to store all the canned goods made by his mother.

Art attended a typical one room rural school, housing grades one through eight. He said that so many of the students were Norwegian who spoke Norwegian as their first language that the school had to hire a Norwegian teacher who could communicate with them. In an aside, Art mentioned that there was only one German family in the community but they had twelve boys, and he went to school with six of them. He noted that by the time he was in seventh and eighth grades, he helped teach the younger children—so he was like an assistant teacher.

In talking about school, Art noted that he was always a pretty good athlete, and he skied a lot, even to school. Practically every Sunday during winter they had ski jumping competition. The big guys built a big ski jump and the young children built a smaller jump next to it so all ages competed. His ski jumping activities started in his early teens, but cross country skiing started even younger. Art said his dad did not buy him skis at first, so he took barrel staves, put straps on them, and made his first skis.

Art said that all the children in his family could speak Norwegian. When asked if he could still speak it, he said, "I can talk Norwegian like a preacher," and he proved it. He went on to say that his older siblings had all been confirmed in Norwegian, and Art prepared to be confirmed in Norwegian too. Then a new minister came to town from Norway, and he was so proud of his English, he said, "No more of this Norwegian!" He insisted that the students being confirmed, including Art, be confirmed in English.

Art became the first person in his family to attend high school when he went to Caledonia High School. Then he launched into the most interesting story. The Holter farm was eight miles from Caledonia, and when Art was a freshman, his mother rented a room for him in town. It did not have electricity, but was located next door to the butcher shop, so he could easily buy meat. He lived by himself during the whole school year.

Art went home for the weekends and sometimes rode the family's old mare, Bess, back to Caledonia on Sunday nights. Then he would pat her on the rump and say "Bess, go on home," and she did.

During his high school years, Art participated in track and basketball. One of his best track events was the high jump. Remember, this was in the late 1920s. Art said that by using the "barrel roll" he was able to clear a height of six feet. This jump involved extending the lead leg up and over the bar with the head and torso facing downward as the bar was cleared. Most people at that time did the "scissors kick" in which the jumper cleared the bar in an almost upright position. He was also a fast runner. In basketball, he was a guard. He pointed out that in those days, the player was allowed only one dribble, so there was a lot of passing as they brought the ball up court. He also pointed out that of the five regulars, three were named Arthur. It sometimes became confusing.

Graduation from high school came in 1928, and Art was set to go to Luther College in Iowa to study to become a minister. He was already registered and was going to board with a cousin who lived there. Then his mother said that the family was going to sell the farm and move to Minneapolis. His father was getting close to retirement age, and with most of the children grown, there was not much help on the farm. Three brothers were already living in Minneapolis, two of which were barbers. A fourth brother was in the army. With an unknown financial situation, Art gave up on the idea of going to college and had to get a job.

His first job was at Sears-Roebuck, a job that lasted a year until he was laid off. However, the family home was only a block from a large bakery, the Excelsior Baking Company. This was at a time when bread was still sold by horse and wagon. Art was told of a job opening at the bakery, and wasted little time in getting down there to apply. His hiring led to a thirty-two year career at the bakery. This was a job he was able to keep during the time of the Great Depression. He eventually became supervisor of the bread department. Then the bakery folded, and he was out of work, but not for long.

After being without a job for about two weeks, his sister informed him that there was an opening at the Federal Reserve

Bank in Minneapolis. Well, Art dashed right down there and "just like that" was hired. He did a variety of jobs during his early time there, including picking up checks from the local banks and bringing them to the Federal Reserve Bank. Art later did some part-time chauffeuring of some of the big shots in the business. Eventually they made him supervisor of the mail department. Art emphasized that two million pieces of mail went through his department every day. (He noted that in 2003 the volume was up to three million pieces a day.) A perk of the supervisor's position was getting a parking spot in the basement of the building, so he never had to pay for parking. He held the job at the Federal Reserve Bank until he retired.

Meanwhile, his personal life progressed. A friend introduced his sister, Bernice, to Art and they started dating. They were married in 1936. They had one daughter, and his wife stayed home to raise the child. When the daughter was old enough and moved out onto her own, his wife got a job and found a new set of friends. One day, Art came home from work and found that his wife had left him, and the marriage dissolved. Art later met and married another woman, Loretta. Loretta and Art had a very nice marriage and raised a wonderful daughter named Vivian. The marriage lasted until Loretta died in 1997.

Recreational sports were always a big part of Art's life. A younger brother got him into the sport of bowling in about 1940. His brother had been bowling for some time and one day asked Art to fill in on the team because it was a man short. All it took was that first time to get him hooked on the sport. He kept improving and soon surpassed many of the bowlers that had more experience, including his brother. At one point he was bowling in five leagues and had a 190 average.

In the meantime, he also played pool. He actually started when he was only eleven years old and still living in Caledonia. Two bachelor brothers were neighbors to his family. One of them would take Art into town when he went grocery shopping so he could have someone to play pool with before returning home. Art continued to play over the next several decades. Not too long ago he played pool with three other fellows at the senior center. They played a game to one hundred. Each ball that was pocketed counted more than the previous ball. If you scratched or went over one hundred you lost all your points and had to start over. Art actually ran the full hundred points to win one to one hundred without missing a shot.

The last sport he took part in was the one that gained him the most fame— horseshoes. He did not take up the sport until the age of forty-seven, and it was because of his success at bowling. According to the story, Art had a longtime friend who was tired of losing to him in bowling. This friend was very good at horseshoes, so he challenged Art to a game. He did not even give Art a chance to warm up, so Art responded by throwing nine straight ringers, and Art was in love with the game. Soon he was beating his more experienced friend regularly.

It was not long before he was in a league and competing in tournaments at the local, state, and national levels. He mentioned going down to Loring Park on a regular basis and taking on all comers. He said sometimes he spent eight hours down there playing horseshoes. Art said, "When I get into something, I stay at it." He even had a horseshoe pit in his yard and said the mayor of Minneapolis (who he thought was Hubert Humphrey) used to stop and play a game of horseshoes every once in a while.

The list of horseshoe accomplishments goes on and on. Over a period of thirty-five years, Art pitched shoes in nineteen states and Canada and attended thirty-five consecutive world tournaments, winning his division two times. During his prime, he averaged seven ringers out of ten pitches, and one time pitched thirty-two ringers in a row! The Minneapolis Park Board chose him as the amateur athlete of the year in 1970. It was the only time a horseshoe player won the award. He became a member of the State Horseshoe Hall of Fame in 1974, followed by induction into the National Horseshoe Hall of

Fame in 1985. He proudly wears his hall of fame ring to this day. Art won a total of 123 trophies over the years.

Art's life has slowed up a bit as he entered his tenth decade. He wore a pacemaker, but other than that, seemed to be in good health. He quit playing horseshoes in his early eighties and quit bowling in his mid eighties. Pool was the last sport he gave up. He had been experiencing dizzy spells and passed out while playing pool not too long before this interview. He still loved to read, a passion he developed in his early days in Caledonia. Art felt that keys to his life came from not smoking, not drinking, and not swearing. It was hard to argue with him.

Anna and Donald (Don) Edson

This is a special couple, partly because their marriage spanned well over sixty years. That and their close vocational association were the reasons this interview was done differently than the others. Don and Anna were interviewed separately for information on their early lives and together for the time covering their marriage.

Anna's Early Life

Anna's mother, Rose Zak, was born in Bohemia (a part of what is now the Czech Republic), and came to the United States when she was seven years old. Her father, Hilding Victor Olson, was born to Swedish parents, Nels and Anna Olson. The elder Olsons had settled in the Mora area.

It was likely that Hilding and Rose met in the Hinkley area of Minnesota. Rose's mother ran a boarding house in Hinkley. By the time Rose came of age, Hilding was working for a lumberyard in Hinkley. They eventually met, married, and moved to the Mora area.

Anna was born near Mora on June 9, 1915, the third of seven children in the family. She was born in a house that was very basic. They relied on kerosene lights, stove heat, and an outhouse. She mentioned that the house still stood and was still inhabited.

When she was five years old, the family moved to Minneapolis and settled in the Seven Corners area near the University of Minnesota. The family had grown to six children by then. Her father worked for a coal company. She remembered her mother as a hard worker, going to a local school at noon to cook lunch for a deaf class. Later, Rose attended night school to study English and sewing. She made most of the children's clothing as well as quilts for the family. As her father kept getting better jobs, the family kept moving. Each move was into a house better than the one before. The downside was that she ended up attending eighteen different schools during her twelve years of primary and secondary education.

A difficult time began when she was eleven and her parents divorced. Divorce was not as well accepted in the 1920s as it is today. Comments and questions from friends made a difficult situation worse. After the divorce, Anna lived with her mother for a time. Her mother remarried and became Rose Taylor. When she was twelve, Anna moved in with her father and two brothers to help with the housekeeping. Anna was grateful that her parents maintained a civil relationship after the divorce.

When she was thirteen, Anna basically went out on her own. Because she had been able to skip a grade or two, she was ready for high school. She enrolled at Roosevelt High School, but things did not go very well. She was so much younger than the other students that it was difficult to fit in.

After six weeks, she transferred to Vocational High School in downtown Minneapolis. She took all the regular classes and specialized in journalism, dress making, and design. During this time, she also worked in homes for room and board for less than two dollars a week. The Depression was on, and hard times became harder. In her senior year, she moved near North High School. Again she worked in a home for room and board, but was paid only fifty cents a week. The pay for a lunch hour job was also cut—to seventy-five cents a week. Anna said, "I wore lots of hand me downs." Nevertheless, she managed, and graduated in 1933. (It is interesting to note that her mother-in-law graduated from North High School thirty years earlier.)

Before the beginning of her senior year, a drastic change occurred in her life. Anna made a commitment to God. She said she "learned how God could help." She prayed daily for her basic needs, such as clothes and car fare. Anna said her needs were always met, but then came graduation. Caps and gowns were not used for graduation in those days. She was so poor that she did not have a dress for graduation and actually asked to get her diploma without going to the ceremony. One day, while she was ironing, she asked the Lord for all the things she needed for graduation. She had faith that the Lord would provide and quoted Matthew 6:33 as proof: "God shall provide all your needs." Not long after that, Anna's employer received a call from a friend who wanted to help someone who needed clothes for graduation. The employer gave her friend Anna's name and sent her to the friend's home. The woman made Anna a beautiful dress and also bought her all the necessary accessories such as shoes and hosiery. Then the woman took her to a hair dresser to have her hair done for the graduation. But that was not all—the woman took Anna back to her home for a wonderful dinner and to get dressed for the big event. Then the woman's husband drove her to the graduation in a limousine. Other students stood in awe when they saw this young lady step out of the limousine driven by the mayor of Minneapolis! Yes, the kindly couple was Mayor William Anderson and his wife.

After graduation from North High, Anna went on to North Central Bible Institute where she took courses in such areas as Bible study, public speaking, and missionary work. After graduation, she spent about two years in missionary work in a rural area near Sheldon, Wisconsin, and also on the Iron Range in Buhl, Minnesota. The next life- changing event took place in 1938, when she attended a Bible camp in northern Minnesota and met Donald, her future husband. She said, "We immediately felt God had brought us together." Donald proposed after only four days, and Anna, of course said yes.

The country was still in the Depression, so money was hard to come by. The engaged couple did not have much money for dating. Anna mentioned that when they had a dime, they went to a small cafe in Minneapolis called the Band Box and bought three hamburgers for the dime. If they had more money, they bought six tokens for forty-five cents and rode the Oak-Harriet street car to the end of the line and back. This gave them affordable and ample time to get to know one another and to plan for the coming wedding. Since neither of their parents were able to finance a wedding, Anna purchased fabric and made her wedding dress and dresses for two bridesmaids and a flower girl at a cost of about five dollars per garment.

Donald's Early Life

Donald started out with an interesting story about his parents. His father, Willis, was born in Iowa; his mother, Aurelia Menard, was born in Minneapolis, and they met in North Dakota! The story went like this: His father was raised in South Dakota. When Willis was twenty-two years old, he went to an open area in North Dakota and homesteaded. About three years after homesteading, a small town called Moffit was started about a mile away. Meanwhile, on his mother's side, his grandparents had six children, all of whom died young. Then Donald's mother, Aurelia, was born healthy, and seven years later, a sister Genevieve also survived. Both children moved with their parents from Minneapolis to an area northwest of Bismarck, North Dakota. As Aurelia was growing up, she decided that she wanted to be a school teacher. She eventually went to Valley City State Teachers College. After graduation, she found work at a school in Moffit, the small town near Willis's farm.

In due course, Willis and Aurelia met and were married in 1912. Donald was the oldest of six children, born on March 16, 1913. He spent the first several years of his life growing up on the farm, then a "strange" event took place that changed his life. When he was fifteen, his parents decided to rent out the farm for a year. The family moved to Bismarck, and just a few blocks away from their house a new church was getting started. One day, he was attending a Sunday evening service and responded to the "invitation" and became a Christian. Even then, he felt an interest in the ministry.

His road to the ministry had a few twists and turns. Donald started high school in Moffit. Then he lived with his aunt while attending school in Bismarck. The following year, the rest of the family moved to Bismarck, and he was back with his family for his junior year. Donald noted that his aunt had been a fantastic piano teacher who studied at the Julliard School of Music. She taught music well into her nineties and died at the age of one hundred five in 2001. After the return to Moffit, Donald finished high school as the valedictorian of a class of five students. Finally he went to Valley City State Teachers College in 1931 and had some of the same teachers as did his mother.

In a related story, Donald said that his father died at the age of sixty-one; his mother was not well, but had a five year old, Robert, to care for. She did not think she could handle it, so gave up the boy to her sister who then raised him, and he became quite successful.

His mother eventually recovered and decided that she wanted to go back to teaching. She returned to Valley City State

Teachers College for more training. Low and behold she met a nice man who, at forty-five years old, was fifteen years her junior. He was head librarian and a teacher at the college. They were married and had twenty-one happy years before she died.

From there, at the age of nineteen, Donald went on to teach for four years in country schools. He said, "It was a special time indeed." The country was in the depths of the Great Depression. Donald was poor and had no car, so he hitchhiked. His first school was in western North Dakota in 1932, and he had an appointment with the president of the school board. This meant hitchhiking to the town of Dodge and then walking an additional ten miles to the president's house. This was only one example of the many long walks he had to make during that period of his life. Donald worked one year at that country school, then taught two years in an area northeast of Bismarck and one year at a school in the southern part of the state. The poor economy meant low pay. Donald's pay was forty-five dollars a month, but he paid twelve dollars a month for room and board. He was grateful to the president of the

Donald Edson's teacher contract of 1933-34

school board for giving him the room when the family still had ten children of their own living at home. One year he did not receive any pay at all until near the end of the school year, when he received his full salary.

Donald told a story about a trip he went on after his third year of teaching. The story is a great example of his spirit of adventure during his early adulthood, a spirit that marked the rest of his life. In 1935, at the age of twenty-two, he bought a 1923 Model T Ford for the grand sum of twenty dollars. The age of the car alone would indicate that it was not in tip-top shape. Nevertheless, Donald decided to drive out to the west coast in that car. In June, after the end of the school year, he convinced a friend, John Hoffman, to join him.

After some preparation, they were ready to depart. Donald said the previous owner had modified the car by moving the gas tank from the back of the car to a position in the front above the steering wheel. Donald added his own personal touch by placing cardboard under the floorboards for insulation. They left Moffit and were no more than ten miles into the trip when the car began burning. Apparently the cardboard caught fire from the exhaust, and before they knew it, flames were advancing. The two men scrambled out of the car and ran across the road, fearing the car would explode. When it did not explode right away, they ran back to try to save some of their belongings. Then they grabbed the burning cardboard from the car and threw it away. Wires from the gauges ran under the gas tank; inspection of the wires showed that the insulation had been burned away, but the wires were still intact.

When the car started, they decided to continue their journey west. At one point along the way, they started their daily drive from a point east of Billings, Montana, and drove all the way to Missoula—an estimated 380 miles. While that may not seem like a great distance by today's standards, it was a tremendous accomplishment by 1935 standards, especially considering the car. Next they drove south and stayed for a time with a couple who had once lived in Moffit. During their stay, they worked to get some money. Then it was on to Washington and Dayton, a small town in the southeastern part of the state. While in Dayton, they worked in a pea canning factory. Unfortunately they were in fresh fruit country and ended up getting sick from eating too much fruit. The trip continued west to the Portland, Oregon, area and then southwest to the town of McMinnville, where they worked picking hops before making the return trip.

On the way home, they stopped in Bend, Oregon, and visited Donald's great uncle, Gus Nelson. Mr. Nelson owned a clothing store and gave Donald a new blue coat before he left town. From Bend, it was on to Yellowstone Park in Wyoming and a shave using water from one of the hot springs. The car broke down near Cody, Wyoming, when gearing bands broke and the car lost some of its braking ability. Luckily, they carried extra bands, and John Hoffman replaced the broken ones. They made it back to North Dakota safe and sound in October, and Donald ended up selling the car for ten dollars. What an adventure!

At the age of twenty-three, with four years of teaching completed, Donald felt the urge to go to Bible college. He returned to Bismarck and talked with the pastor of the small church where he became a Christian. He suggested that Donald attend North Central Bible Institute in Minneapolis, a key suggestion because it brought him to Minnesota rather than somewhere else. He took the train and arrived in Minneapolis in the fall of 1936. The train stopped at the Great Northern Depot near the Mississippi River, and he walked from the train station all the way down Hennepin Avenue to Lake Street and from Lake Street to 13th Avenue and the Bible college. He was able to capitalize on some good fortune. His mother's parents were so happy to have a grandson when he was born that they put money in the bank for his education. Thus he was able to attend Bible college without having to do outside work. Donald graduated in 1938 and was one of four speakers for the graduation ceremony.

During the summer of 1938, Donald attended a Bible camp near Alexandria, Minnesota. He said, "I worked in a bookstore, and I met a beautiful young lady." Both were there as alumni of the Bible college and were attending an alumni meeting. Donald called it a "whirlwind courtship" that lasted four days. They were married two years later on May 11, 1940.

Life As A Married Couple

Married life started off with gusto. Donald did not have just one job but two. He was appointed to the faculty of North Central Bible Institute and also was pastor of the Assemblies of God Church in Cambridge, Minnesota, about thirty-five miles north of the Twin Cities. This was quite a commute for 1940, a commute he made five days a week. They lived in a big room at the back of the church. At first everything was kind of makeshift, but after a while, a young man came by and offered to build a small apartment. He carried out this offer by building a two-room apartment for them at the back of the church. It was also the year of the famous Armistice Day blizzard of November 11. Donald was on his way from Minneapolis when the snow came in through the louvers of the hood and stalled the car. Luckily, another car came by, and he was able to get home to Cambridge. Anna served as an associate minister at the church and took over whenever Donald had to leave. The stress of holding down two positions and the long commute caused them to give up the church in Cambridge, and after about a year and a half, they moved back into Minneapolis and he continued his work at the institute. He also took on the duties of other churches in Minneapolis. The work at North Central Bible Institute lasted for ten years.

They were getting established as World War II was raging. Anna remembered the rationing program for such items as gas, sugar, and meat. A niece was living with them at the time, and they received rationing stamps to cover her. But they also had friends with a larger family, so the Edsons often shared their ration stamps with them.

Their family started growing during this time, but it was not easy. Anna had suffered two miscarriages, and then became pregnant for a third time. According to Donald, "She became awful big." It turned out that she was carrying twins! On August 4, 1947, doctors delivered two boys who had a combined weight of fourteen pounds and eleven ounces! Donald and Eldon were fifty six years old in 2003. Five years later, in 1952, a third boy, Victor, was born. He died from a brain tumor in 1997 at age forty-four.

In 1955, Anna and Donald were on the founding board of a Christian day school in south Minneapolis which grew and prospered. It became a thriving grade and high school known now as Kings Academy. Anna said, "This was a challenging and significant time for us."

As the boys grew, some challenging moments developed. When the boys were little, Anna ran a dressmaking and dry cleaning business in the city. When the twins were six, Eldon developed encephalitis which put him about a year behind his brother in school. By the time the twins graduated from high school, the Vietnam war was going on.

Donnie enlisted in the military right after graduation. Eldon also wanted to go, so he finished up his high school credits during summer school. Anna included his medical history when she filled out papers for him and did not think he would be accepted, but he was. Donnie worked in psychological warfare and Eldon worked as a cook. What was somewhat surprising is that they were both sent to Vietnam at about the same time in 1966. They were nineteen years old, and this was very stressful for his parents, especially when they did not hear from the boys for six weeks at a time. Donnie eventually left Vietnam a little early and spent another year stateside before being discharged. When Eldon came home from Vietnam, he had only about five months of service remaining and was discharged early. Both survived the war without physical wounds and had some exciting but stressful experiences.

About 1964 Donald and Anna became involved with Daystar Christian Ministries. This association called for them to teach and counsel in a Christian community. The community took in people who had various problems, and the people stayed for as long as they needed help.

Their first out-state assignment was at Zion Harbor Camp near Federal Dam, Minnesota, a small town about 35 miles west of Grand Rapids. The Edsons lived there year round, and the campground was used for big meetings during the summer. After a time, they moved back to Minneapolis and worked in the Minneapolis branch of the ministry.

In 1971 they took an assignment in Texas in the area of the Rio Grande Valley. They stayed for eight years, and Donald described it as "a special time indeed!" Anna said, "We had a beautiful home down there with a swimming pool and a great big main house with cabins all around it." The people who came down there for help lived and worked in the compound, and both Anna and Donald counseled during this assignment. When people overcame their problems, most moved on, but some became counselors themselves.

From Texas, they moved to Alpena, Michigan, which turned out to be a short stay. The town was located about 250 miles north of Detroit. They stayed for only six months during a time when the place was winding down.

Then it was on to Tulsa, Oklahoma, to oversee the closing of a community. They stayed long enough to take care of the people there until the property was sold. The residents of the community were absorbed into other ministries around the country.

The next stop was not so short. They went to Indiana and stayed for thirteen years. Daystar Ministries had purchased a large beautiful building that had previously housed a mineral spa resort in Martinsville, Indiana. In 1989, much of the building burned down, apparently from faulty wiring. Although their apartment was not destroyed, the heat from the fire was so intense that it melted glasses in the living room. Eighty-one people were able to escape the building without a fatality. The townspeople really came to their aid with food, housing, and other services. During this time, Donald served ten years as chaplain for the Disciples of Christ in the Kennedy Retirement Center. They stayed in Martinsville, Indiana, for another four years, and he continued his work as a chaplain.

Good fortune often occurs in peoples' lives. Donald and Anna called them "miracles." Some were recounted earlier in their stories, but they had more. They talked about some friends of theirs who lived in the compound while the Edsons were doing their ministry in Texas. The friends sold their car and gave $2,500 to the Edsons to pay down on a motor home.

Donald and Anna took their first trip in the motor home to Guadalajara, Mexico in 1979, where they stayed for two months. They took many other trips in that motor home, criss-crossing the country and traveling to all of the lower forty-eight states but North and South Carolina. By the time they arrived in Indiana, they traded in the first motor home for a second one that was newer and bigger. They used it until about four years ago.

Another incident stemmed from a trip to Mexico. A rear tire blew out on their motor home (the motor home had double tires in the back). There they were in the middle of a desert and in need of help. Donald said that a Mexican man seemed to appear out of nowhere and told them to turn around and go five miles where they would find a gas station. The man said the people at the station would fix the tire.

In another case, a couple that had been ministered to by the Edsons in the 1970s have been sending a pension-like gift every month for many years.

The Edsons said, "Over the years of association with the Daystar Ministries, we saw God work in lives in many wonderful ways and developed many relationships that are still part of our lives, from all over the country and even overseas, which we still maintain."

In 1994, Donald retired at the age of eighty-one, and they returned to Minnesota. They received severance pay from Daystar Christian Ministries and collected social security. They were able to buy a very comfortable mobile home which they still live in. Though never rich in terms of having a lot of money, and in spite of living through some tough times, they are very thankful not to have any debt. They did not even use credit cards.

Anna said they were never rich in material terms, but lived very rich lives when measured in experiences and relationships. They had their marriage vows renewed multiple times. The first time was after they were married twenty-five years. They returned to the church where they were married and had the same preacher renew their vows. They renewed their vows again for their fiftieth anniversary when they were living in Martinsville, Indiana. Then they had their vows renewed again on their fifty-fifth anniversary and their sixtieth anniversary. Anna is working on her third wedding ring. According to both of them, their marriage is for "as long as we both shall live."

Anna mentioned that their biggest challenge currently is to get rid of a lifetime accumulation of books, magazines, pictures, notes, and the like. She said Donald has an office filled with books, records, and memorabilia. For her part, Anna has a sewing room filled with materials and projects. She said, "I still put away things that I am going to do when I get old."

They are happily involved with Abundant Life Community Church in Blaine, and participate in many of the activities at Coon Rapids Senior Citizens Center. They are happy to be alive and together after more than sixty-three years of marriage. All in all, they are two people who have long been in love with the Lord, each other, and their family, and have built a successful partnership in helping others.

Eugene (Gene) Lauro

Much of Gene Lauro's immediate ancestry and early life centered on Ischia, an Italian island north of the Isle of Capri and just west of Naples. Both his father, Buonaventura Lauro, and his mother, Carmella Tuccillo, lived on Ischia. Buonaventura had been married and had seven children with his first wife before she died. Carmella became his second wife. Her father was employed in the forest service and worked on the island to protect the vegetation. The Tuccillos moved moved to the same street, just two buildings from where Buonaventura lived. They eventually met, married, and had Gene who was born on March 16, 1921.

Buonaventura died when Gene was only six. When he died, he left an estate that included a large apartment building. Gene said that a man talked with his father before he died and convinced him to leave an apartment in the building to Gene. His father took the man's advice, and Gene believes it was an act that kept him from being thrown out into the streets. He brought this up because he felt his father's oldest son from his first wife cheated Carmella out of some of her inheritance. Besides getting all the furniture, she was supposed to get 9,000 lira, but the son said he would take the money and she could take the furniture. This experience taught him a lesson he would carry for a long time.

In spite of the sadness of losing a parent, Gene eventually returned to a pretty normal life for a child on Ischia. He rode a bike, played with friends and sometimes explored. One day he was digging near his home and discovered a coin of Napoleon Bonaparte. Napolean apparently sent the coin to a friend who lived on Ischia during the time of his empire. It was a very valuable coin going back to the beginning of the nineteenth century. This became one of his cherished childhood memories.

He has always loved pasta, especially spaghetti. He said there really was not any food he did not like and attributed that to the fact that Italians eat a simple diet.

In spite of the effects of the world wide Depression, his mother always made sure that he had enough to eat. Nevertheless it was a tough time for people to make a living.

He went to school on the island, and a strange thing happened when it was time to go to high school. A priest, who was the director of a Catholic school, came to see Carmella. He asked her why she did not send Gene to the Catholic school. She replied that she could did not have enough money. The priest responded by saying that the religious providence would help, and she should send him to the school. Gene said, "I could kiss the hand of this man," not only for allowing him to go to the school, but also for giving him the opportunity to learn about the literary classics such as The Iliad by Homer, and the ancient civilizations. The priest made Gene excited about learning and he graduated in about 1935.

Once out of high school, he had a decision to make. To stay on the island meant working in one of two areas—fishing or growing grapes. Gene did not like either of the choices; instead, he wanted to learn and to do something in the mechanical or arts areas. So he started out working as a night watchman at a hotel run by his cousin. In the mornings, he also worked in the kitchen. Then another cousin helped him get a job at an electrical power plant on Ischia. He worked a night shift for a period of about two to three years.

During this time, Germans were immigrating to the area to escape the Nazi government. Many were artists who settled on the island. In spite of the fascist government in power in Italy at the time, the Italians did much to help the Germans. He gave one example in which Italians made fake birth certificates for the immigrants, listing them as Catholic rather than Jewish.

As trouble in Europe grew, Gene enlisted in the navy at age fifteen. As he described his military history, he marveled at the coincidences in life and how lucky he was. For example, he wanted to be an air force pilot, but was denied when he enlisted in the navy. Now he is thankful, because so many of the pilots were killed during the war. He gave another example of a friend who went through officers' training school and became a captain. When it came time for a wartime assignment, his superiors wanted him to go to a specific area. He wanted to go somewhere else, but after thinking about it, told his superiors that he would go wherever they sent him. Gene had remembered a previous situation in which superiors had told an officer to report to a certain area, but the officer wanted to go elsewhere. The officer got what he wanted but ended up being killed in battle. Also many of his friends wanted to go to machine gunners school in Naples. They ended up being shipped to North Africa, and they all died when the ship sank in the Mediterranean Sea.

Gene learned well from the tragedy of his friends and chose to say nothing when he was assigned to Salerno for his training.

From there, he was sent to Greece. The orders to go to Greece made him happy because of what he learned about Greek history in school. His destination was Pilos on the island of Peloponnesos. He was placed in a battery on a cliff over the beachhead. The Germans were positioned in the mountains above the cliff, so the Italians took the first hits. After the battle, the Italian troops became prisoners without yet knowing it. They organized at Castle Navarreno, thinking that they were going to be sent back to Italy. In his battery, Gene encouraged the other men to remove the firing pins from their weapons and throw them away. They followed through, making the weapons inoperable and useless to the Nazis. Later the troops found a supply of wine and other liquor in the castle and had a big celebration. Most of the Italian military personnel became drunk. Gene told of one drunken soldier who put a hand grenade in his mouth and ran around. He dropped the grenade, and while it did not go off, it hit his leg and broke it. Gene said he did not get drunk himself because he wanted to keep his feet on the ground—he wanted to be alert.

The day they thought they were going back to Italy was a surprise. The Germans told them they had to get rid of all their clothes except for one jacket, one shirt, one pair of pants, a pair of socks, and a pair of shoes. They had been given three choices. They could go back to Italy and fight with the Germans, they could become prisoners of war, or they could work. They did not want to fight against their own people in Italy and the choice of work turned out to be basically the same as becoming POWs. Not knowing their fate, they chose work. The Italians were then loaded on a train that took them through Macedonia to Belgrade, Yugoslavia, and a large concentration work camp. He gave an example of the torture he saw there— a man being beaten by a rubber covered chain and screaming out in pain.

In Belgrade, his job was to shovel coal. Every day, a truck picked up the prisoners and took them to the railroad station where they had to shovel coal. He remembered seeing a lot of

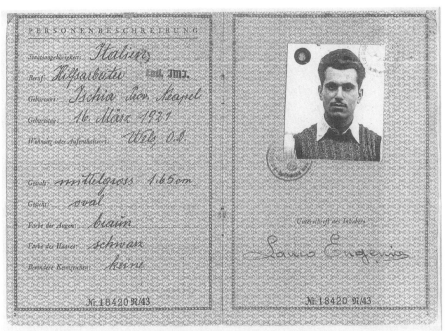

Work card issued by the Nazis during World War II

abuse of prisoners during that time. He even created his own diary of his experiences as a prisoner. However, he did not say anything against the Germans. He felt that if his diary was found, he did not want the Germans to find information that would give them an excuse to kill him. He even drew a plan of the Belgrade camp.

After a period of time, the prisoners were taken to a boat on the Danube River and transported to Vienna, Austria. During the trip, they went through Budapest, Hungary, and some of his friends wanted to jump ship and swim to the other side of the river. They thought they could find friendly Slavic people who might help them get back to Italy. Gene said, "Thank God, I did not." When the Germans found anyone escaping they shot the escapees. He saw more along the way. He recounted a time when he saw some Jewish prisoners forced on a march. When one woman stepped out of line to pick up a pear that had fallen from a tree, she was shot.

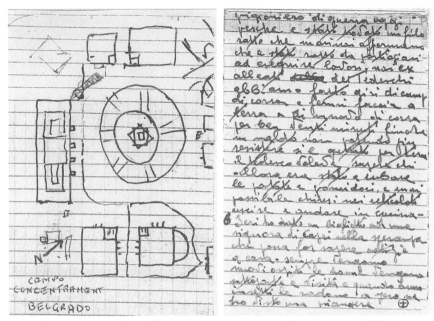

Notes and drawing of Belgrade prison camp by Eugene during WW II

The Italians were placed in a large concentration camp of about 3,000 people. He tried to explain what conditions were like. He said, "Imagine 1,000 people in a room and several Ukrainian girls passing out small pieces of soap." The soap was about one half inch by one and a half inches and about as thick as a piece of cardboard. He tried to get across the idea that when all those people were in close together and did not have a bath for three or four weeks, the smell was pretty bad. A small piece of soap did not do much good with so many people. Gene did admit that he had hidden his own supply of soap. Though he did not explain how he got the soap, he indicated that he was pretty resourceful.

The prisoners settled in at the Linz Camp, but did not have any work. When they first arrived, they were asked, "What can you do?" The prisoners answered that they were cooks because they thought it would be a way to get some food.

One morning, Gene and about twenty to thirty prisoners were gathered and marched from Linz to a camp at Wels,

Austria. They arrived at night, close to the factory where they were to work. They were assigned to make cooking ovens. Maybe the Germans thought that if they were cooks, they could make ovens. Like before, they were kept in the camp except for the time they worked in the factory. They were fed basically the same food every day—boiled carrots and potatoes. Conditions were poor in many ways. For example, the latrine was nothing more than a canal (sic) with a piece of wood over it.

As he discussed the camp at Wels, Austria, a flood of memories came rushing back to him. Some of the memories were of the horrors of the camps, others were poignant, and some had a touch of humor.

Camp conditions caused Gene to discuss the horrors of the war apart from his own experiences. He talked about the torture and death in camps like Auschwitz and Matthausen, the camp closest to the camp he stayed at in Wels. He talked about how the fat from Jews who were executed was used to make soap. Many other gruesome stories stemmed from the death camps, including using hair from people for filling pillows.

The first day at the factory, Gene got a break. A German carpenter in the factory wanted him to nail some boards that were just delivered. As Gene was nailing, the carpenter noticed that he hammered the nails straight and true. So he told Gene to report to him the next morning, and he would work in that area. The next morning, Gene was assigned to a different area instead. The carpenter became so angry that he went to the director and complained loudly. He made such a fuss that Gene was assigned to his area and was not bothered any more. After a time, the carpenter became ill and died. Gene was then given the position as the master carpenter for the factory.

During the time in Wels, Austrian villagers sometimes brought them extra supplies like bread or vegetables. Gene spoke of a beautiful Austrian girl who regularly came by with extra food. He thought she was so beautiful that he decided to give her some coffee in return for a kiss. He gave her the coffee, but when he went for the kiss, she stopped him and said, "I have to go," and left. He never did get the kiss.

He also spoke of another time when he tried to escape with another prisoner. He said they got about fifty kilometers (thirty miles) from the camp and came to a village that seemed deserted. Then they came upon a guard who ordered them to the police station, and from there, they were returned to the camp. He was kept in a small room by himself and it became frightening when planes bombarded the area.

While he was in Wels, another interesting event took place. A young man by the name of Karl came by to have his ski fixed. The tip was broken and when Gene fixed it, Karl suggested that they go skiing. Gene escaped from the camp, met Karl at the train station, and they spent a Saturday and Sunday skiing. Meanwhile fellow prisoners covered for him so the Germans would not find out. Toward the end of the weekend, Gene returned to the camp. As an aside, he said he remembered standing among the beautiful mountains and seeing planes bombarding an area nearby. He was perplexed by how he could experience a moment of peace and beauty while miles away, buildings and people were being destroyed.

During this period of time, he faced a dilemma. He did not want to do any work that would help the war effort. On the other hand, he feared that if he did any sabotage, the Germans would find out and kill him. He ended up not completing the work that he was assigned. The director told him to make some benches for the factory, but he took his hammer and talked to the girls in the factory instead. Also, under his bed, he cut out part of a board that he used for hiding things such as food and items of clothing, and the Germans never found it. In addition, he said he tried to keep up the spirits of the other workers. He continued to work in the factory until the Americans liberated the area.

When the Americans came in, they told the prisoners to stay put; they would get the prisoners back to their homes. While Gene was waiting, he met an Italian GI from Brooklyn named Paul. He asked Paul why he did not speak Italian, and Paul said because his parents did not want him to understand what they were saying. He had good times with Paul.

Not everything was good right after the war. Many of the Jewish prisoners from the death camps such as Matthausen and Buchenwald developed cholera. Prisoners were used to starvation diets, and when they were freed, many ate more food than their bodies could tolerate. Many freed prisoners died. Then he talked about a very personal incident. A starving, sick man came to him, and Gene nursed him along with bits of food. The man was very grateful that Gene had saved his life, and in gratitude gave Gene a silver cigarette holder, one of his few possessions at the time. He said he was from a wealthy family in Vienna and wanted to give Gene something to remember him by. Unfortunately, he never found out the man's name, and he felt sad that in spite of many efforts, he was unable to locate the man. Gene said he just wanted to find the man and feel the joy that the other man also survived.

Gene returned to Ischia and his wife, Gilda, after the war. They married before he went into war and had one boy, named Buonaventura after Gene's father. Gene went to work in the shipyard, but did not make much money. They needed to do something else.

As luck would have it, Gilda's father lived in Buenos Aires. Her father had moved there and two of his six children lived there, so Gilda suggested they move too. So they took care of the visa applications and left for Argentina. Unfortunately, her father died before they reached Buenos Aires.

Gene still had to find work, since his wife soon gave birth to a second child; a boy they named Carlos. Then, just nine months after giving birth, Gilda died from cancer. He had to work two and three jobs to make ends meet. During her illness, she underwent three operations and later was taking morphine to manage the pain. The costs were great. Just the morphine shots cost fifteen pesos a week and he was earning only two pesos on a night job. In the mornings, he went to work for a carpenter, and sometimes worked a third job.

In addition, the children needed care. Luckily Gene brought his mother to Buenos Aires. He said it took her fifteen days to cross the Atlantic. She was then able to watch his children while he worked.

After some time, he worked in a jewelry store. He and a partner repaired things such as eyeglasses and mechanical items. At one point, the jeweler complained that he needed a new punch that was used in fixing watch cases. The ones he had used were made in Germany, and with that country re-covering from the devastation of the war, the punches were no longer available. Gene was able to make a punch to help fix the watch cases. He and a partner paid for a machine that was needed to make the punch. The owner of the jewelry store en-couraged them to go out and open their own repair store, which they did. They eventually added jewelry repair to their busi-ness and Gene became very good at making and fixing watch cases. He went around to jewelry stores to get watch cases to fix, and he also made cases.

About five years after the death of his first wife, and after Gene had established himself in the jewelry business, he met Angelica Pontecorvo. They had worked in the same factory. They eventually married and had a daughter, Claudia.

Several factors caused Gene to leave Argentina. The Peron government was in disgrace, so there was the element of in-stability. In addition, most of the political power in the country was in the hands of just a few families, which meant there was not much chance of reform. His wife even urged the move by telling him many jobs were available in the United States and that pay was good. He also heard that many people had cars in the United States, while he was driving a motor bike.

The next step was to get a visa to come to the United States. Because of the immigration quota laws that applied to Ital-ians, Gene would have had to wait ten years to come on his own visa. However, his wife, a native Argentinean, was eligible right away.

The family arrived in the United States in 1962 and settled in Brooklyn. His half-brother and half-sister already lived in the area. His half-brother asked him what he could do. When Gene told him he could make and repair watch cases, his half-brother took him to the Bulova watch factory. Some of the employees were from Switzerland and could speak to him in German (one of the languages Gene knew) and help him out. When he first started, he earned $100 a week, pretty good pay for the times.

When the word got out that Gene was a jeweler, a nephew of a jewelry store owner named Liberti called him about a jewelry repair job in a shop that was located near Wall Street in Manhattan. The shop repaired jewelry for stores along the east coast from South Carolina to New Hampshire. They even had a customer in Alaska. He did not make a lot of money, about forty-nine dollars a week, but felt it was the right thing to do.

After a couple of years, the owner of the shop, Mr. Liberti, decided to retire. He offered half the business to Gene for about $5,000. Gene only had about $1,000, so he asked his sister-in-law for a loan to cover the rest. The business did very well, and he shocked his sister-in-law by paying her back within a couple of months.

Gene noted that gold was strictly controlled in those days. They saved all of their gold filings and they took those filings to the federal reserve bank once a month. The bank melted the filings down into an ingot and gave it back to them.

A few years later, his partner decided that he wanted to get out of the jewelry repair shop and buy a jewelry store. Again Gene borrowed money, this time to buy out his partner. Again he paid the money back quickly. With the business doing well, he and his wife bought a nursing home, which she ran. This time, he borrowed $21,000 from the bank and said that instead of charging him the going rate of five percent interest, they only charged him four percent.

Expansion of his own business holdings followed. One day, a Jewish customer mentioned that he wanted to retire and sell his store. Gene went to look at the store, which was located in an upscale area of Manhattan. He liked the store and bought it. He now had two stores to run. Gene's son had just returned from Vietnam, and he was given the responsibility of running the second store. Both stores continued to do well, and Gene kept them until he retired.

Meanwhile another change was beginning to take place. His other son was working for the Medtronic Company and living in Minnesota. His daughter was just completing her junior high school education at a Catholic school and was scheduled to go to a public high school. The wife of Gene's partner warned him that it would be difficult for the girl to go from a Catholic school to a public school in New York—it could even be dangerous. After talking it over, she came to live with his son's family and completed high school and college in Minnesota.

Gene's second wife, Angelica, died in 1983, and with his son's family and his daughter's family living in Minnesota, Gene began spending much time in the state. He finally came to Minnesota permanently in 1999. It turned out to be an eventful year because he also suffered a severe health problem. His daughter took him to Mackinac Island for a vacation. During a walk, he found it very difficult to breathe. When his daughter took him to the doctor, the tests showed that he needed bypass surgery and a new heart valve.

Gene did pretty well after moving to Minnesota. He felt good physically, but said the cold weather in the winter bothered him. He went to the local senior center regularly where, he and another person cut stamps from envelopes for the center, but he said he had slowed down. He had been an artist for many years. He especially liked to work with pottery and felt that he created some very nice pieces. He also mentioned that he loved to fly. He made a trip to Germany and Austria in the late 1990s. A highlight was a visit to King Ludwig's

Neuschwanstein Castle near Fussen, Germany. The Disney castles are modeled after it. Gene also returned to Wels, Austria—the sight of the concentration camp where he was imprisoned.

Gene was a man who had to find the creativity and the will to survive a horrible situation during World War II. It appeared that he was able to take what he discovered about himself at that time in history and continue to use it effectively through the rest of his life. Gene wondered about the mysteries of life and how some people escaped dangerous situations and others died. He also worried about the world community. According to Gene, "Jealousy is the biggest enemy of man." He felt that jealousy often caused people to harm others. As of our last in-person interview, he was a man still searching for answers.

A few months after our last conversation, Gene's health declined. He died in the spring of 2004. He will be missed.

Barbara Bester

Barb's father, William James Starkey, was born in St. Paul, Minnesota. Her mother, Margaret Sophia La Rocque, was born in a small town north of Detroit Lakes, called Ogema, which is on the White Earth Indian Reservation. William's mother died when he was twelve years old, and some time after that, the Starkey family moved to northern Minnesota. When William's mother was dying, she asked her sister to marry her husband and raise the children, which the sister did. William and Margaret met and married when they lived in northern Minnesota.

From the late 1800s through the early 1900s the Federal Government mandated an educational program for American Indians which stressed assimilation. Children were removed from their homes at an early age and sent to a boarding school for their education. They were often sent out of state and stayed at the boarding school year round. By the time Barbara started school, many children were accepted at schools closer to home and could return home for the summer. The children were educated in the ways of white culture and at the same time denied access to their own culture. As noted above, the program was mandated, which meant neither the American Indian parents or their children had a say in the matter.

Barb related a story her dad told about the time he went to boarding school in Carlisle, Pennsylvania. The story was about a little girl who came to school at Carlisle, and "all she did was cry, cry, cry." Years later, when William and Margaret met, she told him about being sent away to school when she was only four years old. She was actually two years younger than shown on the records. Barb said, "It's no wonder she cried." It was also interesting that the "little crybaby" turned out to be Barb's mother.

According to Barb's earliest recollection, her father co-owned a small grocery store in the town of Ebro, a small town on the northern boundary of the White Earth Reservation. William and Margaret had twelve children. In order of birth, they were Catherine, Mary Anne, Henry, Margaret, Josephine, Frank, Paul, Agatha, Barbara (born on October 19, 1922), Albert, Joseph, and Anne Marie. Barb is the sole surviving member of the family.

Barb remembered her house in Ebro. She said, "Well, it was a big house, the biggest house in town." They had a water pump inside what they called the cold porch. Barb was sure they had an outhouse and used kerosene lamps for lighting. The family kept cows, pigs, chickens, and horses on their land. She said that when they milked the cows and separated the cream from the milk, they used the cold porch for storage. They also had a small vegetable garden near the house and farther away had a large field where they grew corn and potatoes.

Since Barb was so young during the time in Ebro, she did not have a lot of farm chores, although she did remember standing on a chair to wash dishes. The property was fenced off, and Barb's parents did not allow the children to leave the property. Entertainment was often provided by the family, since her father and brother both played the violin. Her dad also played the bass viol. Barb also recalled taking part in square dancing.

As an aside, she mentioned that when her dad was young and still living in St. Paul, he and his father played music on a river boat owned by a prominent railroad gentleman. She assumed that her grandfather taught her father how to play the violin at a young age.

Barb gave much credit to her mother for helping get the family through the years of the Great Depression. The family had older cousins who worked in the Twin Cities; when they bought new clothes, they sent their old clothes to the relatives in the north. Barb said her mother was an excellent seamstress, and she was able to turn those old clothes into very nice clothes for the children. Not only that, but many of the clothes she made had detachable collars and cuffs, so they could put different ones on a dress or shirt to give it a new look. They often wore underpants made from flour sacks, and when they wore out, the elastic waist was ripped out to be used again. Barb made a very pointed statement by saying, "That's how we got through the Depression, through very frugal living."

Besides being frugal, Barb's parents were also independent. Whenever they moved, they made sure the property included tillable land. They were able to grow most of their own food and canned a lot. Thus they were never without food during the hard economic times. Speaking of food, Barb mentioned that they always had homemade bread, and her mother made nine loaves at a time!

Church was an important part of family life. Barb mentioned that her grandfather, Henry Starkey, was raised in the Episcopal Church, but always attended the Catholic Church with the rest of the family. When his last known relative died, he formally became a Catholic—at the age of seventy!

She mentioned that the family was too large to all fit in the car to go to church. Of course, it meant someone always had to stay home. Sometimes her dad teased Barb when he volunteered to stay home. He said he would "punch the dough" while the others went to church. The teasing comment was his reference to staying home and making bread for the family. Actually, her father went to church quite regularly.

When she was almost seven, Barb and her sister Agatha were sent to the Red Lake Mission School—St. Mary's Mission School. (Her older brothers and sister had attended school in Ebro.) Their admission to the school was an interesting story. Barb's parents were anticipating a move near a town west of Ebro called Lengby. The school the girls were supposed to attend was twenty-two miles away, and they would have to walk two miles to the bus stop every morning and two miles home from the bus stop every afternoon. Given the children's ages and the potential weather conditions, her parents felt the girls would miss too much school. So the parents sought to enroll the girls as outsiders at the mission school. When Barb and Agatha were accepted, their parents also decided to enroll Josephine, Frank, and Paul as well. Thus, the five middle children ended up attending the school.

St. Mary's was a boarding school, and the children basically lived there from September through May. They did not even come home on weekends. Barb and her sister Agatha attended the school through the eighth grade. Her parents made arrangements for them to board at the mission school during her ninth grade year. During the years at the boarding school, the children did more than attend classes. They also took part in doing chores called "details." The younger children did things like peeling potatoes and stacking bread, while the older children did sewing, mending, baking, working with the cream separator, tended the dining hall, and doing laundry. Thus they basically learned life skills along with the classroom learning. On the other hand, nothing in the way of American Indian culture was taught.

Barb finished her secondary education—sophomore, junior and senior years—plus a fourth year vocational at Flandreau Vocational School in South Dakota. She said that if you did not accept your diploma after your senior year, you could attend a fourth year of "vocational" classes without having to pay out of state tuition, which is what she and her sister Agatha did. During her time at Flandreau, she took up commercial sewing and home nursing, as well as doing the regular course work. Both Barb and Agatha took the same path and graduated in 1941. Barb noted that Flandreau School was an Indian school located on Reservation property, but the administration never offered classes in American Indian culture.

After graduating from Flandreau, Barb's life path took some twists and turns. It started when she and Agatha accepted commercial sewing jobs in Chicago. Her mother would not allow the move, so Agatha said she was going to go to Montana to get married. Agatha had a boyfriend from Flandreau who lived in Montana, and she went out there and married him. Meanwhile, Barb went to Lawton, Oklahoma, to take practical nursing. After completing a one-year program, she went to Washington state for a civil service position that she had applied for. She was accepted at an Indian hospital in Nespelem on the Colville Reservation. She worked there for almost three years. It also was the place she learned to drive.

Then it was back to Minnesota to enter the University of Minnesota's Cadet Corps Nursing Program to which she applied and was accepted. It was while attending the University of Minnesota nursing program that she met her future husband Tony. He had recently returned from four and a half years of active duty in the Army Medical Corps and was immediately intent upon getting married. According to Barb, "He presented me with an engagement ring at his family reunion, when all of his family relatives had safely returned from the war. I tried to convince him that I wanted to finish my RN training before I got married but he was determined; we ended up getting married in December of 1945." Tony told Barb that she could always go back for her RN training, but she said whenever the program was to begin, she was pregnant. Finally, she was over thirty years of age, and at that time, people over thirty could not enter the nursing program. Several years later Barb took and passed the Minnesota Board test to be licensed as an LPN.

She continued her career in health care when she took a position at a private hospital in St. Paul, a position she had when she and Tony were married. Then Tony saw an ad in the paper for a couple to work in a rest home. He applied for the jobs and accepted the positions without even telling Barb. When she told the doctors at the hospital that she had to quit, they asked her where she was going to work. According to Barb, when she told them it was a rest home, they said they would hold her job open because she would be back. But in fact, both Barb and Tony liked working in the rest home environment.

Both had backgrounds in the medical field, as Tony had been in the medical corps in the military for several years. Since they liked the work, they decided to look around for a rest home to buy. They came across some owners who had two rest homes. This brash young couple decided to try to buy one of the homes and succeeded! All this happened less than a year after they started working in a rest home. Here she was, only twenty-three years old, and she was a partner in her own business— talk about courage and confidence! The rest home was not large; it had twenty-two beds, and they eventually expanded it to care for thirty-five patients. They ran the rest home successfully for thirty years.

Over the years, rest homes became known as nursing homes, and larger nursing home companies began buying more and more smaller nursing homes. The Besters did not want to expand any more; they chose to transfer their patients to other nursing homes, and they remodeled their building into a boarding house. Their son Joseph ran the boarding house, and Barb and Tony went to work for other nursing homes.

Tony finally retired at age sixty-two. They had purchased twenty acres of land near Prior Lake in 1970, and he was in the process of building a home to live in during their retirement years. He also planted a garden and was working in the garden when he died of a heart attack a short time before his sixty-fourth birthday. They were married for thirty-seven great years and raised a family of eight children. In the order of age they are Yvonne, Rita May, William, Kathleen, Anthony, Joseph, Patricia, and Colette Jean. The youngest child died at the age of twenty-six of kidney disease after being on dialysis for eight and a half years, with Barb doing the dialysis at home. All the surviving children still live in Minnesota and have produced seventeen grandchildren and six great grandchildren, and Barb was very fond of them all.

When her husband died, Barb did not think she wanted to live on the property by herself. She sold the property to her oldest son who finished the house and still lives there. In the meantime, Barb stayed in Minneapolis and continued to work in nursing homes. From her previous ownership of a nursing home, she was also a licensed nursing home administrator. When she retired from nursing home work, she continued doing home health care. Her daughter, Rita, had a place called Senior Assistance which provided nursing care for families who wanted to keep relatives in their own homes. Barb worked for her on an as-need basis—she went wherever she was needed for a period of time.

During the last part of the twentieth century and into the twenty-first century, Barb focused on learning about American Indian culture on her own and through her son, Joseph. He studied Indian spirituality with elders and Indian Culture at the University of Minnesota, developed a good understanding and participated in many cultural events and ceremonies including being a "pipe carrier" and "Sundancer" for over thirteen years. Together they shared their knowledge with a growing community of Catholic Indians and friends at the Blessed Kateri Chapel in the Archdiocesan Office of Indian

Ministry on Park Avenue in Minneapolis. They also shared their culture and songs once a month with the youth at the St. Joseph's Home for Children in Minneapolis.

More recently, Barb made dream catchers. She described a dream catcher as a circle made of red willow bark and man-made sinew. The sinew is woven inside the circle until a tiny hole is left in the middle and a strand is left dangling with beads and a feather attached. According to tradition, the dream catcher was hung above a baby's cradle. It caught the spiritual essences in the air, filtering the good from the bad and only allowing the good spirits through. The dangling sinew with the beads and feather brought the good dreams down to the infant.

In addition, Barb did beadwork. She made necklaces and other articles of beads. Some years ago she combined sewing and beading skills when she made a buckskin dress for her daughter, Patty, for her powwow dancing in the fifth and sixth grades. Her daughter has since handed the outfit on to her daughter, Tiara. Barb also made Tiara a jingle dress; the tin jingles create a musical sound when they clash together. A jingle dress dance, according to tradition, was a gift from the spirits for the Indian maidens. The dress was an integral part of the tradition. Barb's granddaughter Tiara is a very good jingle dress dancer, and recently was a lead dancer at a Mdewakanton Pow-wow.

There was yet another activity in which this creative woman was involved— quilting. She even taught a quilting class. According to Barb, she was asked to show some women at the Indian Ministry in Minneapolis how to quilt. She had quilt pieces already cut for a quilt she was making for herself. She took a few pieces along one day to show them how to get started. After some time, with more and more people showing up to learn quilting, Barb realized that the pieces were no longer hers. When it was finished, she could not find the quilt, so she asked the church pastor where it was. He said it was put away. She planned to hold a raffle for the quilt and use the proceeds to buy more quilting supplies. Instead, it was decided that the quilt be given a place of honor in the chapel of the Indian Ministry where it still hangs.

Some talk was directed to American Indian traditions, such as powwows and their modern day applications. Barb noted that there were powwow seasons, and many Indian schools held powwows regularly. Although many American Indian cultural activities and ceremonies were suppressed for a long time, she felt that a lot of them were being resurrected.

Barb had quite a list of accomplishments. She was able to successfully manage a marriage, a career, and raise a family during some challenging times. She also was able to connect to her American Indian culture and pass some of it on to her children, grandchildren, and others within the American Indian community.

Ferne Krans

Ferne was the daughter of William Hugh Chambers and Emma Dilworth Chambers. William was of Irish descent and Emma was of English descent. Both were born and raised in Canada. Ferne concluded that she came from "good hardy stock."

The Chambers moved to Minot, North Dakota, where they settled in to raise their family. They owned farmland, but lived in the town of Minot where William was a carpenter and Emma was a housewife.

William and Emma had five children, three boys and two girls. What was interesting was that the three boys and the oldest girl were born pretty close together, then there was a gap of eight years until Ferne was born on July 12, 1916. The gap between Ferne and her siblings played a role in her development. Her sister left home when Ferne was in grade school and left her as the only child at home. While discipline and standards of behavior were present, her mother gave her a good deal of freedom, which helped Ferne develop into an assertive and independent woman.

Ferne remembered the home in Minot as being nice. It was a rather large home and had electricity and a coal-burning furnace. They had an icebox for keeping food fresh, as well as a fruit cellar for more long term storage. A coal-burning furnace meant a coal bin had to be filled regularly during fall, winter, and spring when temperatures were cool to cold. The furnace had to be stoked daily during this kind of weather. To keep food cool in the icebox, large blocks of ice had to be placed in it, and as the ice melted, the container for collecting the water had to be emptied. Thus, even in a house that was considered up-to-date for its time, the family had to keep up with a variety of chores to keep it running smoothly. Many of these chores are unknown to our younger people.

Ferne went to elementary and secondary school in Minot. She graduated from high school in 1934. From high school, she went on to a teacher's college in Minot and completed a two-year program. Her great interest was art, and her dream was to become a self-sustaining artist. As a result, many of her classes were in the area of various forms of art. Upon graduation in 1936, she traveled to the Twin Cities to work and attend art school.

Unfortunately, her high school years and post secondary education took place during the Great Depression. Times were tough, and Ferne was expected to do her part. She worked part-time at a Woolworth's store during high school and earned the princely sum of fifteen cents an hour. She also did a lot of babysitting during that time. When she came to the Twin Cities, she worked at a Woolworth's store in Minneapolis and attended the art school in St. Paul.

In discussing her time in the Twin Cities, Ferne talked about getting her driver's license and about her first car. She learned to drive when she settled in the Twin Cities, but a test was not required. As a matter of fact, a girlfriend's dad went to the government center and bought her a license for twenty-five cents. She also bought a car, an old Chevrolet. She did not remember the age of the car, but her description indicated it was from the 1920s. The car was built high off the ground, and the spare tire was located under the back seat. Of course the seat had to be taken out in order to get to the tire. At any rate, she bought the car for eighty dollars, and when she went into the service, she sold it to her brother for $100. Later, he sold it for more than that to someone else. The increases in price were at least partly explained by the fact that cars were not made during much of the war.

When World War II began, Ferne worked at a glider factory at Wold Chamberlain Field. (Today it is Minneapolis/St. Paul International Airport.) Gliders were handmade and quite expensive because they could only be used for one wartime flight. Her job was to rivet torque tubes, and because of the precision needed in getting the tubes uniform, the job required two people. The tubes were required to move the ailerons on the glider wings. Eventually, she was paired with a man, who she trained; and when they received their paychecks, his was larger. Ferne was angry because this man did not work any more hours than she did. She asked why, and the man replied that he was married, and besides, he was a man. She said, "I don't care, you do the same job I do, I taught you how to do it, and then you get more money than I do. How come you are not in the army?" He replied that he had a punctured eardrum and then turned the question around and asked, "If you're so smart, why don't you join the Army?" She said if she went into the military, she would join the Lady Marines. He responded by telling her she could not make it in the Lady Marines. Well, that did it! She enlisted on the way home from work and within a week, she was in the Marines.

Before describing Ferne's experiences in the Lady Marines, it is helpful to understand the history of the organization. Although 305 women served a brief stint in the Marine Corps Reserve during World War I, it was not until World War II that the Marine Corps Women's Reserve was officially organized. On February 13, 1943, General Thomas Holcomb, the Commandant of the Marine Corps, announced its formation. Over the course of the war, more than 22,000 officers and enlisted women joined the Corps as women reserves. They were fully integrated into the Marine Corps and performed more than 200 military assignments. Some of their jobs included the following: clerical, parachute riggers, mechanics, radio operators, mapmakers, and welders. After the surrender of the Japanese, the Women's Reserve was quickly demobilized, and only about 1,000 personnel were still part of the reserve by July of 1946. However, the Marine Corps Women's Reserve continued to function and women played important roles in the Korean War, the Vietnam War, and more recently, wars in the Middle East. The Marine Corps Women's Reserve celebrated its sixtieth anniversary in February 2003. (For readers who would like more information about the Lady Marines, visit the Marine Corps site at: www.usmc.mil/marinelink/mcn2000.nsf/womenmarines.)

Although she did not use the term pioneer, Ferne was one of the pioneers in the Lady Marines. She enlisted on October 12, 1943, and was sent to her parents' home in Minot to await orders. A little over a month later, she was ordered to Camp LeJeune in North Carolina for six weeks of basic training. Ferne said, "In the first place, they got us up at the crack of dawn and we marched and we marched and we marched. Nobody marches like the Marines." She also said they ate things they never heard of before. They also took tests to help determine the type of technical training to take.

Her training started in celestial navigation, which was new in the Marine Corps. Ferne saw that some of her classmates had been teaching college math, and she felt in over her head.

Then she found out that four women a month were being sent for training at the Doall Trade School in Minneapolis. The training involved instruction in the operation and maintenance of contour machines which were used in cutting all kinds of materials. She convinced the lieutenant in charge of the celestial navigation program to allow her to opt out of the program. She then entered the program that allowed her to be sent to the Doall School. After completing the four-week course, she was assigned to the Marine Corps Air Station at El Centro, California, which is located about one hundred miles east of San Diego and about twelve miles north of the Mexican border.

While she was training at the Doall Trade School, she married George Krans. They met when she moved to Minneapolis from Minot and eventually became engaged. Then he entered the Navy and became a submarine sailor. When she completed her training in Minneapolis, she had a seven-day delayed traveling time between her training sight and assignment in El Centro. At about that time, George returned from the Pacific. They were married in just two days—after not seeing each other for two years. They had a one-week honeymoon and then he put her on a train to California. She said, "It was a wild week." He had a thirty-day leave, so he visited his parents in Crosby, a small town in north central Minnesota. He then had to report to New London, Connecticut, for his next assignment. Ferne estimated that they saw each other about twenty days during the first two years of their marriage; such was life during war.

El Centro, which she described as the third hottest place in the world, became her home for the next two years. When she arrived at the base in March of 1944, she found that the people already working there could do the job quicker and better than she. Then one day a captain came by and asked her if she had any work to do. When she answered that she did not have much, he took her across the street to a hanger that included a propeller repair shop and a battery shop. That shop had three big battery chargers, each of which could charge four airplane batteries. The captain told her that the sergeant who ran the shop was leaving and she was now going to be in charge. Ferne knew nothing about batteries, yet her official training consisted of being given a military manual on how to charge batteries. She read the manual, and then a sergeant came in and showed her how to hook up the batteries. That was the job she did for the rest of her military enlistment and earned the rank of corporal.

She mentioned that she got new clothes every month because when battery acid was spilled on cloth, it immediately ate a hole through the cloth. Of course, a Lady Marine could not wear clothes with holes in them. The Marines also ordered special shoes for her called "boon dockers" that would stand up to the acid. In an aside, she mentioned that getting new clothes meant she had to keep sewing stripes on her jackets. Finally, she started painting them on with red fingernail polish. This was not always well received by the men in the Corps, especially the older veterans.

Even though it was hot in El Centro, Ferne said she had a good time. The women were given liberty passes regularly, and they often went to Palm Springs for a weekend and rented a bungalow. They spent much of their time lounging by the swimming pool. They also had opportunities to go across the border to Mexicali and other nearby towns. This woman from farm country in North Dakota was introduced to Mexican food. Ferne was used to meat, potatoes, and cooked vegetables, but came to like the spicy food from south of the border. The Lady Marines even took a trip to Hollywood, and Ferne said she met seven movie stars.

She noted that service personnel ate very well when they were stationed at El Centro. The Imperial Valley was located nearby and was noted for its produce. They had cantaloupe, watermelon, and many other fresh fruits and vegetables.

When World War II ended, Ferne was mustered out fairly quickly, but did not really leave military life because her husband made the Navy his career for over twenty years. After the war, George was stationed at a base outside of San Francisco, and often was gone for weeks at a time. Then, once a year, each submarine was brought in for a complete overhaul that took about six weeks to complete. When that happened, Ferne stayed with George, and when he went back to sea, she returned to her parents home in North Dakota.

Within a few years, the family expanded by two—both boys. Ferne became a stay-at-home mom. Konrad was born first and then came Keith. Both are now in their fifties. Konrad is married and has two children, and Keith also is married.

Frequent moves is a fact of military life and certainly applied to the Krans family. After being based near San Francisco for a few years, George was transferred to the naval base at Honolulu. The island became their home for the next two years during the early 1950s. Ferne's boys started school near Honolulu. San Diego became the next assignment, and they stayed there for nine months before being transferred back to Hawaii. They were scheduled to stay in Hawaii for quite a while, but George put in for a new assignment. He applied to be a recruiter in Minnesota, and to their surprise, he got it very quickly. Ferne said, "So then we came back to Minnesota, which is why I'm still here."

When the Krans returned to Minnesota, they temporarily settled in St. Paul but could not find an apartment to accommodate a family of four. They decided to talk to George's brother, who was in real estate. He advised them to buy a house in one of the booming housing developments of the postwar period. He recommended an Orrin Thompson development that was being built in Coon Rapids, Minnesota. He said if they bought it and another transfer occurred down the road, they could sell it. Ferne and George borrowed $500 from her mother for the down payment and bought the house. The monthly payments were only eighty-six dollars a month, which was less than they were paying for rent in St. Paul.

While George continued working in the Navy, Ferne took a job in a Ben Franklin craft store and worked there for twenty-six years. This was a good match for her because it helped her stay in touch with her love of art.

From the time of her youth, Ferne had been involved in artistic work whether it involved batik, oil painting, acrylic painting, ceramics, or sewing. As a matter of fact, she developed her own little craft business on the side when the family lived in Hawaii. For years she created gifts to be sold in gift shops. She no longer does as much as she used to, but still stays at it.

Her husband developed a heart condition which caused him to retire from the Navy earlier than he intended. He died in 1980.

Though most of her hobby work centers around art, Ferne also likes to read. She said she reads anything. She also has a lot of love and respect for her sons. Both live in Minnesota. The oldest son is a craftsman who makes brass cannons. Her younger son works as a computer consultant and travels quite a bit.

Ferne is still quite an active person. Besides the hobbies already mentioned, she keeps busy doing a variety of things. She often goes to the local senior center and takes advantage of the many programs and excursions that are offered. Although she quit driving a few years ago, that did not stop her from getting around and being active in the community.

Lydia

Lydia's early years were marked by tragedy and change. Her parents were Ramón Flores and Mary Cintron. Both parents were born and raised in Puerto Rico. Ramón worked as a cook during this period. Mary died very young at the age of thirty- four, and Ramón remarried about three months after her death.

Lydia was born in Puerto Rico on September 14, 1933. When she was about one year old, a sister by the name of Socarro was born. Unfortunately, Socarro died at the age of one. Lydia had no memories of her sister because she was only two when her sister died.

Though Lydia was a young child during the 1930s and did not have many personal memories of the time, she did know that the Great Depression was hard on many Puerto Ricans. Many people were poor and did not get enough food to eat. As a result, sickness and death were common. It was her understanding that lack of food was a cause of her sister's death.

Lydia had some memories of her homes in Puerto Rico. They lived in a house with relatives for a time. She said it was a big house with a long porch on two sides. The house was located in the country and had a large sugarcane field that came close to the house. She also remembered a shallow stream that was only a short distance from the house.

The next home was built by her father and a neighbor. It was constructed of wood and had two bedrooms, a living room, a hall, a kitchen, and a small porch in front. Lydia said, "It was a very neat house with running water and electricity." Since Puerto Rico was warm all year, her family did not need a heating system in the house.

As she was growing up, Lydia enjoyed a variety of foods, especially different kinds of fruit. She enjoyed eating avocados and mangoes, and it was a treat having two big trees in the backyard that bore these fruits. Other fruit that was readily available and enjoyed were bananas, guana'banas hearts (a sweet fruit that is bigger than a grapefruit), and guavas. Rice, beans, potatoes, and cabbage were among the other foods she regularly ate.

Lydia enjoyed playing with friends who lived next door to her family. They played games such as hide and seek and volleyball and also enjoyed jumping rope. During quieter times, she enjoyed playing with her dolls and tea set.

Lydia went to public school through eighth grade in Puerto Rico. The school was over a mile from her house, and she remembered walking every day. There were two ways to get to school—walking along the roads or cutting through the sugarcane fields. She tried going through the sugarcane fields once, but it was scary and she did not try it again. English was taught at the school in Puerto Rico, and that is where Lydia learned to read and write the language. Her favorite subject in school was history.

When Lydia's mother died, her aunt promised to take care of her, but the aunt was not quite old enough, so Lydia went to live with another relative. However, when the aunt married, she came back for Lydia. Just after turning fifteen, Lydia went to live with the aunt in New York City.

The move meant that Lydia completed her high school education in New York. She attended a public high school from ninth through twelfth grade, and her favorite high school subject was science. She noted that the school in New York was quite a bit different from schools in Puerto Rico.

Some time later, her father and his new family also came to live in New York City. He worked as a cook when the family lived in Puerto Rico and continued in that line of work when his family moved with him to New York and later to Michigan.

Lydia learned to drive when she was seventeen years old and obtained her license when she was eighteen. However, she never really drove. At first she did not have enough money to buy a car, and later she was fearful because of the congestion in the New York metro area.

Upon reaching adulthood and becoming independent, she continued to live in New York City. At the age of twenty, she married her husband Felipe in 1954. While her husband spent his career working in factories, Lydia was a stay-at-home mom and spent time raising a large family of nine children. Her children are Ricardo, Estaban, Saul, Alex, Benjamin, Ortensia, Minerva, Natalie, and Francis. Lydia had many special memories during the time she was raising her children. Among those that stood out were the births of her children and the annual Christmas seasons.

During the 1960s, she had a serious health problem when she was diagnosed with stomach cancer. Luckily the doctors must have diagnosed it pretty early, for they did not have to operate. Instead she underwent radiation therapy which took care of the cancer, and she was been cancer-free since receiving the treatment.

With a large family, it was hard for Lydia to work full time. She said she tried to improve the economic situation of the family, but did not get a lot of help. Felipe worked, but he had a drinking problem. This meant quite a bit of money was spent on liquor, and he also took a lot of her attention. Finally, in 1978, she made the painful decision to get a divorce. At the time, her youngest child was about twelve years old.

In 1983, Lydia moved to Tucson, Arizona, to be near a daughter who lived there and also to get a change in her life. About a year later, a second daughter moved to Arizona. Lydia made Arizona home for about twenty years before moving to Minnesota. She mentioned that when she lived in Arizona she tried to get a job, but felt she did not get it because of her age. She knew she could handle the work when she applied, but then a man applied after her, and of course, he was bigger. The company ended up hiring the man.

The main reason for coming to Minnesota was the fact that her son, Benjamin, lived in the state. At the time of our interview she lived with a family in St. Paul and worked in the house to help them out.

At the time of the interview, her family was spread out over the United States. Besides the children living in Arizona and Minnesota, she had children in Michigan and Virginia. Her father was ninety-three years old and still lived with his second wife in Michigan. The family continued to grow over the years with the addition of more than eighteen grandchildren. Lydia was able to keep in touch with her children and visited the ones living out of state every once in a while.

Sewing was a hobby that she started in about 1996. However, poor vision caused her to give it up. Recently time has spent at the senior center attached to Our Lady of Guadeloupe Church in St. Paul. She goes to the center two times a week and takes part in many of the activities that are offered.

Lydia is not a rich person in terms of having a lot of money, but she has much more than monetary wealth. She has the wealth of family that she truly loves and she has the knowledge that she tried her best to do what was right for her family. This quiet woman is an easy person to respect.

Lydia is a very private person. She requested that her last name not be used and chose not to be photographed. The request was honored.

Luz Feliciano

Luz's parents were born and lived in Puerto Rico. The family was large, with five boys and six girls, and she described her family as being "poor." Neither parent had the opportunity to get an education. Luz was born in Puerto Rico on February 28, 1928. Her mother died when she was eleven, and this led to a big change in her life as will be noted later.

At first, her father worked on a military base, and later he worked as a farm laborer. Even though the family was poor, they always had enough to eat at their three daily meals. Luz liked most of the food she was given, but rice, beans, and potatoes were among her favorites. For meat, chicken and pork were eaten most often, but the family sometimes ate beef, too. Basically, she said she liked all Spanish food.

Luz went to school in Puerto Rico until her mother died. Since the family did not have a car, she had to walk to school every day. She did not really enjoy school and said, "I went to school to play." Her father took her out of school because he did not like the school curriculum. Besides the basic classes, she learned to sew and cook. These skills became important through most of the rest of her life.

About six months after her mother died, Luz went to New York with an older sister and her husband. At the age of eleven, she was working in a shop sewing dresses for eight dollars a week. From that amount, she gave three dollars to her sister, sent three dollars to her father, and kept two dollars for subway fare and lunches. Even though she was underage, she said she looked older than eleven, and that helped her get a job. She did her sewing in a large room with many other women and worked eight hour days. She did this work for ten years prior to marriage.

During those teenage years to young adulthood, there was not a great deal of time or money for recreation. However Luz often went to movies with her sister and brother-in-law. She also went to dances on Saturday nights.

When she was twenty-one years old, Luz married Faustino Rivera. During their marriage, he worked as a delivery man, and she continued sewing. They had two children, Sandra and Alberto. Faustino ended up leaving her after five years.

Luz took driving lessons during those early years in New York and earned her driver's license. She continued to drive until she developed heart trouble in the late 1990s.

In 1955, a serious accident occurred while Luz was doing a cleaning job. She was cleaning venetian blinds in an apartment when she lost her balance and fell five stories into the courtyard of the building. Though she was lucky to be alive, the injuries included a badly broken right arm, a broken vertebra, and a mouthful of broken teeth. She spent two and a half years in Bellevue Hospital undergoing reconstructive surgery, rehabilitation, and recovery. The labor union took care of her medical bills, and Leonardo Rodriguez came into her life and helped out. In one of the more important surgeries, doctors took bone from her hip and grafted it into her upper arm. That surgery allowed her to use the arm freely. She also had a stainless steel vertebra implanted into her back. She said she had to show a note explaining the vertebra when she went through airport checkpoints. She also noted with a smile that the doctors told her to have her hip checked every ten years to make sure it was strong, but she never did have it checked. She said she has completely healed from the injuries and did not feel any pain from the parts of her body that were injured.

After some time she started seeing Leonardo Rodriguez, and they were married in 1958. As mentioned, he helped her after her first marriage broke up and during her hospital stay. He did things like paying her rent so she could keep food on the table for her children. He worked as a track man for a railroad in New Jersey, and she went back to sewing for her occupation. They continued to live in New York City for most of the thirty-nine years they were married.

Sandra was four and Alberto was two when Luz married Leonardo. Alberto never saw his biological father because he and Luz were already separated when the child was born. As a matter of fact, Faustino denied paternity and never paid child support for Alberto. This, of course, placed greater economic stress on Luz. At any rate, Leonardo helped raise the two children, who considered him their father.

One day, while working in the rail yard, a rail hit Leonardo in the head, severely injuring him. He ended up receiving fifty-seven stitches to close the wound. He eventually made a settlement with the railroad company and received $50,000.

In 1989, they moved back to Puerto Rico, where they planned to retire. They lived in her hometown of Isabella, which was about three hours from his hometown of Bayamien. Instead of retiring, Leonardo spent most of his money to buy a grocery store. Unfortunately the store did not work out. Many of the people who shopped there pleaded that they were poor and asked for credit. Leonardo was too kindhearted to demand payment, and after two years he had run out of money. Then he developed brain cancer and died. Luz said that when he died, people still owed him over $5,000.

After the death of Leonardo, Luz married again. Her new husband was a blind man by the name of Juan Sebastian Acosta. They met and married while she was still living in Puerto Rico. Unfortunately, the marriage did not work out, and they were divorced after two years.

She came to Minnesota after the end of the marriage. The move to Minnesota was dictated by two things. First of all, she had developed heart trouble. She had heart surgery in Puerto Rico, but she needed further surgery that was not available there. Since her two children lived here, she came to Minnesota for the surgery—an angioplasty. At about the same time, doctors diagnosed lung cancer and removed part of her lung. Over the years, this strong woman had six major operations.

While her son and his family live in Minnesota, her daughter lives in New York with her family. Sandra has four children, all girls. She also lost a set of triplets at birth. Alberto and his wife have two children, a boy and a girl. Luz loves all of her wonderful grandchildren.

Luz moved to Minnesota in 1999, and she lives by herself in a senior apartment building in St. Paul. Her favorite hobby is crocheting. She started doing this craft while recovering from the fall she took from the window. On the day of the interview, she wore a beautiful lacy blouse that she had crocheted. She crocheted a variety of things over the years, including tablecloths and bedspreads. Other hobbies include embroidery, sewing dresses for little girls , and watching television.

Kimi Hara

This story starts in Iwate, a prefecture (a territory like a province) on the Island of Honshu in Japan. It was the home region for Kimi's parents, Seiki Taguchi and Matsuye Sato. Her mother, Matsuye, came from the village of Mizusawa, and her father, Seiki, was from the nearby village of Kanezawa. Her parents went to the same schools but did not know each other well because her father was eight or nine years older than her mother.

Seiki came from a family of eight children. The family's business was mainly rice farming as they had several large rice fields that they tended. His parents also raised a breed of horse that was specially trained for civic or governmental duties such as mounts for government guards and parade horses.

The horses were white in color and large in stature, similar to Clydesdales.

Matsuye's family was smaller; she had two brothers and a sister (who died from tuberculosis after reaching adulthood and moving away). Her older brother, Shizu, was director of trains and transportation for the Northern Railway. Her other brother, Shigeo, was an engineer whose life ended prematurely from a train accident. Both brothers were experts at Judo. Shizu was a grade seven black belt and Shigeo reached grade five black belt.

The marriage between Seiki and Matsuye was planned while they were still pretty young and living in Japan. Seiki left Japan in 1905 when he was eighteen years old. He arrived in San Francisco and settled in Seattle, not knowing any English. During those early times, he was able to survive by picking up odd jobs such as picking fruit and working in saw mills. Luckily, he and other immigrant men from Japan were able to find living quarters together where they could pool their resources for daily living and could individually save money. Kimi described her father's existence at the time by saying, "It was a hard, honest living." She could have added that the work was dangerous. She noted that her father cut off his big toe when he was working at a sawmill. Kimi did not remember the details of the accident, but noted that in later years, she and her brothers were fascinated by the incident leading to the missing toe. A brother was even worried Seiki would stumble because he lacked the support of the toe. Seiki further helped himself by taking advantage of an early opportunity to learn English.

Matsuye immigrated to the United States in 1912 with Seattle as her destination. She stayed at the immigration compound for five days from the time of her arrival. She eventually met up with Seiki and they were married in 1912.

In 1913, the Asian Land Act was passed in which Asian immigrants were allowed to go into wooded lands and other areas, cut the trees, and farm the land. The people did not have to pay rent, but they were not allowed to buy the land because they were not citizens. Second generation Asian Americans were eventually able to buy land upon reaching the age of maturity, along with the help of an attorney. This law directly affected the Taguchi family as they attempted to create a livelihood. It should be noted that this law was commonly referred to as the Anti-Asian Land Act because it targeted Chinese and Japanese immigrants. Repeal did not occur until the 1950s.

Seiki and Matsuye settled in the community of Green Lake, located north of Seattle. They found the soil to be fertile and created truck gardens. The gardens were surrounded by water-filled ditches or moats, and water was drawn from the ditches to be used on the plants. Some of the people also had greenhouses on the land. Kimi recalled that most of the field work, such as plowing, relied on horse power. Tractors were not used in the area at that time. She also emphasized how the mostly Japanese community worked together. The neighbors helped each other with plowing and other heavy or time-consuming farm work. The produce was taken to market on the waterfront in Seattle.

Seiki had actually started his truck garden and built his house before Matsuye had arrived in the United States, and they were married soon after she arrived in 1912. Kimi described the houses in the community as "crude." She said they had to dig wells, pump the water, and bring it inside when needed. They did not have indoor plumbing, and heat came from the cook stove in the kitchen and a pot bellied stove in the parlor. It had a Japanese bathhouse attached to the main house and also had a barn for their horses. The bathhouse was heated by wood and had to be stoked every day.

The family began to grow with the birth of Kimi on November 26, 1915. She was followed by brothers Sam on January 22, 1918, Susumu on July 12, 1921, Takeshi on March 27, 1924, and sister Reiko on December 17, 1926.

Kimi's early education took place in Green Lake. She attended a public school that went through grade eight. Her memories included a daily two-mile walk to school through and around neighboring farm fields. She seemed to feel that the school was pretty good. The same teachers seemed to come back each year, creating a sense of continuity. She also noted that there was a teacher for each grade, and all the students seemed to do well. On Saturdays the Japanese students went to the community hall in Green Lake to attend Japanese school. The school was set up mainly to teach children the Japanese language.

When Kimi was about fifteen years old, she learned to drive. Her earliest driving experiences came at the wheel of the family Ford panel truck. She remembered, with a smile, that the truck had a crank start. She also remembered not needing a driver's license in those days. At any rate, it was the start of a long driving career that ended in 2001.

Meanwhile, her father decided to branch out into his own business. In the late 1920s, he and two other men started a wholesale produce market on the Seattle waterfront. One day he was going on a trip to eastern Washington to pick up an order of produce for his market when he suffered a stroke. He was taken to a hospital, a brain tumor was discovered, and he had surgery for the tumor. He never recovered and died on October 31, 1930, at the age of forty-one.

Kimi's mother moved the family to Seattle, which meant giving up the land in Green Lake. Since they did not own the land, they just left it and another family moved in. There were no transactions, and no money was exchanged.

After Seiki died, Matsuye took his place in the wholesale market. She also ran a greenhouse that had been defunct and worked in the greenhouses of others. In spite of some efforts to arrange a new relationship, she never remarried.

Kimi was a freshman in high school when her father died and completed her education at Roosevelt High School in Seattle. During this time, she lived with a Caucasian family and took care of their children. Chores included making breakfast for the children and babysitting, for which she was paid two dollars a week. The pay took care of allowance money for Kimi and two brothers, so it was a help to the Taguchi family. The home was across the street from the high school that was very convenient for her. Kimi was able to return home on the weekends. She concluded her recollection of the experience by saying, "I learned a lot."

Kimi remembered her high school years as a pleasant time. She did not remember Asian American students having any trouble with the white students in the school. She noted that older students were protective of younger students, which made for a nicer environment; most of the students got along really well. Graduation came for Kimi in February of 1933.

The next couple of years were spent doing a variety of things. Kimi and two of her brothers went to Puyallup to pick berries for three summers. They lived in a cabin and brought their own cooking equipment and bedding. The experience was helpful to Kimi for getting money to go on to college, and it helped her mother out. Other jobs from the spring of 1933 to the fall of 1935 included working part-time in the wholesale produce market and working in the home of a doctor's family.

In the fall of 1935, she was off to the University of Washington and enrolled in the nursing program. The program included four quarters at the University of Washington and three years at Swedish Hospital and School of Nursing. She completed her schooling at Swedish, took the licensing exam, and became a registered nurse in October of 1940.

Kimi took a job as an operating room nurse at a local hospital and worked at that until after the attack on Pearl Harbor. She also volunteered to go to area hospitals where first generation Japanese immigrants were patients. Since they did not speak English, she translated for them to help them understand and get adjusted to the medical treatment they were receiving.

Not long after entry into World War II, life in the United States changed radically for Japanese Americans living on the west coast. President Franklin Roosevelt issued Executive

Order 9066 on February 19, 1942. Over 100,000 Japanese Americans were forced from their homes and businesses and were sent to War Relocation Camps (internment camps) in the interior of the United States. Executive Order 9066 was essentially a response to the hysteria and racial prejudice sweeping the country after Pearl Harbor, and it took away the freedom and property of many thousands of innocent people. A provision related to the executive order was made about a week later that said that professional job positions would be made available in the Midwest. The War Relocation Authority would permit Japanese Americans from the west coast to move for the purpose of filling these positions.

The Taguchi family was scheduled to be moved to Idaho for internment, so Kimi's mother encouraged her to look for job opportunities in the Midwest. Under the terms of the executive order, each person going to an internment camp was allowed to bring only what would fit into two suitcases. The camps were all located in isolated areas, and the people were not allowed out. That meant Kimi was the only one left in the family who could earn money and help the family.

With the help of the chief of staff at Swedish Hospital in Seattle, Kimi was able to get a nursing job at St. Mary's Hospital in Rochester, Minnesota, arriving on March 24, 1942. She said the hospital was good because, when it started a cadet nursing program, it took in a lot of Japanese Americans, especially from California. Because so many nurses were going into the war, there was a shortage of nurses on the home front. The cadet program was a government funded program to train nurses to fill the openings created by the war. The nuns at St. Mary's were very grateful to have the cadet program, because it helped fill a shortage caused by nurses and doctors entering the military during the war.

Kimi had to be coerced into taking the position of obstetrics supervisor at St. Mary's, a position that required orienting and teaching new student nurses. She did not want to take the position because she felt she lacked the experience, and she felt she should not take a position without proper training and orientation. Kimi took the position because she realized that they all had to take responsibility. Still, it was contrary to what she learned, which made her reluctant.

She expressed some bitterness toward her circumstances. Hours at the hospital were long and hard, and the pay was low. Even if Kimi would have had the money, she was not allowed to visit her family in the internment camp. On the plus side, Japanese American dietitians, nurses, and a doctor came from the west coast; they were able to create a community, providing support to one another that probably took away some of the loneliness.

Looking back, Kimi felt that there were some positives to her experience in Rochester. She felt the nuns were very bright and the administrator was fantastic. In addition, her mother was able to come to Minnesota with her daughter Reiko after spending about a year in the internment camp. Two of Matsuye's sons were drafted, so the government allowed her to locate with her working daughter, Kimi. Overall, the experience at St. Mary's was hard but positive. However, circumstances dictated that she move to Chicago after a while.

Life was different for the rest of the family. Her brother Sam lived in Alaska, and he was given the job of herding the Japanese Americans from southeast Alaska onto ships for Washington and then for dispersal to internment camps. As that job came to an end, he too was sent to an internment camp. It turned out to be the same one his mother, brothers, and sister were sent to in Idaho. He had contracted hepatitis while working in a cannery at age fourteen, and the ailment kept him out of the military.

Two of her brothers were drafted into the army from the internment camp. Susumu was stationed at Camp Shelby in Mississippi with Kimi's future husband, Sam Hara. Susumu was later stationed at Fort Snelling, and he and Sam ended up in the 442 Regiment which became the most decorated combat unit for its size for the time it was assigned to the European theater. Kimi's other brother, Takeshi, was stationed at the Great Lakes Naval Station near Chicago. Her mother wanted to be near him, so Kimi decided to transfer to Wesley Memorial Hospital in Chicago and took her mother along with to the Windy City. Kimi worked there for nine months. Meanwhile, Reiko stayed in Rochester and lived in a doctor's home so she could finish high school.

While talking about Takeshi, Kimi mentioned that in 1945 he was sent to the language school at Fort Snelling, even though he did not know much Japanese. He was later assigned to the Pacific with the army air corps , and with the end of the war, stayed for the occupation of Japan. It was interesting because he was a very good baseball player and spent his time in Japan playing exhibition games against other American military teams and some Japanese teams.

In an aside, Kimi added an anecdote about Sam's military career that she thought was unfair. Sam had enlisted in the army in 1940 for what was supposed to fulfill his military obligation. It was a program that applied to those at least thirty years of age. As luck would have it, the attack on Pearl Harbor occurred two months after his discharge, and he was called back into the service right away. Before being sent to Camp Shelby and then being sent overseas, he was with the quartermaster depot at Fort Snelling. He was finally discharged on V-J Day at the age of thirty-five, after being wounded in battle.

Speaking more about Sam, she said that her family had known the Hara family for a long time. Sam's father came from the same part of Honshu as Kimi's parents. The elder Hara became a Baptist minister who ministered to the farm families in the Green Lake area and arranged for mission workers to help them adapt to American culture. His influence led Seiko and Matsuye to convert to Christianity in 1925.

Sam Hara was about eight years older than Kimi, so she did not know him well during her teen years. He graduated from West Seattle High School in 1929 and completed training in mechanics in Seattle before trying to get a job during the

Depression. Later, when he was in the army and assigned to Fort Snelling, he and a bunch of friends used to go down to Rochester. It was during that period that Kimi was able to become better acquainted with him. Kimi and Sam were married in April 1945 during the time Sam was going through rehabilitation from his war wound.

After Chicago, Kimi returned to Minnesota and took a job at Fort Snelling Army Hospital. At first, her job involved taking care of Nisei student soldiers who were taking courses in the Japanese language at the Military Intelligence Service Language School in Shakopee. When asked why she came back to Minnesota, she said she liked the state and worked with a group that started new procedures that were needed.

She worked at Fort Snelling Hospital into 1946. After marrying Sam, she had to keep things together while Sam returned to Percy Jones Hospital in Battle Creek, Michigan, to complete his rehabilitation. In 1946, her son Tom was born, and she opened an emergency maternal infant care section at the hospital. The department was set up to help the wives of enlisted men who could not get regular hospital maternity care. Soon they were treating forty to fifty infants a month. It was hard but enjoyable work that built upon her previous maternity experiences in Seattle and Chicago.

The hospital closed in 1946, but Kimi was to continue her work. She said, "I worked at Ripley Memorial Maternity Hospital in Minneapolis for five or six years." During that time she supervised and taught obstetric nurses from several different hospitals. In 1949, while working at Ripley Memorial, Kimi developed tuberculosis, which caused the loss of a lung and required twenty months to recover. She was grateful that her mother was living with them because she was able to keep the household going during Kimi's recovery.

Home life was very stable for the Hara family. Their first permanent residence was in north Minneapolis on Glenwood and Morgan Avenues. At first they did not own a car and relied on the streetcar for transportation. Kimi described the house as "a great place," and the family lived there for eighteen years. During that time, son Tom completed his high school education, graduating from North High School in 1964. He went on to graduate from Johns Hopkins University and earned a law degree from the University of Minnesota. Today, Tom is a successful local attorney.

The Haras moved to a home on Lake Independence which Kimi described as "a beautiful place with 100 feet of lake shore." This was home to Kimi until 1996, when she decided it was just too much for her to care for. By that time, she had hip and knee replacements and could no longer do the yard work required on a big place. It was interesting to note that she continued to live there thirteen years after the death of her husband in 1983.

Sam Hara had been a diesel mechanic for White Trucks for thirty-five years. Being a mechanic was a job he loved, and he continued at it until retiring at age seventy. She noted that he hardly ever got sick and quoted him as saying that he only took sick leave when Kimi had surgery. One day, he did a great deal of yard work in preparation for a visit from his brother. After watching television that night, he suffered a massive heart attack and died.

She moved from Lake Independence to Maple Grove and lived with her son's family for about three or four years. Then she moved into a senior high rise apartment in Brooklyn Center where she has lived since.

In terms of her career, this energetic woman continued her education and volunteerism. She earned a bachelors degree in nursing in 1954 and masters degree in 1957 from the University of Minnesota. She also became a nurse supervisor and a nursing instructor at Fairview Hospital from 1951 to 1957. Her work at Fairview's School of Nursing was part of a program run in conjunction with St. Olaf College in Northfield. During this time, she also was president of the Third District Minnesota Nurses Association (a unit of the American Nurses Association), and Governor Orville Freeman appointed her to the Minnesota Board of Nursing. She later became a staff member of the Minnesota Board of Nursing, including Associate Executive Secretary, until her retirement in December of 1980. From 1957 to 1970, she was Maternal and Child Health Consultant to the Minnesota Department of Health. In her position, she set up prenatal courses throughout Minnesota. That is not all, as she was chosen to serve on a national committee sponsored by the National League of Nursing. The committee was given the task of designing a standardized licensing examination which is still used throughout the country.

Kimi even branched out to help law enforcement organizations. She taught highway patrol cadets what to do in emergency childbirth situations. Then she did police training in different areas under the auspices of the crime bureau. She put this work in context by saying, "It was only on Saturdays, so it did not interfere with other work." Yet this is something she did for twenty years!

In 1970, she took a leave from the Minnesota Board of Nursing to work for the World Health Organization. For eight months, she worked for WHO to inspect nursing programs and schools in Okinawa before the island was to be returned to the control of Japan. The work included making recommendations about how to use the facilities and faculties, and planning curriculum so it fit the laws of Japan. The process included flying to Tokyo for a three day stopover, then going to Manila for a three week orientation, followed by the work in Okinawa, and finally debriefing back in Manila. The work period included several trips to Tokyo to learn about the baccalaureate programs for nurses and to make sure the programs and their recommendations meshed.

Besides everything she did in the area of nursing, Kimi was greatly involved in various Japanese American Organizations. In 1947 she was a founding member of the Twin Cities Chapter of the Japanese American Citizens League. She helped run two-week summer programs for nursing students who came over from Japanese universities. The purpose of the program was to help the students learn current trends in patient care. Kimi gave a lot of credit to the University of Minnesota and Hennepin County for their cooperation in helping to make the program successful.

In 1972, Kimi helped start the Japan America Society of Minnesota (JASM). According to *Asian Pages*, the monthly publication of the society, the purpose of the organization is to "bring the people of Japan and the United States closer together in mutual understanding, respect, and cooperation" (November 15-30, 2003, Vol. 14, No. 6). Her work with JASM included a term as president in 1981-1982. In 2003, Kimi held the position of Emeritus Director of JASM.

In 1976, she was involved in the founding of the Normandale Japanese Garden. Just as she was still involved in the JACL, JASM and other organizations, Kimi was involved in the garden through activities such as fundraising.

Besides the work mentioned for WHO, Kimi has led five groups to Asia. On two of the occasions, she led a delegation of nurses to International Congress of Nurses Conventions. These trips took her to Japan, Singapore, China, Israel, Egypt, and Italy. She also took several trips within the United States as a member of the Minnesota Board of Nursing.

On a more personal level, she had a variety of collections. She had a beautiful collection of Japanese Imari (hand painted porcelain) dishes. There was a collection of sterling demitasse spoons that she said numbered about 300. She also had a number of Bing and Grondahl and Royal Copenhagen Christmas plates. Although she did not have room in her apartment to keep all of these collections, she did have an impressive array of Oriental art on her walls and a beautiful wooden sculpture in her dining room.

Kimi was obviously proud of her family members. In 2003, two brothers and a sister were still living, and her sister lived in the Twin Cities area. She was also very proud of her son and his family. It appeared to be a family that really stuck together.

This energetic woman had accomplished much in her life and had obviously experienced many high points to balance the lows. One of the high points occurred on November 6, 2003, when she received the Japan America Society of Minnesota Mondale award for her contributions to the Japan-America partnership over the years. It was very fitting.

Ernest (Ernie) Abraham

Ernie's father, Edward Gust Abraham, was born in Minneapolis on October 27, 1887. Edward's father, Herman, was born in Berlin, Germany. He married Pauline Pizorski who was also born and raised in Germany. The couple eventually immigrated to the United States and settled in Minneapolis.

Ernie's mother, Artemise Paradise, was born in Frenchville, Maine on April 1, 1888. She was the daughter of Severe Paradise and Leoni Soucy Paradise. Severe was born and raised in Canada, and Leoni was born in Paris, France. Leoni's family migrated to Nova Scotia, Canada, and then to Maine. Severe worked as a lumberjack near the border of Maine. Severe and Leoni were married in Maine and later moved to Minneapolis.

Edward and Artemise met and were married in Minneapolis in July 1913. Edward's side of the family was Lutheran, but he converted to Roman Catholicism before marrying Artemise. Edward worked as a cabinet maker and operated a "trim saw" to cut the wood to the final dimensions. He worked for a company that made cabinets and countertops for stores such as Dayton's and Donaldson's. Edward loved working with wood and was very good at it. On his own time he made tables, cabinets, other pieces of furniture, toolboxes, and many other fixtures made of wood. Some of the items, such as card tables, even included inlaid wood that he cut out with a knife.

Ernie remembered his mother as a very good cook. He thought she made delicious soups. Many days, Ernie came home from school and smelled the fresh bread or biscuits baking in the oven. He loved having a couple of warm slices of bread. His mother also made very good coffee cake, which was a real treat for the children.

The young couple settled on Fourth Street near Ninth Avenue in Northeast Minneapolis. Sheridan School was nearby, as well as O'Connell's Grocery Store on the corner of Fourth Street and Ninth Avenue. The Abrahams were living in that house when Ernest was born on April 27, 1914. The family grew with the birth of Pearl in December 1917, Jeannette in September 1922, and Yvonne in August 1924.

Ernie did not remember a lot about the house, but thought it was modern for the times. He said, "It had an inside toilet, cold water to the kitchen sink, and was heated by a coal stove heater." He added that a combination gas and wood burning stove heated the kitchen.

The year 1914 marked the beginning of World War I. As the war continued and United States involvement became apparent, Edward was at an age to be drafted. However, a teenage accident resulted in his rejection. He was a hunter as a teen, and one year he accidentally shot off the index finger of his right hand while duck hunting. He had been rowing a boat and grabbed his shotgun by the barrel when he spotted some ducks. Unfortunately, the trigger caught on the boat seat and the gun discharged. Many firearms did not have trigger guards in those days.

When Ernie was young, street venders came by the house to sell their wares. The milkman delivered milk to the back door early every morning. Then he came by once a week to collect on the bill. In the winter, the milk froze and pushed a column of cream up, and the kids in the family loved to eat the cream like it was ice cream.

In those days, many families, including the Abrahams, had an icebox to keep food cold during the warm months. The ice man came by twice a week to deliver ice for the ice box. Other venders who came by regularly included those who sold fruit, fish, and meat. All used horse drawn carts or wagons. Junk dealers often came by with their horse drawn wagons to buy paper or other odds and ends. Some, like the meat venders, no longer sold their goods this way by the time Ernie was about five years old.

During those early years of his life, most transportation was powered by horses; even the fire wagons and streetcars were pulled by horses. Plowing snow in the winter was done by horse-drawn plows. The main streets were paved with tar blocks or bricks, and side streets were dirt that was oiled. For people who did not have a new fangled car or a horse and buggy, feet provided the form of transportation. Most family business was done within a few blocks of home. Nearby Thirteenth Avenue Northeast was where the Abrahams did most of their shopping.

When Ernie was about four, the family moved a few blocks to Fifth Street and Twelfth Avenue Northeast. It was a small house with many of the same types of amenities as the previous house. It had cold water to the kitchen sink and bathroom, was heated by a stove, and had gas lights. Baths were taken in a round zinc washtub which was brought into the kitchen. Water had to be heated on the kitchen stove and then poured into the tub. The kids, starting with the youngest, took their baths in the same water.

There were neighborhood friends to play with during those early years, and a lot of time was spent playing in someone's yard or out on the street. Among the games he remembered playing in those early years were tag, hopscotch, kick the can, and marbles. They also enjoyed flying homemade kites and spinning tops. But going to the movies was a real treat. Ernie remembered his parents taking him to the old Main Street Theater to see silent movies. A piano player played music to the movie as the words and pictures flickered on the screen. A favorite actor was William S. Hart, who was considered an action hero. According to Ernie, admission was only five cents in those days, and the action was exciting.

When the Main Street Theater closed, the family started going to the Princess Theater on East Hennepin Avenue. Sunday matinees were choice times for the family. After the movie, the Abrahams would go to the ice cream parlor next to the theater for ice cream sundaes. Ernie said, "Those were days that I enjoyed!"

As gas and electricity became more readily available for transportation, cars became more popular. But many people still relied on electric powered streetcars to get places. Ernie remembered streetcar fare as being five cents, which included free transfers to other cars.

In the early 1920s, the family moved across the street from their second house. Edward and Artemise always rented homes where the family lived. This arrangement necessitated moves more often than if they bought their own home. If the landlord wanted to rent or sell to a relative, the Abrahams had to move. However, the family was poor, and they did what they could afford. At any rate, this was the first house that had both cold and hot water. Not long after they moved in, it was wired for electricity.

Christmases were very special during those early years. Every year, Edward walked to the tree market and brought home a tree. Ernie was able to accompany his father when he was older. The tree was put up and decorated on Christmas

Eve and the presents were put around the tree. Since their early houses did not have electricity, the tree was illuminated by candles during those years. The candles were lit for about an hour on Christmas and then only when guests came over during the season.

As Ernie got older, the types of toys and games changed. He remembered making sling shots with his friends. The key parts were a forked tree branch, a piece of an old leather glove, and a strip of rubber cut from an old inner tube. If he ever got an extra nickel, he bought a metal tube called a bean shooter and shot peas or navy beans through it. This was also about the time that Ernie developed interest in sports such as baseball and football. He was able to take in several minor league baseball games as a member of the "Knothole Gang," which was sponsored by the YMCA.

Ice skating became a favorite winter past time. Ernie learned to skate when he was about seven years old and continued to skate for several winters on the rinks in the public parks near their neighborhood. Building snow forts after heavy snows and sledding were other favorite winter activities.

When Ernie was six or seven, the family took its first vacation to a lake. The destination was Lake George near St. Francis in Anoka County. Since Edward did not have a car, the family rode up with an uncle. The resort included a dance hall and a merry-go-round which Ernie enjoyed. The family fished for pan fish and bass, and fishing became a lifelong passion for him. Ernie said, "I could fish every day and never get tired of it."

Lake fishing did not occur very often, but Ernie and his father did fish along the Mississippi River quite often. One thing they did was fish for bait. His father took a long pole with old fish line and tied a piece of liver to the line. Then he put the liver in the water, and in time, pulled it up with several crayfish attached. When they caught enough crayfish, they would use them for bait.

In 1924 the family got its first radio, a crystal set. Ed and his brother Ted made the set by winding a wire around an old oatmeal box which they attached to a platform. Then they attached what they called a "tickler" to pick up the radio waves. Earphones were required to hear the signal. Sometime later, his father made another crystal set that had two sets of earphones.

The family moved to another house in 1924, this one owned by his grandmother Paradise. This two-story house was located on Sixth Street Northeast. Both floors of the house had the same layout. An unheated porch ran across the back of both floors. The kitchen was in the back with a small pantry off one side which included the cooking stove. The downstairs also included a bathroom, bedroom and living room. A porch ran across the front of the house and wrapped around one side. Though the upstairs was laid out the same, it did not include a stove in the pantry area and the grandmother and children slept upstairs. The house included indoor plumbing and electricity from the time the Abraham family moved in. This was home to Ernie until he married.

Pets became a fixture in the family from the 1920s. The first cat he remembered was a white cat given to him by a friend. This cat ended up having several litters, and the family kept one of the kittens. Ernie noted that the cats loved to play and that play led to a near catastrophe. One Christmas season, the cats were chasing each other around the house when one chased the other up the Christmas tree! Their weight knocked the tree over and several ornaments were broken. Needless to say, Artemise was not very happy. She kicked both cats out of the house and would not let them in for two days.

On another occasion, the white cat was in heat and was attracting several toms. Ernie's mother picked up a piece of coal and threw it toward the tom cats. However, the coal struck the white cat instead—knocking her out! Ernie was devastated thinking the cat was dead, but it came around and turned out to be fine.

Ernie had many other pets during his years growing up. Among those pets were a rooster, rabbits, white rats, pigeons, and a dog or two. As a young boy, he had a dog named Puff, an eighty-pound Chesapeake Bay retriever who loved to go wherever Ernie went, which was okay most of the time. However, Puff was a pain when it was time to go fishing. The problem was that the dog loved to play in the water, which made fishing impossible. Ernie and his father even locked him on their porch when they went, but when Artemise let him out, he made a beeline to the river and ended their fishing.

Ernie had two experiences raising pigeons. The first occurred when he was about nine years old, when a neighbor gave him a pair of pigeons. His father built him a coop, which was later enlarged. Eventually, Edward and his brother Harold decided to go into the squab business and converted the garage into a large coop with an outside fly pen. Soon they began selling to local meat markets. Unfortunately, they were robbed on two occasions and finally gave up.

When the Great Depression hit, the pigeon coop was converted to rabbit hutches and the family started raising rabbits for food. They lived off rabbit meat for a year and a half.

Public parks were very important to the neighborhoods in the 1920s and 1930s. Ernie's father often took him to a nearby park to watch amateur baseball games in the summer, football games in the fall, and hockey games in the winter. The family also attended concerts at city parks on summer evenings. Ernie also took part in park board sports during his early teens. He most enjoyed football, baseball, and hockey.

Ernie attended parochial schools throughout his education. He went to Notre Dame School first. The school no longer exists and the church it was associated with is now called Our Lady of Lourdes. After graduating from eighth grade in June of 1929, he went on to De La Salle High School that fall. He walked to school every day and in all types of weather.

While in high school, he was expected to do daily chores. After school in the winter, his jobs included bringing wood and coal in from a shed in the yard and taking out the ashes from the heating stove. He also did much of the grocery shopping for his mother. This meant regular trips to the grocery and butcher shop to pick up items that his mother needed. Remember, an icebox was not reliable for keeping food fresh for more than a couple of days. When he had rabbits and pigeons, he had to go out to give them food and water. After dinner, it was time to do homework.

The Great Depression was especially hard on this family of six. His father was often laid off for long periods throughout the Depression. He ended up doing work for the WPA in order to get food vouchers. Besides being laid off because of lack of work, Edward missed time because of injuries, and in those days, people did not get paid for sick time or days off for injuries. The Depression years meant they relied mainly on the foods they grew and raised.

During this period of time, Ernie helped the family out by working part-time jobs. He remembered salvaging bricks for his friend's father, working in a greenhouse, selling Sunday papers on the street, and even doing heavy housework for relatives. Most of the money he made went to his parents. Ernie said, "When times were tough, you did what you had to do."

One of the recreational activities he did as a teenager was roller skating. On a Sunday afternoon, he and his friends hopped aboard a streetcar and headed for the roller rink in the Minneapolis suburb of Robbinsdale. The streetcar cost five cents each way and admission to the roller rink was ten cents. With skate rental being another ten cents, they could spend several hours having fun and exercise for thirty cents. He said, "That was a lot of money for us in those days, but it was better than roaming around the streets getting into trouble."

Ernie's second effort at raising pigeons turned into a passion that lasted for several years. In the summer of 1931, a plumber by the name of Cliff Lundblad was working on a new house near the Abraham's. He was a member of the Twin Cities Racing Union Flying Club. One day, he noticed the pigeon coop and fly pen the Abrahams had built for the squabs and invited Edward and Ernie to his house to watch his pigeons return from a race. Ernie was so fascinated by the sport of pigeon racing that he urged his father to get them involved, and Edward agreed. He went about the process of remodeling the rabbit house (the old pigeon coop) into a loft for racing pigeons. Cliff Lundblad then gave them six pigeons to start their operation. He also purchased two more pigeons from racers in St. Paul and gave them to the Abraham's to get the operation started.

The pigeon loft was ten feet by twelve feet and had two levels. The bottom level was for breeding, and the top was for the flying birds. The older birds occupied one half and the younger birds took the other half. They also had bobs or traps attached as places for the birds to land when they came in from a race.

Race stations, where the birds were released, were as close as Owatonna and Albert Lea, Minnesota, and as far away as Topeka, Kansas, and Medford, Oklahoma. In those days, the birds were crated and sent to the release point by train. The day of release depended on the distance of the race. Winners were decided by what was called flying time. The miles were broken down into one sixtieths, and the hours of flying time were broken down into seconds. The flying time was then divided into the distance to determine the flying speed which determined the winners. The first four places from the club received diplomas and prize money. The rest received nothing. Younger birds generally flew the shorter races of seventy-five miles up to 200 miles, while the older birds usually flew races of 300 to 500 miles.

Ernie raised, trained, and raced birds. Because he did not have much money, he had to figure out creative ways to get the proper food for his birds. Feed varied according to the time of year and the stage of the bird—chick, brooding, training, or racing. Of course, fresh water had to be kept on hand at all times.

Early efforts were not encouraging. First, not all the pairs produced broods. Then they lost two birds during the training, and later they lost a bird in their first race. Apparently the bird was attacked by a hawk and severely injured. A farmer found the bird and nursed it back to health. At any rate, the bird returned to the Abraham loft about two months later. It was too damaged to do any more racing, but the bird was kept as a breeder as a reward for its toughness. Later another bird, a hen, was entered in a 200-mile race. She made it home on the same day she was released, but she was a mess. She had two broken legs, all the feathers were off her breast, and her keel was cracked. That bird did not survive.

Most of his birds were identified by the number on the leg band, but every once in a while, a bird with special character earned a name. One memorable bird was Number 149—Ernie and his father called him the Big Train. The name came from his appearance as he powered his big body in a straight line as he flew. The bird did nothing as a yearling. He seemed lazy and never did well in the races. When the Big Train was a two year old, Ernie discovered that he did not like it when other cocks were put into the nesting cage with his hen. That discovery gave Ernie an idea for the next race. Just before crating the Big Train for his next race, a 400 miler, Ernie let him see another cock in the nesting cage with the hen mated to the Big Train. Then the bird was sent to the release point. That bird came back like a house on fire and won the race. Even though they had other successful birds over the years, the Big Train held a special place in Ernie's heart.

Eventually, Ernie started reading a great deal about pigeons and breeding. He learned what to look for in a good pigeon, and he learned how to mate birds that would create the best chances for producing successful offspring. He also gained quite a bit of knowledge regarding training, such as when to start and how to train the birds. These bits of knowledge allowed him to have more success as the years went on.

Even in the 1930s, a top notch bird sold for $1,000 or more. Such prices were way beyond the means of Ernie. As a result, he had to rely heavily on being able to find "bargains'" to add to his stock. To pay twenty dollars for a pair of racing pigeons was a steep price for him. He also needed a keen eye in determining which birds to pair up for mating.

Keeping a loft meant a lot of work. There was not only the daily feeding and watering, but the coop had to be cleaned once or twice a week. The challenges became greater and greater as time went by. Ernie married, had a child, and had a full time job. He no longer lived with his parents, so getting to the loft every day was no longer possible. In addition, his father was getting near retirement age and the costs of pigeon racing were going up. As a result, Ernie and Edward decided to give up racing pigeons in 1942.

Singing was another hobby of Ernie's during his late teens and early twenties. He regularly sang as a member of the choir at Our Lady of Lourdes Church. He also did a little bit of singing with a band led by a friend, Chester Dombrowski.

In September of 1933 he started work for Scott-Atwater Manufacturing Company. At the time, the company made items like plated bowls and trays that General Mills gave away for premiums. Ernie started out as a packer in what was his first fulltime job. However, it was during the depths of the Depression, and for the first few years he was laid off for about four months a year. During those idle periods he worked at whatever jobs he could find. He did some work in construction which included being a hod carrier and cement mixer. He also worked as a stock boy for Dayton's, and later worked heat-treating and painting springs for a company that made furniture springs. Occasionally, he worked for the H. J. Nelson Store and Fixture Manufacturing, which was the same company that employed his father. He worked as a yardman and as a glue man in which he helped glue wooden sections of cabinets together.

Workdays were long and hard during the 1930s, and pay was low. Ernie earned twenty-five cents per hour at Scott-Atwater, and overtime pay was the same as the hourly wage. An example of overtime went something like this: Ernie started his day at 7:00 AM on Friday morning and worked until noon on Saturday with only two lunch breaks during that time.

1933 was also about the time Ernie learned to dance. The young men went to the Northeast Neighborhood House and took dance lessons on Friday evenings. The neighborhood house would then have dances on Saturdays. Since all of this was free, it was hard to pass up. Since he did not have a car, he relied on his friend Audie Emmond who worked for a mortician and was able to borrow the mortician's Cadillac. However, they had to wash it in return for using it.

In May of 1936, he met Dorothy Wyszynski at a dance in the neighborhood. He danced with her a few times that evening, and that was the beginning of their romance. They dated about once a week, usually on Sunday afternoons or evenings.

In the summer, many of the dates were group picnics or evening river cruises. Dances were common dates during the winter months. Ernie called it "the best time of times!" Ernie and Dorothy became engaged on Valentine's Day 1937 and were married about a year later. The wedding took place at Holy Cross Catholic Church on February 26, 1938.

Soon after their marriage they moved into a duplex owned by Dorothy's parents. Her parents lived on the first floor, and the newlyweds lived on the second floor. This was to be their home until 1949.

The family soon expanded with the birth of Lawrence on December 3, 1938. He was followed by Gary on January 12, 1944, Jerome on February 7, 1946, and Cary on September 5, 1959. The kids became known as Larry, Gary, Jerry, and Cary to their parents. To say that the names were sometimes mixed up is an understatement.

The first Christmas in 1938 was special. To start with, Ernie and Dorothy had a newborn. They put up a spruce Christmas tree that went to the ceiling and even managed to buy some lights to put on it. The icing on the cake came when Dorothy gave Ernie a Pflueger Supreme casting rod and reel. It cost more than a week's worth of Ernie's wages, and since he was an avid fisherman, he loved it. As a matter of fact, he still has the outfit, and it is in working condition. There would be many more memorable Christmases to come.

Picnics were common during those first few years of marriage. Ernie and Dorothy often went on these picnics with family members and close relatives. Her mother, Apolonia, and sisters Gertrude, Frances, and Joanne often accompanied them to places like Como Park, Minnehaha Falls, and nearby lakes. They also went on many picnics with Ernie's relatives during this time. Some of the picnics were even the back yard variety at each other's homes. These picnics were usually smaller with just a few family members involved.

All in all, much recreational activity was centered on socializing. It might be through the celebrations of birthdays or just going out to visit friends or relatives. The birthdays always involved the unwrapping of presents and the sharing of birthday cake.

During other visits, people just sat around drinking coffee and eating snacks as they chatted about events in their lives. Other times they played card games like cribbage or 500. Socializing was an important activity for many people before the age of television.

One of Ernie's clearest memories was the Armistice Day Blizzard (November 11, 1940). He said the day started out balmy at about forty-five degrees. When he went to work that day, it was misting, and he wore just a suit jacket. He did not take a hat or gloves since he did not expect the weather to turn bad. The mist turned to rain and then to sleet and finally to snow as the temperature dropped. The snow came down at a clip of about one to two inches per hour. By noon, the snow had accumulated by quite a bit and the wind picked up to over thirty miles an hour, creating huge drifts. He left work at about 2:30 PM with friends Ray Swadener and Chester Dombrowski. Ray drove his old Ford, and they had to stop several times to push the car through drifts before finally arriving at Ray's mother's house. Ernie and Chet had to walk from there. Chet had to go about two blocks, and Ernie had to go about four blocks. By the time he arrived home, he was shivering from the cold and his pant legs were frozen up to his knees. A long warm bath helped him thaw out.

Ernie's draft number also came up in 1940. World War II was going on, and the United States was slowly getting closer to being an active participant. In the fall of the year, he went through a physical and was within seven days of induction. However, the government gave him an exemption because of his work at Scott-Atwater. The company was making presses, dies, and shell casings for the government. Since the work was considered essential for the war effort, he was not called into service.

During those first years of marriage the family did not have a car. As a result, they had to rely on friends and relatives to get around, including trips they took out of town. The first family vacation (without friends or relatives) was to Nokay Lake near Brainerd, Minnesota. In July of 1943, Ernie, Dorothy, and Larry boarded a train for Little Falls, Minnesota. After a layover of about two hours, they boarded a train with open-air coaches for the trip to Brainerd. The owner of the resort picked them up and took them to the lake. The trip was a great success when it came to fishing. They caught many crappies. As a matter of fact, Ernie described the action as the best he had ever experienced up to that time. From that time on, he was hooked on Nokay Lake and made regular trips up there ever since. Fishing trips to Nokay and other lakes around the state became regular summer vacation excursions for many years.

Ernie took up the hobby of bowling in 1943 as well. That first year he bowled on a team sponsored by a funeral home. The next year he bowled in two leagues, one of which was sponsored by his company. By 1945, he bowled in three separate leagues and enjoyed it very much. He continued league bowling until the mid 1950s when bursitis developed and forced him to quit league bowling. He did bowl after that, but it was purely recreational with family and friends.

He purchased his first automobile in 1946, a 1938 Plymouth. It was also the time that he learned how to drive. It was not a very reliable car, and the next year he traded it for a 1942 Plymouth. Again, the car was not very reliable, and he sold it in 1947. Then the family took a train to Detroit and bought a 1940 Oldsmobile, which served the family for several years.

Lake vacations continued during these years, with a trip to a different lake each summer. These trips were often taken with Laurent and Myrtle Paradise and their two children. Lorry was a cousin of Ernie. Sometimes other relatives and Ernie's father came along. Most of the time these vacations were filled with fun and laughter as the families enjoyed the fishing, swimming, and other northern Minnesota activities. Sometimes memorable experiences occurred.

In 1948, the family went to Little Pine Lake near the town of Cross Lake, Minnesota. Dorothy caught a large crappie and entered it in a fishing contest in town. She ended up winning a picnic kit as a prize. On the down side, nine-year-old Larry was bitten near the eye by an insect and the eye swelled shut. He ended up being taken into town to be treated by a doctor.

The next year, the family went to Mitchell Lake. As the story went, three-year-old Jerry was found floating in a stream that flowed into the lake. His cousin Judie went after him to get him out of the water, and she went under too. Luckily her sister Carol and Jerry's brother Larry were nearby and pulled them out.

Jerry had some more bad luck on a 1953 trip to Little Cormorant Lake near Detroit Lakes, Minnesota. The family stopped at a gas station for gas and rest room breaks on the way to the lake. When Jerry got out of the restroom, the car was gone. The family had driven off without him! When they discovered their mistake, they came back for him and found him walking down the street. He was trying to walk to the lake! The last of these lake vacations took place in 1957 and all were filled with fond memories.

The Abraham's moved into their first single-family home in 1949. They bought a lot in the Minneapolis suburb of Robbinsdale and had a two bedroom house built. They did the painting on the outside to save some money. They were able to move in just before Thanksgiving of that year. Ernie and his father turned the attic into a large bedroom for the three boys in 1952. The knotty pine bedroom was twelve feet by thirty feet with storage closets on each side. It included built in bunk beds for Gary and Jerry, and Larry had a full-sized bed.

The spring and summer of 1950 was spent landscaping, which included the addition of fifty truckloads of fill to raise the level of the backyard. The last addition was a large vegetable garden which supplied a lot of fresh vegetables during the summer and canned vegetables for the winter.

The first out-of-state trip for the Abraham family took place in December of 1954 when they traveled to Florida. They decided on the spur of the moment to visit Dorothy's sister Joanne, brother-in-law Bob Lundquist, and their son Bobby in Sanford, Florida. They had a fun visit with trips to Cypress Gardens, Silver Springs, Marineland, and Daytona Beach. Of course, they had a wonderful Christmas celebration.

Other out-of-state trips followed. In 1957 the family joined with the R. F. Wisniewski family (R. F. was Dorothy's brother-in-law, and Gert her sister). The two families drove to Mackinac Island near the Upper Peninsula of Michigan. The Victorian theme of the island was fantastic! The next year, the family drove to southern California to visit some of Ernie's cousins. The trip included stops at Yellowstone Park and Calico Ghost

Town near Death Valley, California. During the early 1960s, Ernie and Dorothy made trips to Mississippi and Oklahoma to visit their son, Larry, who was a pilot in the Air Force. In 1963, Ernie, Dorothy, Jerry, and Cary took a second trip to California, this time to visit Ernie's sister Yvonne and her family. Several other car trips were taken in the upcoming years. These trips took Ernie and Dorothy to both coasts and many points in between.

The first family pet was a parakeet named Poncho. Poncho was a very friendly bird, but gave the family quite a surprise when they returned from their 1954 Florida trip. Dorothy's sister and brother-in-law were taking care of the bird. When the Abrahams went over to get the bird, R. F. Wisniewski brought out a small box. When the box was opened, it was full of parakeet eggs! Poncho was a female! By 1957, Ernie was involved in breeding parakeets. Ernie was always interested in genetics and tried to develop new colors in parakeets. He gave up after about two years without accomplishing his goal, but he did come up with some brilliantly colored birds. Over the following years, other pets followed, including three successive miniature poodles and several tanks of tropical fish.

During the late 1950s, several changes had occurred in the Abraham family. Larry had been gone for three years after joining the Air Force, and Cary became the newest member of the family when he was born in 1959. In 1960, the family moved to another house in Robbinsdale. This house was next door to the Lundquist's and across the street from the Wisniewski's. This house remained their home through the years that the three youngest children grew to adulthood, went to college, and married.

Then in 1961, Ernie took a big step. He quit his job as a tool and die maker for Scott-Atwater after twenty-eight years and took the same position at the Honeywell Corporation. He went on to work seventeen years for Honeywell, finally retiring on April 27, 1979. As luck would have it, Scott-Atwater was bought out by the McCulloch Corporation, and by 1963 the plant in

Minneapolis was closed and operations were moved to California. Honeywell was a big corporation with plants all over the world. Ernie worked at several plants in the Twin Cities area including St. Louis Park, New Brighton, Hopkins, and Golden Valley. He took great pride and joy in his work.

In the 1970s, Ernie and Dorothy were able to expand their travels to Europe, Asia, and the Caribbean. By that time, Larry was a pilot for Trans World Airlines (TWA) and was able to get discount tickets for his parents. Using these tickets allowed them to travel to several European countries as well as to places such as Israel, Greece, India, Thailand, and Hong Kong. One of the trips allowed Dorothy to visit relatives in Poland, a real treat for her. They were also able to take an enjoyable trip to Hawaii and continued to travel in the continental United States. Several trips were taken to visit the Wisniewskis who had moved to the suburban Detroit area.

As noted earlier, Ernie became involved with tropical fish. It all started in 1976 when the oldest son, Larry, bought his youngest brother, Cary, a fifty-five gallon fish tank and all the necessary apparatus. When Cary went to college, Ernie took over the maintenance of the aquarium. Of course, he was not satisfied with having just one tank of tropical fish. One day, a swordtail gave birth to some babies, and Ernie said, "This got me started on raising fish." So he bought more tanks and started raising fish and selling them to a local pet store. Soon he started thinking about genetics and tried to breed a new color line into the swordtails. He started with two green-tailed swords and through crossbreeding ended up getting some albinos. Unfortunately, a disease hit the tank and killed off the albinos. The incident really discouraged him, and he eventually shut down the aquariums and gave up working with fish.

Retirement meant the opportunity for a variety of activities. One of the first things Ernie took up was walking. He chose an out and back route from his house that totaled about five miles. He always timed his walk to make sure he was keeping up a good pace. Eventually arthritis in his knees caused him to quit this activity.

A major activity during the 1980s included redecorating their home. Of course there were the typical things like painting and wallpapering, but the big job had to do with the woodwork. Ernie stripped, restained, and varnished all the cabinets, doors (and door frames), and wood trim in the house. Ernie said, "I handled each piece nine times." He also painted the outside trim and installed storm doors on the front and back.

Golf was another major retirement activity. Ernie honed his game at the Theodore Wirth par three course that was nearby. However, he also played executive courses and full length courses in the northwest suburban area. He sometimes played with sons Gary, Jerry, or Cary, sometimes with friends or relatives, and sometimes by himself. No matter who he played with, he enjoyed the often frustrating game.

In the spring of 1988, Ernie and Dorothy moved one more time. This time it was into a townhouse in Maple Grove. Things did not start well because the movers did not show up, and the family and relatives had to scramble to get everything moved. Nevertheless, the townhouse turned out to be a comfortable retirement place without the stress of outdoor work.

Different kinds of trips continued in the late 1980s and early 1990s. Ernie and Dorothy took their first Caribbean cruise in 1987 with their in-laws. This cruise was followed by Caribbean cruises in 1988, 1990, 1991, and 1993. Ernie joined his four sons and wives on an Alaskan cruise in the summer of 2002 and another Caribbean cruise in the spring of 2004.

Fishing trips again became important getaways for Ernie in the 1980s and after. He never stopped fishing, but most of his fishing had been on day trips to lakes in Minnesota. Several fishing excursions were to Bob and Joanne Lundquist's lake home just outside of Pequot Lakes, Minnesota. In 1988, he joined sons Gary and Jerry and grandson John on a Canadian fishing trip. Although the fishing was not as good as expected, Ernie hooked a fish that was big enough to break his rod. In 1990 Ernie went with his three youngest sons on their first Canadian fly-in fishing trip. The walleye fishing was great and Ernie was hooked on this type of trip. For the second time, he experienced a rod breaking under the pressure of a large fish. This trip was followed by ten more trips during the 1990s and early 2000s. Sometimes the fishing was spectacular, sometimes it was okay and a couple of times it was poor, but each trip was memorable. Ernie summed it up this way, "Fishing is my favorite hobby. To me, nothing can be better than sitting on a lake; everything is so quiet and relaxed. You have a fishing pole in your hand and you can look around at the beautiful scenery."

A difficult period of time began in 1991 when Dorothy was diagnosed with stomach cancer. She had surgery in the fall to remove the cancerous areas and then developed an infection during recovery that kept her hospitalized for sixteen days. Unfortunately, the cancer returned and she died in July of 1993. Ernie and Dorothy had been married for fifty-five years, and her passing was a big blow to him.

Ernie struggled through the next year on his own, but made it. He continues to live by himself in the townhouse. During this time he has done all his own laundry, housework, and cooking. Besides fishing, he continues to take trips around the country with various family members.

Ernie also helped himself by continuing two other hobbies that he practiced before Dorothy's death. One hobby was woodworking. He made planter boxes, duck shaped planters, crayon boxes, wooden teddy bear banks, shadow boxes, and shelves. He even made beautiful nativity mangers for his sons' families. He said, "Working with wood was like play for me." He also took up yarn crafts. He started with little magnetized figures for refrigerator doors and worked his way up. He made it a tradition to make Christmas gifts for his sons' families and often for his grandchildren and in-laws. He made everything from ornaments, to tissue boxes and napkin holders, to Christmas villages.

As Ernie entered his ninetieth year, he cherished the time he had with his four sons and their families. Having come from a poor background, he was thankful for the successes attained by his children. As noted earlier, Larry was a commercial pilot for TWA and is still flying. Gary is a retired psychologist who worked in Minnesota and Washington. Jerry is a retired teacher, and Cary works as a sales representative for a medical device manufacturer. Ernie has seven grandchildren and six great grandchildren and enjoys the times he visits with them.

This independent man still finds ways to stay active mentally and physically. Housework and crafts help keep him going physically, while reading and doing the daily crossword puzzles keep his mind sharp. He also has a deep commitment to his church, which keeps his spirit alive.

Order Form

Please copy this page, add the necessary information, and mail it to:

Jerry Abraham
12305 Heather St. NW
Coon Rapids, MN 55433

Please enclose personal check or money order, payable to: Jerry Abraham

Voices From Minnesota $22.00 each US
ISBN 1-930374-13-5   ($33.00 each Canadian)

Qty. _____   Total: _____

MN residents add 6.5% sales tax ($1.43 / book) _____

Shipping & Handling: Add $2.50 for first book
$1.00 for each additional book _____
(Canadian residents please add $6.00)

Total enclosed _____

Name: _____

Address: _____

City: _____ State: _____ Zip: _____

Phone: _____ Email: _____

You can also order this book and others from our secure web site at:
www.DeForestPress.com for immediate delivery.

Or, you can mail your order with check or money order,
payable to DeForst Press, to:

DeForest Press
P.O. Box 154
Elk River, MN 55330